# The River Nene

## A guide for river users

Northampton to The Wash
including the Grand Union Canal
(Northampton Arm to Gayton Junction)

**ROGER GREEN**

# The River Nene

## Summary of distances, locks and estimated times

### Cruising downstream

| Location | Miles | Locks | Hours |
|---|---|---|---|
| Gayton Junction | 0·0 | 0 | 0·0 |
| Northampton Junction | 4·8 | 17 | 4·8 |
| Whiston Lock | 7·2 | 8 | 5·0 |
| Wellingborough Embank | 5·5 | 5 | 3·5 |
| Upper Ringstead Lock | 7·9 | 5 | 3·9 |
| Thrapston Bridge | 4·9 | 3 | 2·3 |
| Upper Barnwell Lock | 8·8 | 5 | 4·0 |
| Fotheringhay Bridge | 7·9 | 4 | 3·3 |
| Wansford Station | 8·0 | 4 | 3·6 |
| Peterborough Embank | 8·8 | 3 | 3·5 |
| Dog-in-a-Doublet Lock | 6·1 | 1 | 1·7 |
| **Totals** | **69·9** | **55** | **35·6** |

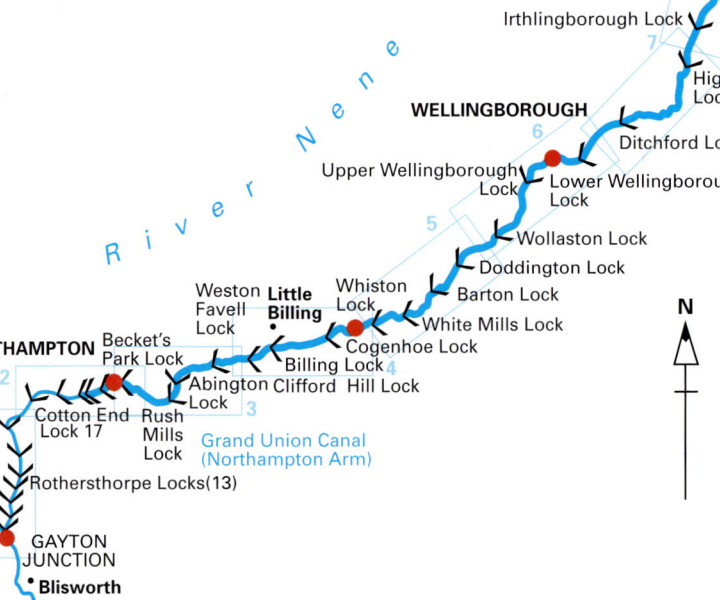

### Cruising upstream

| Location | Miles | Locks | Hours |
|---|---|---|---|
| Dog-in-a-Doublet Lock | 0·0 | 0 | 0·0 |
| Peterborough Embank | 6·1 | 1 | 1·7 |
| Wansford Station | 8·8 | 3 | 3·5 |
| Fotheringhay Bridge | 8·0 | 4 | 3·6 |
| Upper Barnwell Lock | 7·9 | 4 | 3·3 |
| Thrapston Bridge | 8·8 | 5 | 4·0 |
| Upper Ringstead Lock | 4·9 | 3 | 2·3 |
| Wellingborough Embank | 7·9 | 5 | 3·9 |
| Whiston Lock | 5·5 | 5 | 3·5 |
| Northampton Junction | 7·2 | 8 | 5·0 |
| Gayton Junction | 4·8 | 17 | 4·8 |
| **Totals** | **69·9** | **55** | **35·6** |

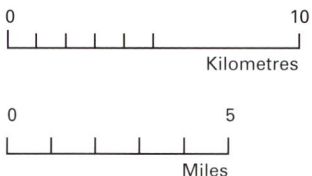

Published by
**Imray, Laurie, Norie & Wilson Ltd**
Wych House, St Ives,
Cambridgeshire PE27 5BT, England
www.imray.com
2020

All rights reserved· No part of this
publication may be reproduced, transmitted or used in
any form by any means –
graphic, electronic or mechanical, including
photocopying, recording, taping or
information storage and retrieval systems or otherwise –
without the prior permission of the publisher.

© Imray Laurie Norie & Wilson Ltd 2020
© Commentary – Roger Green 2020
© Previous editions 2006-2016 – Iain Smith
All photographs © Roger Green unless credited

British Library Cataloguing in Publication Data
A catalogue record for this book is available from the
British Library.

ISBN 978 178679 163 4

CAUTION
Every effort has been taken to ensure the accuracy of this
book. It contains selected information and thus is not
definitive and does not include all known information on
the subject in hand; this is particularly relevant to the
plans which should not be used for navigation. The
author and publisher believe that its selection is a useful
aid to prudent navigation but the safety of a vessel
depends ultimately on the judgement of the navigator
who should assess all information, published or
unpublished, available to him.

This work has been corrected to April 2020

Printed in the UK by Sudbury Print Group
Reprinted in June 2022 by Sudbury Print Group

# Contents

Preface  *6*
River Nene navigation  *7*
Changing river conditions  *16*
The Inland Waterways Association  *17*
Using the River Nene guide  *18*
   Moorings and facilities  *22*
   Canoeing  *25*
   Locks  *28*
   Low bridges and structures  *31*
   Distances, locks, estimated times and dimensions  *32*
   Useful contacts and links  *34*
   Key partners  *36*

**1 GRAND UNION CANAL – NORTHAMPTON ARM**  *39*

**2 RIVER NENE – NORTHAMPTON TO WELLINGBOROUGH**  *51*

**3 RIVER NENE – WELLINGBOROUGH TO WADENHOE**  *75*

**4 RIVER NENE – WADENHOE TO STIBBINGTON**  *105*

**5 RIVER NENE – STIBBINGTON TO DOG-IN-A-DOUBLET**  *135*

**6 TIDAL RIVER NENE – DOG-IN-A-DOUBLET TO THE WASH**  *163*

Appendix  *168*

Index  *170*

# Preface

The River Nene has many outstanding qualities as those who walk and boat along the river will vouch. It can exhibit tranquil beauty as you navigate its meanders, water meadows, lock structures and neighbouring villages and towns. It can also be quite ferocious and always needs to be respected.

I hope that this edition will appeal to all users of the river, not just boaters, but also provide a useful reference for those who enjoy walking, canoeing and cycling around the Nene valley.

This latest edition of the *The River Nene* guide has involved a considerable amount of fieldwork, local knowledge and discussions with many river users. Just like the river, some of the information will change over time, and whilst every effort has been made to check details river users are advised to make their own real-time checks before relying too much on local services.

I am really pleased that the Inland Waterways Association have agreed to support this project and continue to campaign for access to our waterways. The adoption of the Northampton Arm by the IWA Northampton Branch and involvement with plans for a more modest version of the Fens Waterways Link are examples that will benefit all waterway users.

I would also like to thank Iain Smith (previous author) for allowing me to use his wealth of historical text, Sue Cant (Environment Agency) for checking details and updating sections of text, Dick Whitehouse (Friends of the River Nene) for providing the information about canoeing access and advice and Chris Howes for allowing me to use some of his photos to supplement my collection.

*Roger Green*
*April 2020*

Autumn at Ringstead

# River Nene navigation

The River Nene is the tenth longest river in the United Kingdom and is navigable for 91 miles (147 km), from Northampton to the Wash. Linking the navigable rivers of East Anglia with the Grand Union canal and the national canal network, this important river rises at sources near Badby, Naseby and Yelvertoft.

Navigation starts at Northampton and extends to the sea, entering The Wash between two towers, at Guy's Head, known as 'the lighthouses'. The river is tidal downstream of the Dog-in-a-Doublet Lock near Peterborough.

Originally a commercial navigation it is now used almost entirely for recreation. Boat traffic is increasing on this attractive waterway, but it is still quiet compared with other navigations such as the canals and Great Ouse.

Take your time to explore this very beautiful waterway ... don't rush it. With views throughout, it passes through Northamptonshire, the county of 'squires and spires', Cambridgeshire and Lincolnshire, flowing through industrial towns such as Northampton and Wellingborough, the cathedral city of Peterborough, and the Dutch style waterfront architecture of Wisbech. Farmland, fenland, wetland areas of special scientific interest, castle mounds, and quintessential English villages (like Wadenhoe and Fotheringhay) built from local limestone are just some of the delights that await you.

Human history in the Nene Valley dates back at least 5,000 years. Bronze age settlements, Roman remains, birthplace of the last Plantagenet king and the site where Mary Queen of Scots was executed at Fotheringhay, quiet country churches, and mills that once produced paper, leather or flour - all this, and more, can be seen as you navigate the river.

*Neen* or *Nen*? Well, you may or may not get it right as pronunciation of the river's name varies by locality. Generally, it is pronounced 'Nen' from Northampton to Thrapston and 'Neen' from Thrapston to Peterborough. Either way, you will be quickly corrected by locals and boaters.

## Navigation Authority

**The Environment Agency (EA)** is the navigation authority for the River Nene from the confluence with the Northampton Arm of the Grand Union Canal in Northampton to Bevis Hall, just upstream of Wisbech.

## Boat licensing and registration

All vessels kept, used, or let for hire on the River Nene must be registered for use with the Environment Agency. This includes vessels in marinas and on privately owned moorings.

Depending on the type of craft, to obtain a boat registration you may need:

- insurance
- a Boat Safety Scheme (BSS) certificate

You must renew your registration each year for the waterway you want to keep or use your boat on. Annual registrations expire on 31 March regardless of when they start on EA waterways and 31 December for Gold licences.

Visitor registrations are available for shorter periods; 1 day, 7 days, and 31 days. The Environment Agency advises that you should allow two weeks for your application to be processed. Registration costs for powered boats are based on boat length. A registration charges sheet can be found at www.gov.uk/register-a-boat

To renew your boat registration, contact the boat registration team:

Environment Agency boat registration team
PO Box 544, Rotherham, S60 1BY
Email boatreg@environment-agency.gov.uk
☏ 03708 506 506
Minicom (for the hard of hearing)
☏ 03702 422 549
Monday to Friday, 8am to 6pm

Visitor registrations may also be purchased from Northampton Marina or from one of several outlets along the river. You should contact the Boat Registration Team for the most up to date details of these outlets.

## Reciprocal arrangements with other navigation authorities

A River Nene registration also covers use of your boat on the River Great Ouse. Reciprocal arrangements with other Navigation Authorities include:

- A Gold Licence, available from either the Agency or the Canal and River Trust (CRT) permits craft licensed by either Authority to navigate the other's waters. (CRT is the navigation authority for the Northampton Arm.)
- Cambs Conservators

You must purchase a reciprocal licence before venturing onto these waterways, from:

**Canal and River Trust**
Boat licencing team
PO Box 162, Leeds, LS9 1AX
☏ 0303 040 4040

**Cam Conservancy**
Clayhithe Office, Clayhithe Road, Waterbeach, Cambridge, CB25 9JB
☏ 01223 863785

At present you do not need to register or have a licence to boat on the **Middle Level** network. This will change shortly as the Middle Level Bill takes effect when boat registration will be required.

## Legislation

Boat owners navigating Recreational Waterways within the Environment Agency's Anglian waterways should acquaint themselves with the following legislation, particularly local byelaws and registration requirements (The Order 2010).

*The Anglian Water Authority Act* 1977

*The Recreational Waterways (General) Byelaws* 1980

*The Environment Act* 1995

*The Environment Agency (Inland Waterways) Order* 2010

Copies can be obtained from the Environment Agency at WaterwaysAnglian@environment-agency.gov.uk

## Speed limits

A speed limit of 7mph (11kph) applies throughout the navigation except for one mile downstream of Peterborough. This derestricted stretch is clearly signposted. Elsewhere, the Agency seek to enforce this limit, to prevent unsocial behaviour. Even within this limit, boaters should travel at an appropriate speed in the interests of safety and to protect wildlife. Powered vessels should also slow down and maintain a steady course when approaching manual or sailing craft or swimmers. Care must especially be taken when overtaking other vessels or turning as well as near bridges and sharp bends, where vessels travelling upstream must give way to those going downstream.

## Navigation keys

Vessels navigating the River Nene need a navigation key, often called an *Abloy* key to operate the locks and to access sanitary facilities and water points. Navigation keys can be purchased from the Boat Registration Team, Northampton Marina or one of several outlets along the river. Proof of registration is required when purchasing a navigation key.

## Windlass

As well as a navigation key you will need a windlass to fit a 1¼ inch square when operating the locks on the River Nene.

## Environment Agency marina

**Northampton Marina**, immediately upstream of Northampton Town Lock (Becket's Park Lock), is operated by the Environment Agency. This popular marina provides a warm welcome and ideal first stopover for visiting boats travelling to and from the national canal network. Its facilities include:

- All berths are on rise and fall, non-slip pontoons and walkways within a secure site
- Residential, permanent and visitor moorings. Winter moorings are popular but subject to availability.
- Electricity and drinking water to all mooring berths, security lighting, toilets, washrooms, showers, pump-out and chemical toilet disposal, rubbish collection, laundry, BBQ area with picnic tables and wild flower meadow
- Fully manned site

- Short stay vehicular access and parking for off-loading by boat users
- Long term parking by arrangement with Northampton Borough Council in close by town centre car parks
- Easy access to town centre facilities and attractions

The marina is well signposted from the river. For full details and current fees:

www.northamptonmarina.co.uk

☏ 01604 604344 or ☏ 07867 580129

Funding has been obtained though the Heritage Lottery Landscape Partnership Scheme, to deliver access from and to the River Nene as part of the Nenescape project (*see page 37*). The Environment Agency is a key partner. Boaters should start seeing new moorings and improvements, funded by the scheme, from summer 2019 onwards for the next five years.

## Private marinas

There is a growing number of developing private marinas, in addition to those that have been established for many years. Marina details can be found on the maps/text pages.

## Visitor/short stay moorings

The Environment Agency provides **visitor moorings** at 10 locations on the river. These are shown on the map pages. There is no charge for the use of these moorings, but the maximum period of stay is limited to 48 hours within any period of three consecutive days.

In an emergency or periods of high flows (Strong Stream restrictions) please let the Environment Agency know that you are there, permission to stay longer than would normally be allowed is unlikely to be refused in such circumstances.

Visitor moorings provided by the Environment Agency are a mixture of fixed level and floating pontoons. All provide a safe haven for boats and boaters in times of high flows.

**Overnight mooring** at lock landing stages is generally prohibited, except in an emergency, during times of high flows, and with the permission of the Environment Agency.

For safety reasons, boats must not be moored within 36m of any locks, sluices, weirs or water intakes except when navigating through a lock. In some cases, such as the Dog-in-a-Doublet Tidal Lock & Sluices, Bedford Road Sluice (Northampton) and Weston Favell (Northampton), mooring is prohibited for 100m on both sides of the structure.

### Other visitor and short stay moorings

Local councils, businesses and boat clubs all provide short term moorings for boaters.

**Friends of the River Nene (FOTRN** - *see p.36*) membership allows access to 10 mooring sites. With annual membership in the region of £12, it is well worth joining FOTRN before embarking on your journey.

The location of these moorings are shown on the map/text pages.

There also several permissive moorings on the river, these are noted on the map/text pages.

## Water points and sewage disposal

The Environment Agency provides water and sanitary facilities along the River Nene.

The EA toilet pump-out facilities at Northampton Marina and Wellingborough Embankment are token operated, tokens can be purchased from Northampton Marina.

Peterborough City Council provides drinking water, pump-out and chemical toilet disposal at Peterborough Embankment.

Elsewhere along the waterways, these facilities are available at most marinas and some boat clubs.

These are marked on the map/text pages.

## Public slipway

There is a public slipway at Potters Way, Peterborough, provided by Peterborough City Council. A key is required to access the slipway, which is available from the Visitor Information Centre at Peterborough City Council and with whom you should also check the details of the height restriction along Potters Way.

Visitor Information Centre
41 Bridge Street Peterborough PE1 1HA
☏ 01733 452336

Monday, Wednesday, Thursday and Friday, 0900–1700
Tuesday 1000-1700
Saturday 1000–1600
Sunday and Bank Holidays closed

The Environment Agency slipway at Wellingborough is currently closed and awaiting improvements to the public highway access before it can be reopened.

EA water point

## River Nene locks

There are 38 locks on the River Nene from **Northampton Town Lock 1** (also known as **Becket's Park Lock**) to the **Dog-in-a-Doublet tidal lock 38** downstream of Peterborough.

All the River Nene locks have steel pointing/mitre gates at the upstream end and 6 of the locks have steel pointing/mitre gates at the downstream end as well. 31 locks have vertical gates at the downstream end and 1 lock has a radial gate at the downstream end. This type of lock is almost unique to the navigable rivers of East Anglia and an important heritage feature. They are known as 'Guillotine Gate Locks' and the majority are electrically operated. Except for the Dog-in-a-Doublet, the Nene locks are unmanned.

**Ditchford Lock** is unique in that it has a radial gate at its downstream end. There were once many more radial lock gates on the River Nene but today the only one remaining is at Ditchford.

Each Nene lock is 83ft 6ins (26m) long and 15ft wide (4·6m) with a minimum depth of 4ft (1·2m). To make allowances for adverse conditions, the maximum dimensions for craft should be regarded as:

Length 78ft (23m)
Beam 13ft (3·9m)
Draught 4ft (1·2m)
Headroom 7ft (2·1m)

Craft approaching these maximum dimensions may have difficulties.

All Nene locks have plentiful bollards for use and ladders placed on the left-hand side near the guillotine when proceeding downstream and another near the mitre gates on the left-hand side when proceeding upstream.

Ditchford Lock radial gate

## Using guillotine or radial gate locks

Guillotine gate locks and Ditchford radial gate lock should be left with the pointing/mitre gates closed and the vertical lift/radial gate raised and locked. This is because the height of the upstream pointing gates is set to maintain water levels for navigation in the upstream reaches. In times of higher than normal flows, water weirs over these pointing gates and is a sign that river conditions are changing.

Yellow zones in the lock pen mark the location of underwater cills. Never moor within these zones as these are where sinking is possible if water overtops the upstream gates.

Where a lock has a manually operated winding wheel, a lockable bolt retains the handle for the lock operation. This is released by inserting the EA *Abloy* navigation key. The bolt should be securely pushed into the operating wheel after use and the spring-loaded lock fully pushed home.

The vertical gates and paddle mechanisms should always be operated with care. Children should not be allowed to operate them.

Manually operated winding wheel Chris Howes

Always check with the person responsible for the boat in the lock that they are secured and prepared before opening any paddle or vertical gate. This is particularly important when locking upstream as top-gate paddles can create a strong current. Boat owners are advised to use side fenders when inside the lock pen and to open the upstream paddle slowly, to avoid creating turbulent water within the lock pen and possible damage to your boat.

## Caution

If the pointing doors are found chained back (open) and the vertical gate partially lifted, ie the lock is 'reversed', no attempt to navigate should be made. Warnings are sited upstream and downstream of locks to indicate when a lock is reversed.

Should there have been heavy rain in the area it is probable there will be a rapid change in water condition eg rise in level, increase in current, change in colour. With any such change in conditions the Agency will almost certainly be operating sluices to regulate water levels and extreme care should be taken when approaching locks or other structures.

At several locks the river may overtop the mitre gates (*see photo opposite*) even when flows are normal. Boaters should take care and be aware that this may make manoeuvring into locks interesting.

All locks with guillotine gates should be left empty with the guillotine gate raised. At locks with mitre gates at both ends both sets of gates must left closed.

## Lock procedures

### Entering the lock from a higher level

- Lower the vertical gate
- Open paddles slowly in the pointing doors to fill the lock pen
- Open the pointing doors when water levels are equal, and enter the lock
- Lower the paddles and close the pointing doors
- On manually operated locks raise the vertical door a few inches only. This is stiff at first, to prevent rapid opening of the door; vessels can be difficult to control if water surges forward. The vertical gate should be fully raised once the water level in the lock pen has fallen. Powered locks automatically allow two minutes for water to level.

### Entering the lock from a lower level

- After entering the lock, lower the vertical gate
- Open paddles slowly in the pointing doors to fill the lock pen
- When levels permit, open the pointing doors
- After leaving the lock, lower the paddles and close the pointing door
- Finally, raise the vertical gate fully.

Irthlingborough Lock Chris Howes

THE RIVER NENE 13

## Low headroom bridges

There are 70 fixed bridges along the River Nene between Northampton and Wisbech, several of which have low headroom. Low headroom bridges are those that offer less than 2·7 metres air draught in normal river conditions. These are listed on the bridge headroom table on page 31 and shown on the map/text pages.

Inverted gauge boards adjacent to these low headroom bridges give guidance on available headroom. When travelling with the flow, care should be taken when approaching bridges and proceed only when you are sure that there is enough air draft for your boat to pass through safely.

Headroom at bridges on the tidal section of the river will always vary. Please seek advice from the Dog-in-a-Doublet lock keeper before attempting to pass underneath any bridges on the tidal reaches.

## Passage to and from the tidal River Nene

Passage into the tidal river downstream of the Dog-in-a-Doublet lock must be made by prior arrangement with the lockkeeper. Registered craft may pass through this lock every day from 0730 hours until official sunset time. Boat owners should telephone the Navigation Duty Officer to make arrangements for passage in advance of their arrival.

Navigation Duty Officer
☎ 07384 249151

The river is tidal for 25 miles downstream of the Dog-in-a-Doublet Lock, which is five miles below Peterborough. This stretch can be treacherous, especially during spring tides. Passage should only be attempted if you are sure of your own capabilities as well as that of your boat.

For information regarding the passage of craft or moorings in the port of Wisbech and down to the sea apply to

The Port Manager
Port Office
Wisbech
☎ 01945 588059 / 01406 351530

Craft should proceed through Wisbech with care. The banks are lined with steel and concrete piling, there is stone in the bed, and there is a strong run on the flood and ebb tide, particularly at the lower stages.

## Navigation closures and restrictions

The Environment Agency posts advance information on closures and restrictions to the navigation of the river on the information boards at each lock. This information is also published on Northampton Marina's website www.northamptonmarina.co.uk, on Twitter @PaulSeparovicEA, and held by the marinas and boat clubs along the river.

## Water levels

Water levels naturally fluctuate and cannot be guaranteed. Care should be taken when:

- Approaching any of the river controls, weirs, sluices, locks etc, should there be any significant flow on the river
- When stopping overnight or leaving a boat for a considerable length of time, i.e. over winter (where boats are permitted to remain in the water)
- In a flood situation, do not moor in shallow water or with a tight rope or chain as water levels may fluctuate. If the level drops and a craft is moored aground or in shallow water, it may be damaged. If the level rises and mooring ropes or chains are tight, the boat may take on water, be pulled under or even broken free.

The Environment Agency disclaims liability for any damage caused to craft moored on the river, as a result of fluctuating water levels.

## Reversed locks

The Nene is susceptible to a rapid rise after heavy rain, due to its nature and catchment area and river users are advised to pay close attention to weather forecasts. If you observe any of the following changes - a rapid change in water condition, rising water levels, an increase in flow and current, water cascading over lock pointing doors, as well as a change in water colour - the Environment Agency will almost certainly be operating sluices to regulate water levels.

**Boaters should take extreme care and seek suitable mooring at the earliest opportunity.**

**If the pointing doors of a lock are found chained back (open) and the vertical gate partially lifted, no attempt to navigate should be made.**

These locks are 'reversed' and being used to discharge flood water from the system. You should not approach a reversed lock but moor up safely a distance away, contact the Environment Agency to let them know where you are, tune into the local weather forecast and wait for conditions to return to normal.

Warning signs are displayed upstream and downstream of locks and red warning lights (visible from a distance) deployed on the top of the guillotine gate frames to indicate when a lock is reversed.

There are eight locks that are 'reversed' on the River Nene in times of high flows: **Doddington, Titchmarsh, Wadenhoe, Lower Barnwell, Cotterstock, Warmington, Elton** and **Yarwell**.

The Environment Agency is working on mitigation measures that will allow them to cease this practise and divert excess water via alternative routes.

# Changing river conditions

## River Advice for Boaters (Strong Stream Advice)

Boaters are encouraged to sign up to receive Environment Agency River Advice for Boaters (also known as Strong Stream Advice). This free service advises boat users that conditions are such that it is strongly recommended against attempting to navigate and that locks are 'reversed'.

To receive SSA notifications, email or write to ask to be added to the service:
Anglian Waterways
Environment Agency, Ceres House, Searby Road, Lincoln,
LN2 4DW

waterwaysssaanglian@environment-agency.gov.uk

You can request to receive SSA by many different methods including automatic voice message, text, pager or email.

Please note that automated warnings can be generated any time of the day or night.

When River Advice for Boaters (RAB) is issued/Strong Stream Advice (SSA) is in force, signs and/or red flags are deployed to inform users on the River Nene of changing river conditions. These are located at the top and bottom locks of the Northampton Arm of the Grand Union Canal, Stanground Lock Peterborough, the Dog-in-a-Doublet tidal lock, all reversed locks, visitor moorings and Northampton Marina.

Several marinas and boat clubs (in association with the Agency) raise red flags when RAB is issued/SSA is in force.

These flags not only inform club members and marina users against attempting to navigate but are of value to other river users as well.

## Floodline service

River users can also telephone the Agency's Floodline Information Service to hear the recorded message informing users whether River Advice for Boaters has been issued.

To do this complete the following steps:

1. Call Floodline ① 0845 988 1188. You will be welcomed to Floodline and offered different touch tone options.

2. Choose option '1' to listen to pre-recorded information for flood warnings currently in force.

3. Simply enter the River Nene quick dial SSA number 032112 when prompted.

Strong Stream Advice signage at Wadenhoe Lock

# The Inland Waterways Association

The Inland Waterways Association (IWA) was born from necessity back in 1945, when two forward-thinking canal enthusiasts, Tom Rolt and Robert Aickman, realised there was a need to protect the waterways of Britain, which were being abandoned and filled in at an alarming rate in favour of new road and railway networks. At a meeting in August 1945, at Tardebigge, near Bromsgrove on the Worcester & Birmingham Canal, plans for IWA were agreed between the two men and the Association was officially set up in February 1946. In November of that year, the first ever Bulletin was issued informing members that the Stratford Canal, Kennet & Avon and Suffolk Stour were the targets of the first IWA campaigns.

On the Stratford Canal, Rolt successfully challenged Great Western Railway (GWR), the then owners of the Stratford Canal, at Tunnel Lane, Lifford Bridge at Kings Norton. GWR had replaced a former drawbridge with a new bridge that was too low to allow boat passage along the canal, despite a statutory right of navigation existing. A question in Parliament and a notice of intention to navigate, forced GWR to lift the bridge to allow Rolt, in his narrowboat Cressy to pass.

The successes of these early actions gave IWA the confidence needed to start campaigning far and wide, further buoyed by the rise of leisure boating, which swelled membership numbers during the 1950s, 60s and beyond.

Today, IWA speaks for all users of the inland waterways network, which includes 6,500 miles of rivers and canals across England and Wales as well as the Scottish Canals. IWA works tirelessly to help protect and restore these waterways through its lobbying and campaigning activity, whether on a government level, with changes to legislation or the introduction of new transport initiatives, or on a more local level with council-led planning issues or decisions from navigation authorities. Local campaigning is undertaken by IWA's network of branches across the country.

Through its Waterway Recovery Group, IWA works with canal restoration trusts around the country, providing a volunteer workforce, expert engineering and planning advice and information on how to raise the necessary funds. Over 500 miles of canal have been restored and put back to water in the course of IWA's history, with many more currently undergoing restoration.

In this region the IWA is represented by the Northampton and Peterborough branches. Both meet regularly, and welcome new members. To learn more about the IWA's illustrious history, current campaigns, or to find out some of the many benefits of membership, please visit www.waterways.org.uk. The site will also give you up to date contact details for your local branches.

# Using the River Nene Guide

## Map pages

18 detailed maps of the canal and river, showing the main features of the navigation, local facilities, services and features of interest. The maps are marked with 'mile markers'.

### Map symbols

| Symbol | | Symbol | |
|---|---|---|---|
| | Navigation Authority (EA/CRT) | - - - - | Footpath |
| | Friends of the River Nene (FOTRN) | - -●- - | Long distance footpath |
| | Town and Borough Council | | Drinking water |
| | Marina berths | | Chemical disposal point |
| | Boat clubs | | Toilet pumpout |
| | Private or permissive | | Shower |
| ◆ | Mile marker | | Refuse bin |
| | Slipwaybank | | Fuel |
| | Direction of stream | | Shop |
| | Lock | | Public house |
| / | Weir | | Café/restaurant |
| | Winding hole | | Railway station |
| - - - - | Power cable | | Church |
| ▲▼ | Canoe portage point | i | Information |
| | Canoe access for launching | ✉ | Post Office |
| | Footbridge | | Telephone |

18 THE RIVER NENE

## Distance and feature tables

Each map has a section of text to provide more information. The table at the start of the section provides a summary of distance, locks, time, facilities and services.

| Headings | Definition | | | | | | | | |
|---|---|---|---|---|---|---|---|---|---|
| Miles | Number of miles from previous location | Single | Mitred | Vertical powered | Vertical manual | | | | |
| Locks | Number of locks for each map section | | | | | | | | |
| Lock type | Single, mitre, vertical, and whether powered | ▲ | ◁ | ☐ | ☐ | | | | |
| Estimated time | Based on miles/locks. Average from several sources | | | | | | | | |
| Bridge <2.7m | Restricted headroom for some boats | EA | FOTRN | Marina | Council | Boat club | Private | | |
| 48hr | Overnight/short stay visitor moorings | ⚓ | ⚓ | ⚓ | ⚓ | ⚓ | ⚓ | | |
| Long stay | Long stay or permanent leisure mooring | ⚓ | | ⚓ | | ⚓ | | | |
| Water point | Drinking water on tap within hose reach of bank | 🚰 | | | | | | | |
| CDP | Chemical disposal point for cassette toilets | ⤓ | | | | | | | |
| Pumpout | DIY or marina-operated waste tank emptying | ⛽ | | | | | | | |
| Refuse | Basic rubbish disposal - may offer recycling | 🗑 | | | | | | | |
| Diesel | Bankside sale of 'red diesel' requiring declaration | ⛽ | | | | | | | |
| Shops | Local general food store to wide range of shops | 🛒 | | | | | | | |
| Pub | Serving drinks and possibly food | 🍺 | | | | | | | |
| Café | Snacks to full restaurant meals | 🍴 | | | | | | | |
| Post Office or bank | PO counter services, also includes banks | £ | | | | | | | |
| Portage | Purpose-built and sited low launching platform | ▲▼ | | | | | | | |
| Access | Parking with suitable location for launching | 🛶 | | | | | | | |

*A note about timings – the timings included in this guide must be treated with caution! Bearing in mind factors such as boat speed, wind strength and direction, flow on the river, whether travelling up or down stream and waiting and operation times at locks it is not a defined art. I have used an average of times derived from our own experience with a narrowboat, and data from Waterway Routes, Canal Planner, Pearson's and Imray.

*A note about National Grid References and Postcodes – on the lock details, bridge headroom, canoeing and throughout the guide in various places I have used grid references wherever possible. Together with postcodes this provides clear positional data for emergency and breakdown services and a good way of identifying meeting places or places to explore.

## Navigation notes

Detailed notes about the course of the river, information about some of the backwaters and weirs and key things to look out for as you travel along the river.

## Moorings and facilities

This section aims to provide the boater with key information about location of moorings, marinas, drinking water and sanitation and refuse facilities. Contact details are included for marinas.

## Victualling services

We all want to know where the next meal is coming from and we can shop, drink and eat – this heading tries to identify where these essential services are located within reasonable reach of moorings on the river.

**Note that facilities do change and it is always worth checking in advance to avoid disappointment.**

## Nature reserves and features

Environmentally, the Nene valley is an important route for migrating birds, situated on the 'route' from the Humber estuary to the north and the Exe estuary to the south. The 'necklace' of lakes formed in the valley by the gravel extraction, together with the river and its flood plain, are important bird feeding and breeding areas and there are several important nature reserves close to the river. There are also several country parks where conservation supports education and outdoor adventure. The notes for each section provide details of location and contact information.

## Walking and exploring

Exploring the river on foot is becoming more popular, not only for those looking for a long-distance walk challenge, but also for families who want to enjoy what the river and Nene valley have to offer.

The map/text pages provide enough information to help walkers plan possible excursions. For serious walkers and explorers, and to provide more enriched information, I would strongly advise using an Ordnance Survey 1:25000 Explorer map. These are readily available in paper and digital form. Sheets 223, 224 ad 227 cover the route from Gayton Junction to Dog-in-a-Doublet.

Specific maps and guides are available for our key long-distance routes i.e. Grand Union Canal Walk, Hereward Way and Nene Valley Way. www.nenevalley.net has plenty of downloadable walking maps and leaflets that cover sections of the trails and shorter riverside walks that are well worth exploring.

## Cycling

Cycling opportunities in the Nene valley continues to develop with convergence of National Cycle Routes, Green Wheel and several routes around Northampton. Country parks at Stanwick and Nene Park provide shorter routes and links to some of the regional trails. www.nenevalley.net website has plenty of downloadable cycle routes and maps for villages around the River Nene.

## Canoeing

Canoeing is an increasingly popular activity on the River Nene and there are canoe hire centres mentioned in this guide and suggested places for accessing and launching canoes are listed. The River Nene is a beautiful river to explore by canoe, and canoeists have the added advantage of being able to explore areas where larger craft cannot, for example the backwaters. Most locks and some backwaters now have canoe portage platforms provided by the EA and several sites have low enough banks to make launching and retrieval manageable.

Boaters are advised to pass unpowered craft slowly and with care. In a large boat with higher freeboard it is not always easy to know whether you have been seen or which course you are intending to take. Clear hand signals can help for canoes and small boats that are much lower in the water.

All canoes must be properly registered for use on the River Nene, either directly with the Environment Agency or via British Canoeing
www.britishcanoeing.org.uk

Dick Whitehouse, a Friends of the River Nene member, is an expert and knowledgeable canoeist with many years of boating experience on the river Nene. Most of the information about canoeing, used in this guide, originated from Dick. Further helpful and more detailed information about the sites mentioned can be found at:
www.friendsoftherivernene.co.uk/friendswithcanoes.html

The tables on pages 26–27 and the text/map pages indicate the location of portage platforms, access and suggested launching points.

## Local history

Local historical context provides enrichment and a wider understanding of how the Nene valley has developed over the centuries. These detailed notes provide the user with background information from several respected publications.

Mural plaque at Gayton Junction

# Moorings and facilities

It is often said that moorings and facilities are scarce on the River Nene. This might have been the case until recently. Since 2014 there has been considerable improvement due to:
- Friends of the River Nene establishing 12 moorings for members
- Northampton Marina now fully developed with excellent moorings and facilities
- Boat Clubs welcoming affiliated members
- New marinas at White Mills, Lilford Lodge and Sibson in addition to existing marinas at Oundle, Willy Watt, Blackthorn Lake and Billing

| | |
|---|---|
| 🖈 | Navigation authority (EA, CRT) |
| 🖈 | Friends of the River Nene (FOTRN) |
| 🖈 | Town and Borough Council |
| 🖈 | Marina berths |
| 🖈 | Boat clubs |
| 🖈 | Private or permissive |

We should soon begin to see further improvement in moorings and facilities when The Nenescape Landscape Partnership Scheme begins to deliver some of the proposed projects outlined in the Waterspace project.

Regular boaters on the river may well have what they think are their own 'secret' mooring spots – these are not listed for obvious reasons!

If you anticipate wanting to use moorings and facilities at any of the river Nene boat clubs or private moorings (shaded in yellow and brown), remember to make contact first to seek permission.

Environment Agency pump-out facilities at Northampton Marina and Wellingborough Embankment require a token to operate. Tokens are available from the marina office at Northampton. Remember that Wellingborough facilities are closed from November to April.

Several refuse sites shown in the guide are not specifically for boaters but are sites where public rubbish bins are available.

Water point details

| Map | Location | Moorings & facilities ||||||| 
| | | 48hr | Long stay | Water point | CDP | Pumpout | Refuse | Diesel |
|---|---|---|---|---|---|---|---|---|
| 1 | Gayton Junction | ✓ | | ✓ | ✓ | | ✓ | |
| | Gayton Marina | ✓ | ✓ | ✓ | ✓ | ✓ | ✓ | ✓ |
| 2 | Cotton End Moorings | ✓ | | | | | | |
| | Northampton Junction | ✓ | | | | | | |
| 3 | Town Quay Moorings | ✓ | | | | | | |
| | Northampton EA Marina | ✓ | ✓ | ✓ | ✓ | ✓ | ✓ | |
| | Midsummer Meadow EA | ✓ | | | | | | |
| | Weston Favell EA | ✓ | | | | | | |
| | Northampton Boat Club | ✓ | | ✓ | ✓ | | | |
| 4 | Clifford Hill Lock 5 | ✓ | | | | | | |
| | Billing Marina | ✓ | ✓ | ✓ | ✓ | ✓ | ✓ | ✓ |
| 5 | White Mills Marina | ✓ | ✓ | | | | ✓ | ✓ |
| | Hardwater Road Bridge | ✓ | | | | | | |
| | Doddington Field Bridge | ✓ | | | | | | |
| 6 | Wellingborough Embank | ✓ | | ✓ | ✓ | ✓ | ✓ | |
| 7 | Ditchford FOTRN | ✓ | | | | | | |
| | Glebe Farm moorings | ✓ | | ✓ | ✓ | | | |
| | Rushden Lakes FOTRN (opening delayed) | ✓ | | | | | | |
| | Irthlingborough EA | ✓ | | | | | | |
| 8 | Stanwick Lakes FOTRN | ✓ | | | | | | |
| | Little Addington FOTRN | ✓ | | | | | | |
| | Blackthorn Lake Marina | ✓ | ✓ | ✓ | ✓ | | | |
| | Willy Watt Marina | ✓ | ✓ | ✓ | ✓ | ✓ | ✓ | |
| 9 | Woodford Marina | | ✓ | ✓ | ✓ | | ✓ | |
| | Woodford FOTRN | ✓ | | | | | | |
| | Thrapston Bridge EA | ✓ | | ✓ | | | | |
| | Islip Dave FOTRN | ✓ | | | | | | |
| | Islip Mill EA | ✓ | | | | | | |
| 10 | Middle Nene Cruising Club | ✓ | | ✓ | | | | |
| | Titchmarsh EA | ✓ | | | | | | |
| | Peartree Farm FOTRN | ✓ | | | | | | |
| | Kings Arms, Wadenhoe | ✓ | | ✓ | | | | |

| Map | Location | Moorings & facilities ||||||||
|---|---|---|---|---|---|---|---|---|
| | | 48hr | Long stay | Water point | CDP | Pumpout | Refuse | Diesel |
| 11 | Lilford Lodge marina | | ● | ● | | | | |
| | Barnwell Boat Club | ● | | ● | ● | | | |
| | Upper Barnwell Lock 26 | | | ● | | | | |
| | Oundle Cruising Club | ● | | ● | | | ● | |
| | Oundle Marina Village | ● | ● | ● | ● | | ● | ● |
| 12 | Oundle Bridge | ● | | | | | | |
| 13 | Fotheringhay Bridge | ● | | ● | | | | |
| | Castle Farm | ● | | | | | | |
| | Elton Boat Club | ● | | ● | ● | | | |
| | Elton Permissive | ● | | | | | | |
| 14 | Queens Head Arm | ● | | | | | | |
| | Yarwell Mill | | ● | ● | ● | | ● | |
| | Yarwell Lock 33 | | | ● | | | | |
| | Wansford Bridge | ● | | | | | | |
| | Stibbington Boatyard | ● | | ● | | | | |
| 15 | Wansford Station EA | ● | | | | | | |
| | Sibson Marina (due to open 2020 with full facilities) | ● | | ● | ● | ● | ● | ● |
| | Peterborough Cruising Club | ● | | ● | ● | | ● | |
| | Alwalton Lock 36 & FOTRN | ● | | | | | | |
| 16 | Overton Lake | ● | | | | | | |
| | Peterborough Yacht Club | ● | | ● | ● | | ● | |
| | Orton Lock EA | ● | | | | | | |
| | Thorpe, Boathouse cut | ● | | | | | | |
| 17 | Peterborough Embankment | ● | | ● | ● | ● | ● | |
| 18 | Dog-in-a-Doublet Lock 38 | ● | | | | | | |
| 19 | Guyhirn A47 Road bridge | ● | | | | | | |
| | Wisbech Yacht Harbour | ● | | ● | ● | ● | ● | ● |

24 THE RIVER NENE

# Canoe access and portage

| Map | National Grid Ref | Postcode | Address | Upstream | Downstream | Parking and launch access | Comments |
|---|---|---|---|---|---|---|---|
| 3 | SP 748597 | NN1 1ET | St James Mill Road East, Nhampton | | | 🛶 | |
| | SP 758599 | NN1 1HF | Northampton Lock 1 | ▲ | ▼ | 🛶 | |
| | SP 763600 | NN1 5LA | Midsummer Meadow Car Park | | | 🛶 | |
| | SP 776597 | NN4 7AA | Nene Whitewater and Canoe Club | | | 🛶 | Hire/launch |
| | SP 777593 | NN4 7YB | Rush Mills Lock 2 | ▲ | ▼ | 🛶 | Emergency pick up |
| | SP 780597 | NN1 5RN | Abington Lock 3 | ▲ | ▼ | 🛶 | Emergency pick up |
| | SP 792604 | NN3 9HZ | Weston Favell Lock 4 | ▲ | ▼ | | |
| 4 | SP 804606 | NN7 1AL | Clifford Hill Lock 5 | ▲ | ▼ | | Portage on backwater |
| | SP 812610 | NN7 1NH | Billing Lock 6 | ▲ | ▼ | | Portage on backwater |
| | SP 811614 | NN7 1NH | Billing Aquadrome | | | 🛶 | |
| | SP 813612 | NN7 1NH | Billing Mill | | | 🛶 | |
| | SP 831613 | NN7 1NA | Cogenhoe Lock 7 | ▲ | ▼ | | |
| 5 | SP 846617 | NN6 0EP | Whiston Lock 8 | ▲ | | | |
| | SP 856622 | NN6 0RB | White Mills Marina | | | 🛶 | Campsite, café & launch |
| | SP 857620 | NN7 1NP | White Mills Lock 9 | ▲ | ▼ | | |
| | SP 859619 | NN7 1NP | Station Road, Grendon | | | 🛶 | |
| | SP 867627 | NN29 7TD | Earls Barton Lock 10 | ▲ | ▼ | | |
| | SP 875636 | NN29 7TD | Doddington Lock 11 | ▲ | ▼ | | |
| | SP 875637 | NN29 7TD | Hardwater Road, Gt Doddington | | | 🛶 | |
| 6 | SP 888645 | NN29 7PF | Wollaston Lock 12 | ▲ | ▼ | 🛶 | Launch into backwater |
| | SP 899662 | NN8 2ED | Upper Wellingborough Lock 13 | ▲ | ▼ | | |
| | SP 900667 | NN8 2DT | Wellingborough Embankment | | | 🛶 | |
| | SP 909671 | NN8 1RJ | Lower Wellingborough Lock 14 | ▲ | | | |

| Key to symbols on pages 25-27 | |
|---|---|
| 🛶 | Canoe access |
| 🛶 | Canoe hire |
| ▲ | Upstream portage platform |
| ▼ | Downstream portage platform |

## Canoe portages and access locations

| Map | National Grid Ref | Postcode | Address | Upstream | Downstream | Parking and launch access | Comments |
|---|---|---|---|---|---|---|---|
| 7 | SP 932682 | NN9 5PN | Ditchford Lock 15 | ▲ | ▼ | | |
| | SP 931682 | NN8 1RL | Glebe Meadows, Ditchford Lock | | | 🛶 | |
| | SP 939679 | NN10 6FA | Rushden Lakes - Canoe2 hire | | | 🛶 | Hire/short breaks on Nene |
| | SP 955700 | NN9 5QQ | Higham Ferrers Lock 16 | ▲ | | 🛶 | |
| | SP 957705 | NN9 5QF | Station Road, Irthlingborough | | | 🛶 | |
| 8 | SP 960714 | NN9 5QF | Irthlingborough Lock 17 | ▲ | | | |
| | SP 968723 | NN9 6TQ | Stanwick Lakes | ▲ | ▼ | | On backwater |
| | SP 967744 | NN14 4DT | Upper Ringstead Lock 18 | ▲ | ▼ | | |
| | SP 973751 | NN14 4DU | Lower Ringstead Lock 19 | ▲ | ▼ | 🛶 | |
| 9 | SP 993768 | NN14 4EH | Denford War Memorial | | | 🛶 | |
| | SP 990786 | NN14 4FG | Thrapston Bridge EA mooring | | | 🛶 | |
| | SP 991791 | NN14 3JN | Islip Lock 22 | ▲ | | | |
| 10 | TL 014809 | NN14 3ED | Titchmarsh Lock 23 | ▲ | ▼ | | Backwater |
| | TL 021815 | NN14 3NZ | Aldwincle Bridge, Thorpe | | | 🛶 | |
| | TL 011833 | PE8 5ST | Wadenhoe, Church St car park | | | 🛶 | |
| | TL 013833 | PE8 5XD | Wadenhoe, Mill Lane | | | 🛶 | |
| | TL 011832 | PE8 5ST | Wadenhoe Lock 24 | ▲ | | | |
| 11 | TL 025837 | PE8 5SG | Lilford Lock 25 | | | | |
| | TL 025839 | PE8 5SG | Lilford Bridge | | | 🛶 | Emergency pick up |
| | TL 037869 | PE8 5PB | Upper Barnwell Lock 26 | ▲ | ▼ | 🛶 | Plus 2 on backwater |
| | TL 038873 | PE8 5PA | Oundle Marina | | | 🛶 | |
| | TL 041873 | PE8 4DN | Lower Barnwell Lock 27 | ▲ | ▼ | | |
| 12 | TL 053877 | PE8 5LB | Ashton Lock 28 | ▲ | ▼ | | |
| | TL 045888 | PE8 4DE | Nene Extreme, Oundle Wharf | | | 🛶 | Canoe hire |
| | TL 046902 | PE8 5HH | Cotterstock Lock 29 | ▲ | ▼ | | |
| | TL 049093 | PE8 5HH | Cotterstock Bridge | | | 🛶 | |
| 13 | TL 044922 | PE8 5HU | Perio Lock 30 | ▲ | ▼ | | Portage on backwater |
| | TL 060930 | PE8 5JA | Fotheringhay Bridge | | | 🛶 | |
| | TL 061930 | PE8 5HZ | Castle Farm mooring, Fotheringhay | | | 🛶 | Campsite & launch |
| | TL 072920 | PE8 6TJ | Warmington Lock 31 | ▲ | ▼ | | |
| | TL 084 939 | PE8 6RG | Elton Lock 32 | ▲ | | 🛶 | |

## Canoe portages and access locations

| Map | National Grid Ref | Postcode | Address | Upstream | Downstream | Parking and launch access | Comments |
|---|---|---|---|---|---|---|---|
| 14 | TL074972 | PE8 6PZ | Rutland Canoe Hire, Yarwell Mill | | | ✓ | Canoe hire |
| | TL 074972 | PE8 6JX | Yarwell Lock 33 | | | ✓ | |
| | TL 075992 | PE8 6JH | Wansford Bridge | | | ✓ | |
| | TL 077995 | PE8 6LJ | Wansford A47 picnic area | | | ✓ | |
| 15 | TL 094979 | PE8 6LR | NVR Wansford Station mooring | | | ✓ | EA mooring platform |
| | TL 109973 | PE8 6LY | Water Newton Lock 35 | | | ✓ | |
| 16 | TL 143984 | PE6 7AB | Milton Ferry Bridge | | | ✓ | North bank by bridge |
| | TL 143978 | PE3 6HN | Ferry Meadows, Peterborough | | | ✓ | |
| | TL 143978 | PE2 6FD | Nene Park Watersports Centre | | | ✓ | Canoe hire & launch |
| | TL 166971 | PE2 7DZ | Orton Lock 37 | | ▼ | ✓ | |
| 17 | TL 195982 | PE2 8AD | Peterborough Embankment | | | ✓ | Low bank near Key Theatre |

Canoe2 canoes approaching Wadenhoe Norman Church, River Nene  Dave Joyner, courtesy of Canoe2.co.uk

# Locks

| Map | National grid reference | Postcode | Lock name and number | Upstream | Downstream | Rise/fall (metres) |
|---|---|---|---|---|---|---|
| 1 | SP 722560 | NN7 3JG | Rothersthorpe Top Lock 1 | ▲ | ◁ | 24·33 |
| | SP 723561 | NN7 3JG | Rothersthorpe Lock 2 | ▲ | ◁ | |
| | SP 723562 | NN7 3JG | Rothersthorpe Lock 3 | ▲ | ◁ | |
| | SP 724563 | NN7 3JG | Rothersthorpe Lock 4 | ▲ | ◁ | |
| | SP 724564 | NN7 3JG | Rothersthorpe Lock 5 | ▲ | ◁ | |
| | SP 725565 | NN7 3JG | Rothersthorpe Lock 6 | ▲ | ◁ | |
| | SP 725566 | NN7 3JG | Rothersthorpe Lock 7 | ▲ | ◁ | |
| | SP 725566 | NN4 9QS | Rothersthorpe Lock 8 | ▲ | ◁ | |
| | SP 725567 | NN4 9QS | Rothersthorpe Lock 9 | ▲ | ◁ | |
| | SP 726569 | NN4 9RN | Rothersthorpe Lock 10 | ▲ | ◁ | |
| | SP 726569 | NN4 9XF | Rothersthorpe Lock 11 | ▲ | ◁ | |
| | SP 726571 | NN4 9XF | Rothersthorpe Lock 12 | ▲ | ◁ | |
| | SP 726574 | NN4 9XF | Rothersthorpe Bottom Lock 13 | ▲ | ◁ | |
| | SP 724581 | NN4 9QT | Wootton Lock 14 | ▲ | ◁ | 2·07 |
| 2 | SP 729591 | NN4 8JX | Hardingstone Lock 15 | ▲ | ◁ | 1·90 |
| | SP 743595 | NN4 8SJ | Hunsbury Lock 16 | ▲ | ◁ | 2·08 |
| | SP 752596 | NN4 8ES | Cotton End Lock 17 | ▲ | ◁ | 1·53 |
| | Grand Union Canal Northampton Arm total rise/fall | | | | | 31·9 |

## Northampton Arm lock details

The locks on the Northampton Arm are standard canal narrow locks:

Length  21·9m (72ft)
Width   2·1m (7ft)

The top gates are all single gates ▲ operated from the towpath side and have ground paddles on each side at the top of the lock.

The bottom gates are all mitre gates ◁ with gate paddles.

In general, the locks are easy to operate, fill and empty without too much delay. Depending boat traffic and potential leakage the pounds between some of the locks can be quite low, but usually passable. The locks nearer the town are fitted with security locks, operated with a Canal and River Trust Watermate Yale key (not all the security locks are in use).

The total rise/fall for the 17 locks is 31·9m giving an average fill depth of 1·88m.

## River Nene locks

| Map | National Grid reference | Postcode | Lock name and number | Upstream | Downstream | Rise/fall (metres) |
|---|---|---|---|---|---|---|
| 3 | SP 758599 | NN1 1HF | Northampton Lock 1 | ◁ | ◁ | 1·22 |
| 3 | SP 777593 | NN4 7YB | Rush Mills Lock 2 | ◁ | ◁ | 1·57 |
| 3 | SP 780597 | NN1 5RN | Abington Lock 3 | ◁ | ◁ | 1·01 |
| 3 | SP 792604 | NN3 9HZ | Weston Favell Lock 4 | ◁ | ☐ | 1·17 |
| 4 | SP 804606 | NN7 1AL | Clifford Hill Lock 5 | ◁ | ☐ | 1·02 |
| 4 | SP 812610 | NN7 1NH | Billing Lock 6 | ◁ | ☐ | 1·27 |
| 4 | SP 831613 | NN7 1NA | Cogenhoe Lock 7 | ◁ | ☐ | 1·35 |
| 5 | SP 846617 | NN6 0EP | Whiston Lock 8 | ◁ | ☐ | 1·08 |
| 5 | SP 857620 | NN7 1NP | White Mills Lock 9 | ◁ | ☐ | 1·37 |
| 5 | SP 867627 | NN29 7TD | Earls Barton Lock 10 | ◁ | ☐ | 1·42 |
| 5 | SP 875636 | NN29 7TD | Doddington Lock 11 | ◁ | ☐ | 1·24 |
| 6 | SP 888645 | NN29 7PF | Wollaston Lock 12 | ◁ | ☐ | 1·76 |
| 6 | SP 899662 | NN8 2ED | Upper Wellingborough Lock 13 | ◁ | ◁ | 1·61 |
| 6 | SP 909671 | NN8 1RJ | Lower Wellingborough Lock 14 | ◁ | ◁ | 0·81 |
| 7 | SP 932682 | NN9 5PN | Ditchford Lock 15 | ◁ | radial | 1·81 |
| 7 | SP 955700 | NN9 5QQ | Higham Ferrers Lock 16 | ◁ | ◁ | 1·47 |
| 8 | SP9 60714 | NN9 5QF | Irthlingborough Lock 17 | ◁ | ☐ | 2·36 |
| 8 | SP 967744 | NN14 4DT | Upper Ringstead Lock 18 | ◁ | ☐ | 0·60 |
| 8 | SP 973751 | NN14 4DU | Lower Ringstead Lock 19 | ◁ | ☐ | 1·26 |
| 9 | SP 980769 | NN14 4JB | Woodford Lock 20 | ◁ | ☐ | 0·89 |
| 9 | SP 992769 | NN14 4EH | Denford Lock 21 | ◁ | ☐ | 1·15 |
| 9 | SP 991791 | NN14 3JN | Islip Lock 22 | ◁ | ☐ | 1·34 |
| 10 | TL 014809 | NN14 3ED | Titchmarsh Lock 23 | ◁ | ☐ | 1·87 |
| 10 | TL 011832 | PE8 5ST | Wadenhoe Lock 24 | ◁ | ☐ | 1·49 |
| 11 | TL 025837 | PE8 5SG | Lilford Lock 25 | ◁ | ☐ | 1·23 |
| 11 | TL 037869 | PE8 5PB | Upper Barnwell Lock 26 | ◁ | ☐ | 0·78 |
| 11 | TL 041873 | PE8 4DN | Lower Barnwell Lock 27 | ◁ | ☐ | 1·11 |

## River Nene locks (continued)

| Map | National Grid reference | Postcode | Lock name and number | Upstream | Downstream | Rise/fall (metres) |
|---|---|---|---|---|---|---|
| 12 | TL 053877 | PE8 5LB | Ashton Lock 28 | ◁ | ☐ | 1·30 |
| | TL 046902 | PE8 5HH | Cotterstock Lock 29 | ◁ | ☐ | 1·61 |
| 13 | TL 044922 | PE8 5HU | Perio Lock 30 | ◁ | ☐ | 1·06 |
| | TL 072920 | PE8 6TJ | Warmington Lock 31 | ◁ | ☐ | 1·76 |
| | TL 083939 | PE8 6RG | Elton Lock 32 | ◁ | ☐ | 1·73 |
| 14 | TL 074972 | PE8 6JX | Yarwell Lock 33 | ◁ | ☐ | 2·07 |
| | TL 074982 | PE8 6JT | Wansford Lock 34 | ◁ | ☐ | 1·45 |
| 15 | TL 109973 | PE8 6LY | Water Newton Lock 35 | ◁ | ☐ | 1·51 |
| | TL 130963 | PE7 3UZ | Alwalton Lock 36 | ◁ | ☐ | 1·85 |
| 16 | TL 165972 | PE2 7DZ | Orton Lock 37 | ◁ | ☐ | 1·24 |
| 18 | TL 271992 | PE6 0RW | Dog-in-a-Doublet Lock 38 | ◁ | ☐ | Tidal |
| | River Nene (Northampton to The Wash) total rise/fall | | | | | 51 |
| | Gayton Junction to The Wash total rise/fall | | | | | 83 |

## River Nene lock details

The locks on the River Nene are interesting and sometimes challenging, the lock chambers are a standard size along the river:

Length 23·7m (78ft)

Width 3·9m (13ft)

All 38 locks have a pair of steel mitre gates ◁ at the upstream end fitted with low-geared gate paddles.

There is a variety of downstream gates:
- 6 locks with a pair of mitre gates ◁◁
- 31 locks with a vertical (guillotine) gate ☐. Six of these locks have manual wheels to lift and lower the vertical gates ☐
- 1 lock with a radial lifting gate

An EA *Abloy* navigation key is required to operate all powered and manual vertical gates.

Several Nene locks have heavy gates and paddles that require numerous turns to raise and lower. The manual hand wheel locks are well balanced but still require some physical exertion to operate. Despite this the locks are usually in scenic surroundings and make the effort worthwhile!

The total rise/fall for the 38 locks from Northampton to Dog-in-a-Doublet is 51m giving an average fill depth of 1·34m.

# Low bridges and structures

Bridges and lock structures with a headroom less than 2·7 metres at normal river levels. Inverted gauge boards before, and at, bridges will give a more accurate headroom figure when levels fluctuate.

| Map | Grid reference | Postcode | Bridge name | Headroom (metres) | |
|---|---|---|---|---|---|
| 4 | SP 805607 | NN7 1AL | Clifford Hill Lock Bridge | 2·65 | |
| | SP 814610 | NN7 1NH | Billing Causeway Bridge | 2·40 | |
| | SP 824611 | NN7 1NR | Glebe Way Field Bridge | 2·60 | |
| 5 | SP 851619 | NN6 0RB | Whiston Farm Bridge | 2·60 | |
| | SP 876636 | NN29 7TD | Doddington Lock | 2·50 | |
| | SP 876637 | NN29 7TD | Hardwater Road Bridge | 2·40 | |
| | SP 880641 | NN29 7TE | Doddington Footbridge | 2·30 | |
| 6 | SP 901665 | NN8 2EA | Mills Road Bridge | 2·30 | |
| 7 | SP 933683 | NN9 5PN | Ditchford Lock | 2·50 | |
| | SP 955698 | NN10 8NP | Kings Meadow Lane Bridge | 2·60 | |
| | SP 956706 | NN9 5QF | Ithlingborough Bridge | 2·90 | use largest arch and beware sharp turn |
| 8 | SP 968723 | NN9 6TQ | Stanwick Lakes Footbridge | 2·50 | |
| 9 | SP 981769 | NN14 4JB | Woodford Lock | 2·65 | |
| | SP 781769 | NN14 4JB | Woodford Old Rail Bridge | 2·60 | |
| | SP 992792 | NN14 4EH | Denford Farm Bridge | 2·60 | |
| 10 | SP 997799 | NN14 3EN | Mill Lakes footbridge | 2·40 | |
| | SP 020814 | NN14 3NZ | Thorpe Road Bridge | 2·60 | |
| | TL 016831 | PE8 5SN | Achurch Footbridge | 2·60 | |
| 11 | TL 038870 | PE8 5PB | Barnwell Rd Bridge | 2·20 | |
| 12 | TL 053887 | PE8 5LB | Ashton Lock | 2·60 | |
| | TL 053887 | PE8 5LB | Ashton Lock Footbridge | 2·65 | |
| | TL 050881 | PE8 4HN | Ashton Footbridge | 2·50 | |
| | TL 046902 | PE8 5HH | Cotterstock Lock | 2·65 | |
| 13 | TL 060930 | PE8 5JA | Fotheringhay Bridge | 2·10 | only 3·9 metres wide |
| | TL 072920 | PE8 6TJ | Warmington Lock | 2·45 | |
| 14 | TL 084949 | PE8 6RJ | Duck Street Footbridge | 2·60 | |
| | TL 072962 | PE8 6QB | Wilgar Bridge | 2·60 | |
| | TL 075973 | PE8 6JX | Yarwell Lock | 2·40 | |
| 17 | TL 189981 | PE2 9NR | Peterborough Rail Bridge | 2·50 | |

# Locks, dimensions, distances and estimated times

## Number of locks

| | Gayton Junction | Northampton Junction | Whiston Lock | Wellingborough Embank | Upper Ringstead Lock | Thrapston Bridge | Upper Barnwell Lock | Fotheringhay Bridge | Wansford Station | Peterborough Embank | Dog-in-a-Doublet Lock |
|---|---|---|---|---|---|---|---|---|---|---|---|
| Dog-in-a-Doublet Lock | 55 | 38 | 30 | 25 | 20 | 17 | 12 | 8 | 4 | 1 | |
| Peterborough Embank | 54 | 37 | 29 | 24 | 19 | 16 | 11 | 7 | 3 | | 1 |
| Wansford Station | 51 | 34 | 26 | 21 | 16 | 13 | 8 | 4 | | 3 | 4 |
| Fotheringhay Bridge | 47 | 30 | 22 | 17 | 12 | 9 | 4 | | 4 | 7 | 8 |
| Upper Barnwell Lock | 43 | 26 | 18 | 13 | 8 | 5 | | 4 | 8 | 11 | 12 |
| Thrapston Bridge | 38 | 21 | 13 | 8 | 3 | | 5 | 9 | 13 | 16 | 17 |
| Upper Ringstead Lock | 35 | 18 | 10 | 5 | | 3 | 8 | 12 | 16 | 19 | 20 |
| Wellingborough Embank | 30 | 13 | 5 | | 5 | 8 | 13 | 17 | 21 | 24 | 25 |
| Whiston Lock | 25 | 8 | | 5 | 10 | 13 | 18 | 22 | 26 | 29 | 30 |
| Northampton Junction | 17 | | 8 | 13 | 18 | 21 | 26 | 30 | 34 | 37 | 38 |
| Gayton Junction | | 17 | 25 | 30 | 35 | 38 | 43 | 47 | 51 | 54 | 55 |

## Lock dimensions

| | Grand Union Canal Northampton Arm | River Nene Northampton to Peterborough | River Nene Peterborough to Wisbech | River Nene Wisbech to The Wash |
|---|---|---|---|---|
| Distance | 4.8 miles | 57.3 miles | 19.3 miles | 11.4 miles |
| Length | 21.9m | 23.7m | 39.6m | 79.2m |
| Beam | 2.1m | 3.9m | 6.1m | 12.2m |
| Draught | 0.8m | 1.2m | 1.9m | 5.1m |
| Headroom | 2.1m | 2.1m | 2.1 | unlimited |
| Locks | 17 | 37 | 1 | 0 |

## Distance in miles

| | Gayton Junction | Northampton Junction | Whiston Lock | Wellingborough Embank | Upper Ringstead Lock | Thrapston Bridge | Upper Barnwell Lock | Fotheringhay Bridge | Wansford Station | Peterborough Embank | Dog-in-a-Doublet Lock |
|---|---|---|---|---|---|---|---|---|---|---|---|
| Dog-in-a-Doublet Lock | 70 | 65.1 | 57.9 | 52.4 | 44.5 | 39.6 | 30.8 | 22.9 | 14.9 | 6.1 | |
| Peterborough Embank | 63.8 | 59 | 51.8 | 46.3 | 38.4 | 33.5 | 24.7 | 16.8 | 8.8 | | 6.1 |
| Wansford Station | 55 | 50.2 | 43 | 37.5 | 29.6 | 24.7 | 15.9 | 8 | | 8.8 | 14.9 |
| Fotheringhay Bridge | 47 | 42.2 | 35 | 29.5 | 21.6 | 16.7 | 7.9 | | 8 | 16.8 | 22.9 |
| Upper Barnwell Lock | 39.1 | 34.3 | 27.1 | 21.6 | 13.7 | 8.8 | | 7.9 | 15.9 | 24.7 | 30.8 |
| Thrapston Bridge | 30.3 | 25.5 | 18.3 | 12.8 | 4.9 | | 8.8 | 16.7 | 24.7 | 33.5 | 39.6 |
| Upper Ringstead Lock | 25.4 | 20.6 | 13.4 | 7.9 | | 4.9 | 13.7 | 21.6 | 29.6 | 38.4 | 44.5 |
| Wellingborough Embank | 17.5 | 12.7 | 5.5 | | 7.9 | 12.8 | 21.6 | 29.5 | 37.5 | 46.3 | 52.4 |
| Whiston Lock | 12 | 7.2 | | 5.5 | 13.4 | 18.3 | 27.1 | 35 | 43 | 51.8 | 57.9 |
| Northampton Junction | 4.8 | | 7.2 | 12.7 | 20.6 | 25.5 | 34.3 | 42.2 | 50.2 | 59 | 65.1 |
| Gayton Junction | | 4.8 | 12 | 17.5 | 25.4 | 30.3 | 39.1 | 47 | 55 | 63.8 | 70 |

## Estimated times (hours)

| | Gayton Junction | Northampton Junction | Whiston Lock | Wellingborough Embank | Upper Ringstead Lock | Thrapston Bridge | Upper Barnwell Lock | Fotheringhay Bridge | Wansford Station | Peterborough Embank | Dog-in-a-Doublet Lock |
|---|---|---|---|---|---|---|---|---|---|---|---|
| Dog-in-a-Doublet Lock | 36 | 30.8 | 25.8 | 22.3 | 18.4 | 16.1 | 12.1 | 8.8 | 5.2 | 1.7 | |
| Peterborough Embank | 33.9 | 29.1 | 24.1 | 20.6 | 16.7 | 14.4 | 10.4 | 7.1 | 3.5 | | 1.7 |
| Wansford Station | 30.4 | 25.6 | 20.6 | 17.1 | 13.2 | 10.9 | 6.9 | 3.6 | | 3.5 | 5.2 |
| Fotheringhay Bridge | 26.8 | 22 | 17 | 13.5 | 9.6 | 7.3 | 3.3 | | 3.6 | 7.1 | 8.8 |
| Upper Barnwell Lock | 23.5 | 18.7 | 13.7 | 10.2 | 6.3 | 4 | | 3.3 | 6.9 | 10.4 | 12.1 |
| Thrapston Bridge | 19.5 | 14.7 | 9.7 | 6.2 | 2.3 | | 4 | 7.3 | 10.9 | 14.4 | 16.1 |
| Upper Ringstead Lock | 17.2 | 12.4 | 7.4 | 3.9 | | 2.3 | 6.3 | 9.6 | 13.2 | 16.7 | 18.4 |
| Wellingborough Embank | 13.3 | 8.5 | 3.5 | | 3.9 | 6.2 | 10.2 | 13.5 | 17.1 | 20.6 | 22.3 |
| Whiston Lock | 9.8 | 5 | | 3.5 | 7.4 | 9.7 | 13.7 | 17 | 20.6 | 24.1 | 25.8 |
| Northampton Junction | 4.8 | | 5 | 8.5 | 12.4 | 14.7 | 18.7 | 22 | 25.6 | 29.1 | 30.8 |
| Gayton Junction | | 4.8 | 9.8 | 13.3 | 17.2 | 19.5 | 23.5 | 26.8 | 30.4 | 33.9 | 36 |

# Useful contacts and links

This is not intended as a complete list of potential contacts or organisations. It merely provides a personal list of key contacts that we have found useful when cruising on the River Nene and compiling this guide.

## Navigation Authorities

**Canal and River Trust, Milton Keynes**
☎ 0303 0404040 *incident report line*

**Environment Agency Incident Control**
☎ 0800 80 70 60  *24-hour service*

**Environment Agency National Enquiries**
☎ 03708 506506

**River Nene EA Inspectors:**
Northampton to Lower Ringstead
☎ 07760 422263
Woodford to Peterborough
☎ 07920 087741

**Dog-in-a-Doublet Lock, tidal passage**
☎ 01733 202219 or 07384 249151

**Port of Wisbech, Wisbech**
☎ 01945 588059
☎ 01406 351530

**Port of Sutton Bridge**
☎ 01406 351133

**Flood line**
☎ 0845 9881188
*Quick dial* 032112

**Middle Level Commissioners**
☎ 01354 653232

**Stanground Lock-keeper**
☎ 07824 600470

## Slipways

**Billing Marina**
☎ 01604 408181

**Middle Nene Cruising Club**
(club members)
☎ 07795 124020

**Northampton Boat Club** (club members)
☎ 07505 127163

**Oundle Marina Village**
☎ 01832 272762

**Peterborough City Council**
*(Public Slipway)*
☎ 01733 863775

**Peterborough Cruising Club**
(club members)
☎ 07759 034764

**Peterborough Yacht Club**
(club members)
☎ 01733 231170

## Navigation key and visitor licence agents

**Northampton Marina**
☎ 01604 604344

**Peterborough Visitor Information Centre**
☎ 01733 863775

**Yarwell Mill Leisure Parks Estates**
☎ 01780 782344

**Dog-in-a-Doublet Lock Keeper**
☎ 01733 202219

## Marina services

| | |
|---|---|
| Gayton Marina | ☎ 01604 858685 |
| Northampton Marina | ☎ 01604 604344 |
| | ☎ 07867 580129 |
| Billing Marina | ☎ 01604 408181 |
| White Mills Marina | ☎ 01604 812057 |
| Blackthorn Marina | ☎ 07985 181358 |
| Willy Watt Marina | ☎ 01933 622038 |
| Lilford Lodge Marina | ☎ 01832 272230 |
| Oundle Marina Village | ☎ 01832 272762 |
| Stibbington Boatyard | ☎ 07850 218364 |
| Sibson Marina | ☎ 07544 636844 |

## River Nene Boat Clubs and Friends

Please check boat club websites for latest telephone numbers, as officers and numbers frequently change

**Association of Nene River Clubs**
www.anrc.org.uk

**Barnwell Boat Club**
www.barnwellboatclub.co.uk

**Elton Boat Club**
www.eltonboatclub.co.uk

**Friends of the River Nene**
www.friendsoftherivernene.co.uk

**Middle Nene Cruising Club**
www.middle-nene-cc.co.uk

**Northampton Boat Club**
www.northamptonboatclub.org

**Oundle Cruising Club**
www.oundlecruisingclub.co.uk

**Peterborough Cruising Club**
07885 483464

**Peterborough Yacht Club**
www.pycnew.weebly.com

## Other marine services

**Nene Valley Boats**
01832 272585
www.nenevalleyboats.co.uk

**Nene Marine**
07539 228258
www.nenemarine.co.uk

**River Canal Rescue**
01785 785680
www.rivercanalrescue.co.uk

## Tourist and visitor information

**East Northamptonshire Council, Oundle**
01832 274333
www.east-northamptonshire.gov.uk/visitors

**Northampton TIC**
01604 367997
www.visitnorthamptonshire.co.uk

**Peterborough TIC**
01733 452336
www.visitpeterborough.com

**Northamptonshire County Council**
0300 126 1000
www3.northamptonshire.gov.uk/

**Peterborough City Council**
01733 863775
www.peterborough.gov.uk

**Stanwick Lakes**
01933 625522
www.stanwicklakes.org.uk

**Nenescape Landscape Partnership Scheme**
01536 526451
www.nenescape.org

**NeneValley**
01832 742064
www.nenevalley.net

**Nene Valley Railway**
01780 784444
www.nvr.org.uk

**Wildlife Trust for Beds Cambs & Northants**
1604 405285
www.wildlifebcn.org

## Other organisations and services

**British Canoeing**
www.britishcanoeing.org.uk

**Inland Waterways Association**
www.waterways.org.uk

**National Association of Boatowners**
www.nabo.org.uk

**Canal Planner AC**
www.canalplan.org.uk

**Waterway Routes**
www.waterwayroutes.co.uk

**Jim Shead's waterways information**
www.jim-shead.com

# Key partners

## Environment Agency

The Environment Agency (EA) has responsibility for navigation on the River Nene. The agency is involved as partners in Nenescape Landscape Partnership Scheme and liaison with landowners and organisations with interests in developing the Nene Valley for residents, visitors and particularly river users.

Northampton marina website www.northamptonmarina.co.uk is the gateway for boaters to access information about EA activities:

- Navigation keys and visitor registration
- Handy guide for facilities on the River Nene
- Information for boaters – emergency and planned closures
- Sign-up for Strong Stream Advice (SSA)
- The Boater's Handbook

## Friends of the River Nene

Friends of the River Nene (FOTRN) was established in September 2014 by a group of enthusiastic boaters looking to improve facilities on the River Nene. Membership has grown significantly to over 600 members. The main improvements include the establishment and maintenance of 10 overnight bankside moorings for members. This is a real bonus for river users as previously mooring spots were scarce or almost non existent in many places. A *Moorings* booklet has recently been sent out to members providing useful information regarding location and access to local services. FOTRN also provides useful information and advice for boaters, including a separate tab for canoeists at www.friendsoftherivernene.co.uk

## Wildlife Trust for Bedfordshire, Cambridgeshire and Northamptonshire

A local wildlife charity supported by over 1000 volunteers and over 36,000 members that protects and cares for wildlife and wild places across Bedfordshire, Cambridgeshire and Northamptonshire. The trust manages most of their reserves in the Nene Valley with a key focus on 'Living Landscapes' that connect these smaller sites together in a bigger, more joined up area helping wildlife to move freely through the countryside without barriers.
www.wildlifebcn.org

## Nenescape

This National Lottery Heritage funded project in partnership with the Environment Agency will bring together groups from along the River Nene between Northampton and Peterborough to celebrate, protect and conserve the natural and built heritage of the landscape. The River Nene Regional Park is leading the project in partnership with a wide range of organisations.

The river valley has hidden gems – ancient mill sites, wintering bird habitats, nationally important Roman archaeology and buzzing wildflower meadows to name a few – but this special and underappreciated collection is under threat from fast population growth. There are, however, many passionate organisations and individuals in the area working to look after the landscape and Nenescape will support their projects by increasing access into the landscape, sharing skills and knowledge across partners and ensuring that the river is resilient to increasing visitor numbers.

## nenevalley.net

'*Commanding some of Britain's most spectacular views and stunning landscapes, the impressive Nene Valley is an oasis of tranquillity with exciting opportunities for new outdoor experiences*'

www.nenevalley.net is an excellent website developed by the Environment Agency as part of their 'Enabling Access from Waterway to Land' project which aims to improve physical access onto the river, as well as increase the information available to boaters and other visitors to the area.

The website also provides lots of information about Nene-based activities and opportunities with downloadable maps and leaflets for those wanting to explore deeper into the Nene Valley, including:

*Wildlife* Nature reserves and parks within reach of the river

*Adventure* Visitor attractions, boating, cycling, fishing and walking

*Places to visit* Arts, market towns, museums and historic houses

*Food and drink* Local food and drink, restaurants, tea rooms and farmers' markets

Northampton Arm near M1

# 1

# GRAND UNION CANAL NORTHAMPTON ARM

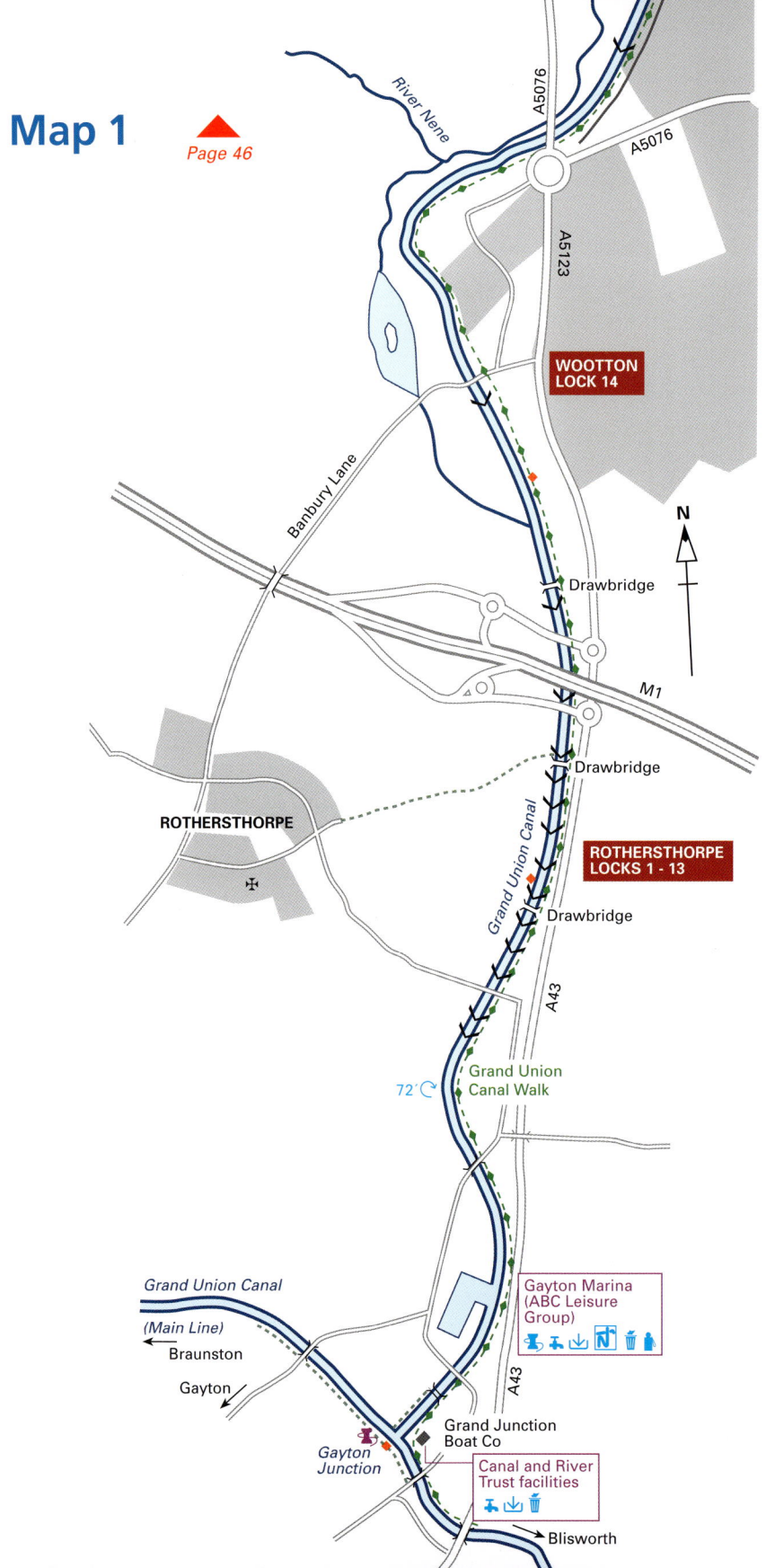

# Map 1

## Gayton Junction to Wootton Lock 14

*Grand Union Canal Northampton Arm*

| Map 1  Gayton Junction (GR 719550) to Wootton Lock 14  (GR 724581) | | | | | | | | | | | | | | | | | | | |
|---|---|---|---|---|---|---|---|---|---|---|---|---|---|---|---|---|---|---|---|
| Location | Miles | Locks | Lock type | | Est. time hours | Bridge < 2.7m | Moorings and facilities | | | | | | | Victualling | | | | | Canoe |
| | | | | | | | 48hr | Long stay | Water point | CDP | Pumpout | Refuse | Diesel | Shops | Pub | Café | PO or Bank | Portage | Park & access |
| Gayton Junction | 0·0 | 0 | | | 0·0 | | ♨ | | 🚰 | ⤓ | | 🗑 | | | | | | | |
| Gayton Marina | 0·2 | 0 | | | 0·0 | | ♨ | ♨ | 🚰 | ⤓ | ⛽ | 🗑 | 🛢 | | | | | | |
| Rothersthorpe Top Lock 1 | 0·5 | 1 | ▲ | ◁ | 0·3 | | | | | | | | | | | ☕ | Milton Malsor | | |
| Rothersthorpe Lock 6 | 0·3 | 5 | ▲ | ◁ | 1·2 | | | | | | | | | | | | | | |
| Rothersthorpe Lock 10 | 0·2 | 4 | ▲ | ◁ | 0·9 | | | | | | | | | | | | | | |
| Rothersthorpe Lock 11 | 0·1 | 1 | ▲ | ◁ | 0·2 | | | | | | | | | | | | | | |
| M1 crossing below Lock 12 | 0·1 | 0 | ▲ | ◁ | 0·0 | | | | | | | | | | | | | | |
| Rothersthorpe Bottom Lock 13 | 0·2 | 2 | ▲ | ◁ | 0·5 | | | | | | | | | | | | | | |
| Wootton Lock 14 | 0·4 | 1 | ▲ | ◁ | 0·3 | | | | | | | | | | | | | | |
| **Map 1 totals** | **2·0** | **14** | | | **2·5** | | | | | | | | | | | | | | |

THE RIVER NENE

## Navigation notes

The Northampton Arm of the Grand Union Canal was opened in 1815. It created a key link between the River Nene, which first became navigable as far as Peterborough in 1761, and the main canal network. The original plan was to dig a canal directly from Leicester to Northampton but costs and engineering difficulties meant that the original idea was abandoned. In 1805 a railway was built to link the Grand Union main line with Northampton. In 1815 the Northampton Arm replaced the railway, the track bed provides much of the towpath. Presumably it must have been cost, but why build the Arm to narrow beam dimensions when the canal main line and the River Nene navigation were able to accommodate wide beam craft?

The navigation from the Grand Union Canal to Cotton End Lock measures 4.7 miles with a rise/fall of 39 metres. Gayton Junction is 92 miles from the sea and 58 metres above sea level.

The arm leaves the Grand Union Main Line at Gayton Junction. A towpath follows the west bank as far as Arm End bridge, where the path crosses the canal to then follow the right bank; as the canal continues north-east to run close to the A43 trunk road. After 0·2 miles **Gayton Marina** is reached after which the canal turns again, moving away from the A43 where it is crossed by a second minor road, at Sandlanding bridge.

**Rothersthorpe Locks** are viewed by many as a gateway, either into the Anglian region waterways or out on to the canal system. Whichever way you are travelling 'The Arm' and particularly the Rothersthorpe flight provide that element of excitement and anticipation regarding what lies ahead. There are 13 locks in the Rothersthorpe flight, between them climbing/falling 24 metres within 1·6 miles.

**Rothersthorpe Top Lock 1** soon comes into view around the next bend just after a full-length winding hole. The view from here extends over the

Northampton Arm Bridge

## Moorings and facilities

### Blisworth Marina
Located near Gayton Junction on the opposite side of the canal provides short and long-stay moorings with all facilities.
☎ 01604 858043

### CRT
24hr and 14-day visitor moorings can be found along the towpath near the junction.

### Grand Junction Boat Company
can provide all aspects of service and repair including mechanical, electrical, plumbing, including a crane out facility and chandlery.
☎ 01604 858043

### Gayton Marina
Facilities include: water, pump-out, chemical toilet disposal facilities, overnight and long-term moorings, toilets, showers, recycling facilities, a power hook up, diesel and a hire fleet.
ABC Leisure Group ☎ 01604 858685

### Mooring
Opportunities within the Rothersthorpe lock flight are limited due to short pounds. As the pounds get longer below and above the main flight there are several places where mooring is possible alongside the towpath.

**The Greyhound**, at Milton Malsor, is a traditional English country pub with a restaurant. The pub dates from the 16th century, and forms part of the Milton Malsor Conservation Area ☎ 01604 858449.

Northamptonshire countryside, now being developed on the outskirts along the main arterial routes. Despite this sprawling, and mostly isolated, development there remains a vista of interest and anticipation as the boater looks down the flight as far as the M1 motorway.

These locks are generally easy to use with well-greased paddles and relatively light gates. As the boater descends or ascends there is plenty of interest along the route. Three traditional wooden lift bridges (locked open) add nostalgic thoughts of earlier days when they would have provided key links between villages and farmland.

The condition of the 'arm' has improved considerably during the last few years. The empty pounds between several of the locks and the very narrow, shallow channel encroached by reeds are for now mostly a memory. Thanks for this must go to the **Canal and River Trust** (CRT) for diverting resources to improve this key link between the Anglian waterways and the canal system. Contact them if you do happen to come across an empty pound. Credit must also go to the **Northampton Branch of the Inland Waterways Association** who have also made an important, supportive and innovative contribution, welcomed by transient boaters, walkers and cyclists. The mosaic trail, bridge murals and tidy lock sites all add to the interest and pleasure of the 'arm'. The Northampton branch are often joined by volunteers from commerce and local businesses.

THE RIVER NENE

Northampton Arm Rothersthorpe locks

Several local schools have also been involved in helping to design and construct these environmental improvements.

After the first two locks, the canal is crossed by the Rothersthorpe Road leading to Rothersthorpe village before it runs close again to the A43. The next three Rothersthorpe locks are passed in quick succession before a drawbridge crossing, and then a further five before a second drawbridge crosses the flight.

The M1 slip road to junction 15A passes overhead after lock 11. Lock 12 must be negotiated before the M1 itself crosses near to the Rothersthorpe motorway services area, before the downstream slip road is reached. On a dull day this dingy, large concrete arched bridge creates a somewhat depressing vista. However, the recently painted canal murals underneath the M1 bridge provide much needed interest and welcome colour.

Most boaters have a smug grin when passing under the M1 and its slip roads, particularly when the traffic is stationary, and motorists and lorry drivers look down with envy.

Following **Rothersthorpe Bottom Lock** there is a further drawbridge and the canal turns to the north-west, moving away again from the A5123. Banbury Lane bridge crosses just after **Wootton Lock 14**, already the fourteenth on the navigation and 0·4 miles from Rothersthorpe Bottom Lock. The canal then passes a lake/reservoir on the west bank before curving to the north east. At this point, the River Nene can be seen coming from the northwest to run parallel to the canal for a short distance before both are crossed by the A5123/5076 road bridge. The National Lift Tower and the clock tower of St Crispin's Hospital, both landmarks of Northampton, are visible from the canal path.

**44 THE RIVER NENE**

## Nature reserves and features

Apart from the natural beauty of the canal and the surrounding countryside there are no officially recognised reserves. The hedgerows provide excellent habitats for small birds and mammals. Ducks and the occasional swan enjoy the canal, particularly when boaters provide them with a slalom course when opening paddles.

## Walking and exploring

The **Grand Union Canal Walk** begins its journey at Brentford and wends its way up the towpath through to Birmingham. At Gayton Junction the walk diverts to include the Northampton Arm where it follows the towpath into Northampton.

The towpath is in a good state as it follows the canal down the arm and there are several footpaths available for exploring the villages of Rothersthorpe to the west and **Milton Malsor** to the east.

## Cycling

The towpath is used regularly by leisure cyclists and commuters as a traffic free route in to Northampton and to link up with other routes.

## Canoeing

Due to the number of locks and short pounds 'the arm' is rarely frequented by canoeists or small boats but several sites provide access and parking for launching.

## Local history

**Rothersthorpe** village 13th-century Church of St Peter and St Paul contains a late 16th century pulpit.

**Hunsbury Hill Country Park** can be reached from the towpath immediately after Wooton Lock along a footpath from Banbury Lane Bridge, about 1 mile. A key feature of the park is the Iron Age hill fort dating between the 7th and 4th centuries BC. The deep ditch, which is now overgrown, has survived to the present day. Running beside the fort and through the park is the ancient Banbury Lane drover's road which was used to bring sheep and cattle from Wales to the market at Northampton. In Victorian times the area became an ironstone quarry and a quarry face can still be seen along the southern boundary of the park. The history of this period has been preserved by the Northampton Ironstone Railway Trust.

Mural under M1 bridge

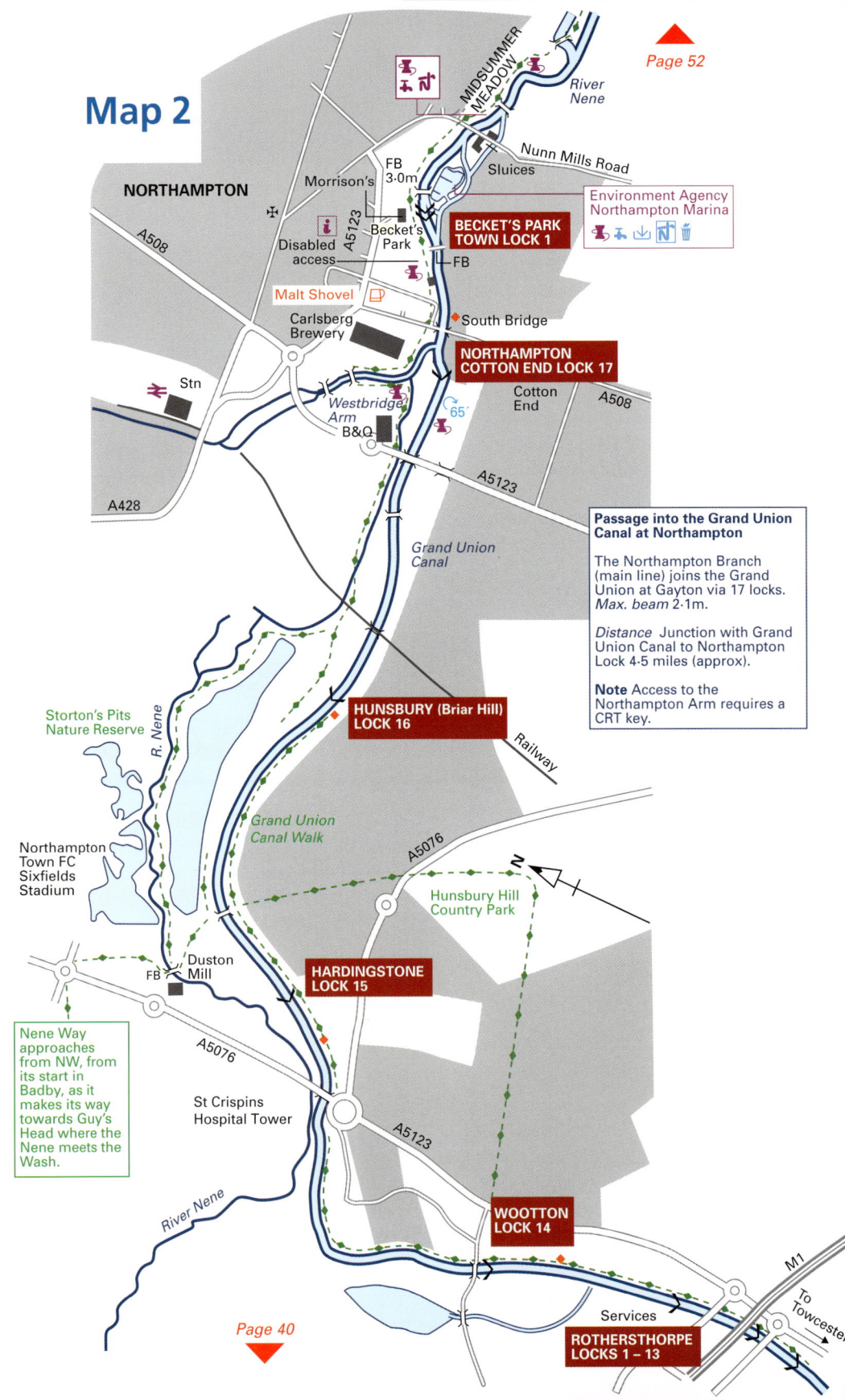

# Map 2

# Wootton Lock to Northampton Junction

*Grand Union Canal Northampton Arm*

**Map 2** Wootton Lock 14 (GR SP 724581) to Northampton Junction (GR SP753597)

| Location | Miles | Locks | Lock type | Est time hours | Bridge < 2·7m | Moorings and facilities |||||| Victualling ||||| Canoe ||
|---|---|---|---|---|---|---|---|---|---|---|---|---|---|---|---|---|---|---|
| | | | | | | 48hr | Long stay | Water point | CDP | Pumpout | Refuse | Diesel | Shops | Pub | Café | PO or Bank | Portage | Park & access |
| Banbury Lane Bridge | 0·0 | 0 | | 0·0 | | | | | | | | | | | | | | |
| Upton Country Park Footbridge | 0·7 | 0 | | 0·2 | | | | | | | | | | | | | | |
| Hardingstone Lock 15 | 0·3 | 1 | ▲ ◁ | 0·3 | | | | | | | | | | | | | | |
| Duston Mill Bridge | 0·3 | 0 | | 0·1 | | | | | | | | | | | | | | |
| Hunsbury Lock 16 | 0·8 | 1 | ▲ ◁ | 0·4 | | | | | | | | | | | | | | |
| Cotton End Mooring | 0·6 | 0 | | 0·1 | | 🍺 | | | | | | | | | | | | |
| Cotton End Lock 17 | 0·0 | 1 | ▲ ◁ | 0·2 | | | | | | | | | 🧺 | | | | | |
| Northampton Junction | 0·1 | 0 | | 0·0 | | 🍺 on Westbridge Arm | | | | | | | | on Badby Arm | | | | 🛶 |
| **Map 2 totals** | **2·8** | **3** | | **1·3** | | | | | | | | | | | | | | |

THE RIVER NENE  47

## Navigation notes

The navigation on the canal, after the A5123/5076 road bridge, is joined by the route of the disused railway line which follows the course of the Grand Union as it turns through **Hardingstone Lock 15**, about one mile from Wootton Lock, where the footpath from Duston Mill (showground and special events site) crosses the canal.

The canal and the adjacent Nene turn east and then southeast to pass by Hunsbury Hill Country Park on the right bank before the canal approaches **Hunsbury Lock 16**, 0.9 miles from Hardingstone Lock, where a footpath crosses the canal to head northeast and join the Nene Way alongside the Nene. Hunsbury Hill Iron Works used the canal at this point for importing iron ore from quarries in the Blisworth area.

Northampton Arm lift bridge

The disused Blisworth to Northampton branch line still runs parallel to the navigation, but the canal and river are next crossed by a second railway line heading northeast to Northampton Station.

The canal then formally joins the River Nene at **Cotton End Lock 17**, 0.6 miles from Hunsbury Lock and just after the A5123 Towcester Road bridge crosses. Note that there is a change of navigation authority at this point from CRT to EA, which means a new lock key is required. The Grand Union Canal therefore connects the River Nene and its onward connections to the Midlands waterway network and in turn links that network to the Wash. The absolute upstream limit of the river navigation lies at West Bridge in Northampton Town. The maximum beam width for the Grand Union Canal is 7ft.

The upper reaches of the Nene flow north to **Duston Mill**, where it is crossed by the footpath leading to the mill. Duston Mill reservoir, a balancing reservoir built to accommodate surface water drainage from new development to the west of Northampton and designed to be used for water-based leisure activities is located here, on the right bank, adjacent to **Storton's Pits Nature Reserve**, which can be crossed on foot.

The Nene then turns east past the Sixfields Stadium, home of Northampton Town FC and is now accompanied in its journey by the Nene Way long distance footpath.

The river joins the Grand Union Canal and forms the Nene navigation downstream of Cotton End Lock where there is also a connection to the Westbridge Arm of the river. The northern and western branches of the

## Moorings and facilities

Overnight mooring is possible in several places between Hunsbury lock and Cotton End Lock. There is a winding hole just before Cotton End lock.

There are moorings alongside B&Q on the Westbridge Arm to the left of Northampton Junction – however they are often taken up by non-continuous cruisers!

Town Quay moorings, near the yellow footbridge, provide good access to Morrison's (200m) and town centre services.

> If you are unable to wait for **Morrisons** or other town centre shops there is a **Co-op** food shop and a fish and chip shop quite close to the canal on St Leonard's Road, Briar Hill

Nene unite in the southwestern suburbs of Northampton just above the Town Bridge and almost opposite the junction with the Grand Union Canal.

## Nature reserves and features

**Storton's Pits** is a 22-hectare Local Nature Reserve managed by the Wildlife Trust for Bedfordshire, Cambridgeshire and Northamptonshire. This site on the bank of the River Nene has old gravel pits, meadow and fen ditch. Around 350 invertebrate species have been recorded, including some which are rare. Water birds include snipe, teal, tufted duck and the uncommon water rail. There is access from Edgar Mobbs Way.

**Duston Mill Meadow** is adjacent to the north-west corner of Storton's Pits reserve. It is important for dragonflies and butterflies.

## Walking and exploring

**The Grand Union Canal Walk** continues along the towpath following the route of the Northampton to Blisworth branch line as it approaches the end of the 'arm'.

**The Nene Way,** established by Northamptonshire County Council, runs near the Nene for 70 miles from Badby, near Daventry. From Dunston Mill it follows the river Nene on its right bank as it turns southeast and, then south, as the footpath from Hunsbury Lock links with the Nene Way. The Nene Way then crosses the Nene to run on the left bank.

## Cycling

The towpath continues to provide a key route as it approaches the town.

## Canoeing

**St James Mill Road, Northampton**
GR: SP 748597 provides free on street parking with access to the Badby Arm of the Nene down a walk/cycle way down to the river. Paddling downstream you reach the Naseby Arm of the Nene and Carlsberg Brewery opposite the junction with the canal arm.

THE RIVER NENE 49

Northampton Arm Mosaic

## Local history

People have lived in **Northampton** for over 5,000 years and excavation at Briar Hill in the late 1970s found a large circular earthwork enclosure, where Neolithic farmers held tribal ceremonies. By 1800 BC the Nene Valley from here was an important trade route.

Overlooking the town is **Hunsbury Hill**, whose name derives from 'bury' a fortified place and 'Hun' the name of a tribal leader, now partly covered by a modern housing development and Hunsbury Hill Country park. Hunsbury thrived under the Danes and became an important commercial centre.

The Nene was, in former times, very important for the transport of grain and, close to the South Bridge, still stands Latimer's and Crick's Grain Store, which has now been converted into flats. Soon after the river became navigable up to Northampton dozens of barges began to transport coal, grain and general goods.

In 1998 areas of the town and St James and Far Cotton, were seriously affected by flooding and a scheme by the Environment Agency to provide an improved level of protection for these areas to a one in 200 year return period (0·5% chance of flooding each year) was subsequently completed, which included channel widening up and downstream of the South Bridge, and realignment of the bank opposite the Carlsberg Brewery, so that the northern arch of the South Bridge has an unobstructed entry.

# 2

# NORTHAMPTON TO WELLINGBOROUGH

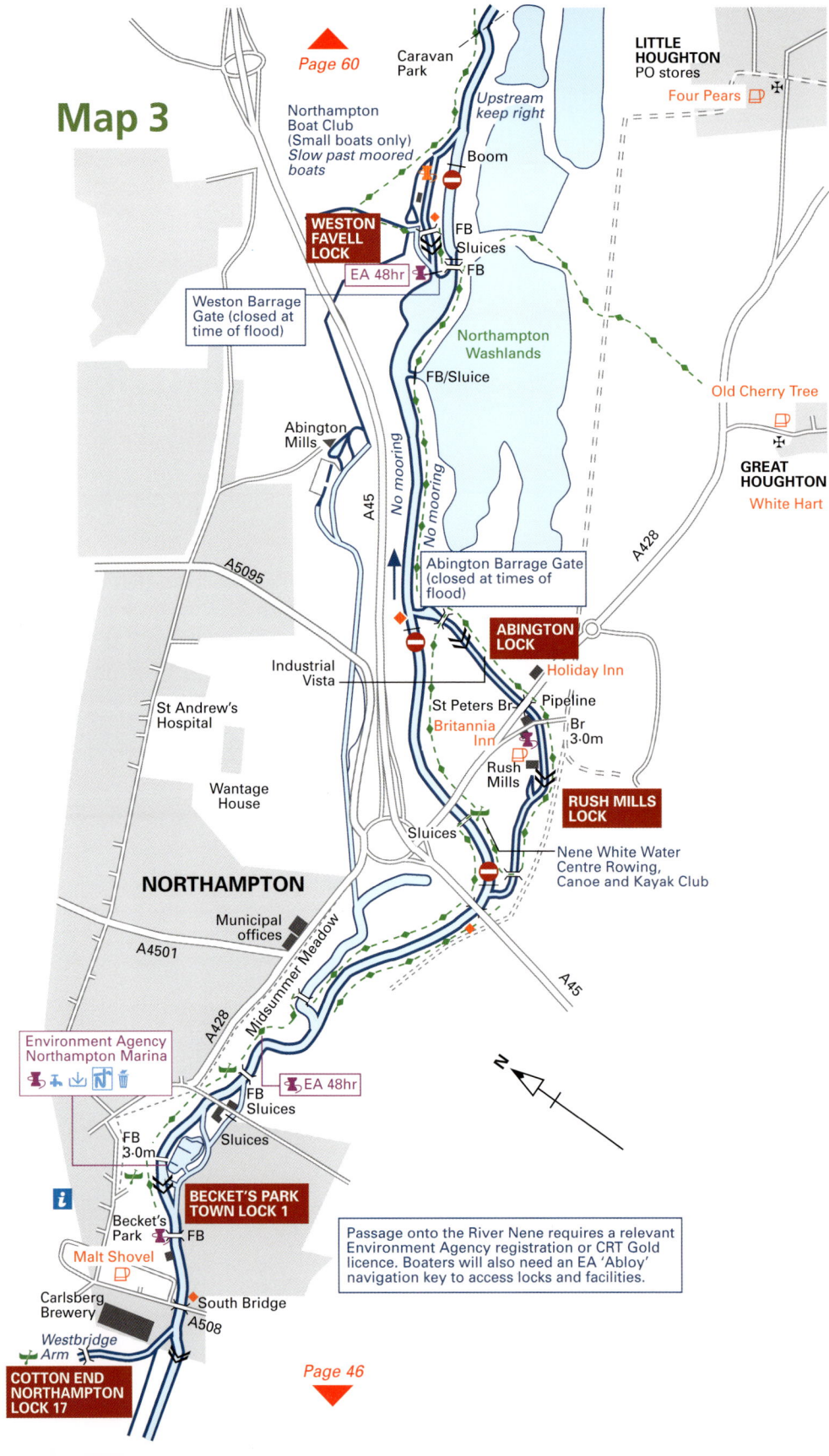

# Map 3

## Northampton Junction to Northampton Boat Club

| Location | Miles | Locks | Lock type | Est. time hours | Bridge < 2.7m | Moorings and facilities | | | | | | Victualling | | | | Canoe | |
|---|---|---|---|---|---|---|---|---|---|---|---|---|---|---|---|---|---|
| | | | | | | 48hr | Long stay | Water point | CDP | Pumpout | Refuse | Diesel | Shops | Pub | Café | PO or Bank | Portage | Park & access |
| Town Quay Moorings | 0·4 | 0 | | 0·1 | | 48hr | | | | | | | Shops | Pub | Café | £ | | |
| Northampton EA Marina | 0·1 | 0 | | 0·0 | | 48hr | Long stay | Water point | CDP | Pumpout | | | Shops | Pub | Café | £ | | |
| Northampton Lock 1 Becket's Park | 0·1 | 1 | ◁◁ | 0·4 | | | | | | | | | | | | | ▲▼ | ✿ |
| Midsummer Meadow EA | 0·5 | 0 | | 0·2 | | 48hr | | | | | | | | | | | | ✿ |
| Rush Mills Lock 2 | 0·8 | 1 | ◁◁ | 0·6 | | | | | | | | | | Pub | Café | | ▲▼ | ✿ |
| Abington Lock 3 | 0·4 | 1 | ◁◁ | 0·5 | | | | | | | | | | | | | ▲▼ | ✿ |
| Weston Favell EA mooring | 1·0 | 0 | | 0·3 | | 48hr | | Weston Favell shopping centre | | | | | | | | | | |
| Weston Favell Lock 4 | 0·2 | 1 | ☐ | 0·4 | | | | at Great Houghton | | | | | | Pub | Café | | ▲▼ | |
| Northampton Boat Club | 0·1 | 0 | | 0·0 | | 48hr | | Water point | CDP | permission required for use of facilities | | | | | | | | |
| **Map 3 totals** | **3·5** | **4** | | **2·5** | | | | | | | | | | | | | | |

THE RIVER NENE 53

## Navigation notes

Once through Northampton Cotton End Lock 17 the boater leaves the narrow Northampton Arm and enters the much wider and, at times livelier, River Nene. Carlsberg Brewery comes into view, immediately on the left bank just before South Bridge. The complex comprises of 8 hectares and looks spectacular when lit at night. The buildings were designed by Danish architect Knud Munk and won the 1975 Financial Times Award for Industrial Architecture.

**South Bridge**, the crossing for the A508, provides a splendid welcome to Northampton. It was built in 1818, widened and strengthened later to accommodate trams that ran until 1934. Wathen Wigg footbridge (named after the curate allegedly responsible for establishing Northampton Saints rugby club) crosses the Nene from the embankment to link with the south bank. This was once a thriving commercial centre but has today been redeveloped as can be seen by the modern apartment buildings now constructed here on both banks of the river. This is part of the major regeneration of this part of the town, which includes the former Avon factory complex, which is now the new waterside campus for the University of Northampton.

On the skyline is the 131 metre-high tower built by Express Lifts, in 1982, to test and research new technology. The lift tower became surplus to requirements in 2008, but the tower remains and has been listed. The tower now provides a testing facility, for health and safety equipment and emergency escape system tests. A recent initiative to use the tower as the home of the National Abseiling Centre has played a part in the regeneration of the tower.

**Becket's Park** is on the left bank. Just upstream of it the Nene splits, with the right-hand southern channel looping round the south side of the Marina to rejoin the main channel in three distinct minor channels.

The main Nene passes through **Town Lock No.1** at **Becket's Park**, 0·5 mile from Cotton End Lock 17, which was the last lock to be constructed, in 1761, and the first to be replaced, when the Nene navigation was restored in the 1930s.

A recent addition is curved, rustic steel footbridge that passes over the downstream tail of the lock. It provides pedestrian access between the new university site with the town. I can't help thinking that the builders forgot to paint it!

Becket's Park footbridge

Until April 1969, there was considerable narrow boat traffic on this stretch carrying grain between London and Whitworths' Mill at Little Irchester, Wellingborough. Willow Wren boats *Flamingo* paired with the butty *Beverley* were probably the last pair to make this run.

At **Midsummer Meadow** the Nene channel splits again. The minor left-hand channel here formed part of the original course of the Nene. A footpath crosses Midsummer Meadow to continue across this channel and then along both sides of the main channel, which itself turns southeast and crosses under the A45 road bridge. Once under the A45 road bridge, the Nene divides again. The northern channel is a flood relief channel and there is no entry for powered vessels. **The Nene White Water centre and Rowing Club** use part of the relief channel. The navigation channel turns south and then southeast. The Nene Way footpath joins on the south bank. A bridge and power line cross just upstream of Rush Mills Lock, which is just over a mile from Becket's Park Lock. **Rush Mills lock** has mitre gates at each end.

After the **Britannia Inn** (which offers short term moorings and food), a road bridge crosses the channel, the east bank of which is tree lined while the west has more of an industrial vista. The Nene is then crossed first, by a pipeline and then, just downstream, by the A428 at St Peter's Bridge. Here by the A428 is the **Holiday Inn**.

The Nene Way footpath continues along the east bank as the channel turns north to **Abington Lock**, 0.4 miles from Rush Mills Lock. The two channels of the Nene then rejoin, the navigation having been crossed by a path, at the Abington Barrage Gate, an important flood defence structure, closed at times of flood. The channel then continues in a northeasterly direction. There are warning notices to explain to the nervous boater that sirens will sound, and lights will flash before the barrage gate closes – I bet we are not the only crew to put on a bit more throttle to get through with a little more haste than usual.

Weston Favell mooring

## Moorings and facilities

### Town Quay visitor moorings
Conveniently situated for victualling at Morrisons, a short walk from the moorings. The town centre shops and the Dearngate Theatre are only a 10-minute walk up the hill.

### Northampton Marina
This popular marina provides a warm welcome and ideal first stopover for visiting boats travelling to and from the national canal network.
Its facilities include:

- All berths are on rise and fall, non-slip pontoons and walkways within a secure site
- Residential, permanent and visitor moorings. Winter moorings are popular but subject to availability
- Electricity and drinking water to all mooring berths, security lighting, toilets, washrooms, showers, pump-out and elsan disposal, rubbish collection, laundry, BBQ area with picnic tables and wild flower meadow
- Fully manned site
- Short stay vehicular access and parking for off-loading by boat users
- Long term parking by arrangement with Northampton Borough Council in close by town centre car parks
- Easy access to town centre facilities and attractions
- The marina is well signposted from the river. Full details and current fees online

www.northamptonmarina.co.uk
☏ 01604 604344 or 07867 580129

### Environment Agency 48-hour visitor moorings
incorporating a disabled access platform, can be found on the adjacent Midsummer Meadows, the view from these moorings is a little restricted due to the raised bank. The town centre is about 0·5 miles distant from the Park and is well signposted. Mooring is not permitted between Abington and Weston Favell visitor moorings.

### Environment Agency 48-hour visitor mooring
within the Northampton Washlands. Also doubles up as an emergency mooring when the Washland is being used to store flood water. The moorings are close to the Weston Favell barrage gate, near a split in the river and near to the Environment Agency sign. The mooring pontoon rises and falls with changing water levels.

During times of flood, navigation may be closed by barrage gates near Abington and Weston Favell locks. Lights and sirens give warning that the gates are moving – under no such circumstances should boaters attempt to pass through these gates. If you are within the Washlands you should moor at the emergency/visitor mooring.

### Northampton Boat Club
On Weston Mill Lane this has a limited number of visitor moorings and the club house, situated downstream of the lock, on the left bank, although the slipway is for the use of members only.
☏ 01604 711735

**Northampton** has a good selection of shops, banks, restaurants, hotels, museums and a theatre

**Malt Shovel Tavern**
Bridge Street
☎ 01604 234212
The traditional pub has a wide range of real ales and food is available.

**The Britannia Inn**
Bedford Road (Chef & Brewer) ☎ 01604 630437)
Stands adjacent to Rushmills lock and welcomes boaters for drinks and meals.

**Holiday Inn**
☎ 08704 007214
Next to the river on the A428 near St Peters Bridge.

**Great Houghton** has two pubs:
Old Cherry Tree
☎ 01604 761399
providing drinks and food just off the A428.

**The White Hart**
☎ 01604 762940 provides drinks and food on the High Street.

**Weston Favell shopping centre** on Wellingborough Road is about 1 mile from Weston Favell lock by public footpath. Shops/services include bank, chemist, coffee shop, clothes shop and electrical store. Bus services hourly from here to Northampton.

Northampton Marina

The A45 trunk road runs close to the left bank for a short distance, before turning away to the northwest. The Nene Way continues along the south east bank.

The river widens out past the sluice leading into the flood storage **Northampton Washlands,** on its approach to Weston Favell Lock and then, upstream of the lock, divides again, this time into three channels. There is no entry to the southernmost right-hand channel, with lakes on its right bank, but a footpath leads to **Great Houghton** and north to **Little Houghton**. The navigable channel, the centre of the three, turns east, but Weston Barrage Gate, a flood defence structure, prevents entry in times of flood. The EA floating visitor moorings are to the north of the lock entrance.

**Weston Favell Lock,** 1·1 mile from Abington Lock, comprises an electrically powered vertical gate. The entrance to the Washlands is via Abington Lock with exit via Weston Favell Lock. The Riverside Business Park development lies to the northeast. A footbridge crosses immediately downstream of the lock.

## Nature reserves and features

### Barnes Meadow Nature Reserve
An area of 20 hectares is managed by the Wildlife Trust for Bedfordshire, Cambridgeshire and Northamptonshire. The site includes a stretch of the River Nene, meadows and a redundant arm of the river. There are many dragonflies, grass snakes, grey herons, kingfishers and great crested grebes. GR:SP 770597

### Northampton Washlands Scheme
This controls floodwaters and protects development to the east of Northampton. The Washlands consist of channels and storage lakes and can hold up to 500 million gallons. The area has since become of national importance for large numbers of lapwing, golden plover and other migrating birds and there are footpaths through the lake area.

## Walking and exploring

### The National Abseiling Centre
The Express Lift tower now hosts a permanent abseil that features 'The Big One' 122 metres on the exterior of the building and smaller abseils at 46–61 metres in the interior of the tower. It is popular for charity fundraising and group events.

**Delapre Abbey,** south of the river, from Town Quay, stands the site of one of only two Cluniac monasteries in England. The park, abbey and visitor facilities are open to the public. Check website for opening times and days
www.delapreabbey.org

### Grand Union Canal Walk
Ends at Becket's Park Lock 1.

**The Nene Way** takes over as the prominent long-distance walking route, closely following the course of the river from Northampton to Billing Lock.

There are several local footpaths near Weston Favell that provide routes (around one mile) into the villages of Great and Little Houghton.

## Cycling

### Norbital
An 18-mile circular cycle route that circumnavigates Northampton, passing through residential, commercial and historic vistas, crossing the river close to Rush Mills lock.

### National Cycle Route 6
This route from London to Keswick passes through Northampton and crosses the river via the A45 close to Rush Mills lock.

## Canoeing

**Becket's Park** provides vehicle access, between the tennis courts and Morrisons car park, to Northampton Marina and 30mins parking for unloading. This is an ideal spot for canoe launching from the portage platforms either side of the lock. Cars can park in the multi-storey car park opposite the entrance.

**Midsummer Meadow** pay and display car park has a height restriction of 2·25m and permits overnight parking.

## Local history

**Becket's Park** is named after Thomas à Becket, who was famously Archbishop of Canterbury between 1162–70 and was murdered in Canterbury Cathedral by knights, who saw themselves as carrying out the wishes of Henry II. The problems between King and Archbishop had boiled over, at an earlier stage, at the Council of Clarendon in 1164, held at Northampton, when Becket escaped through a gate in the old town wall, the site situated in the northern corner of Becket's Park.

By the 11th century, **Northampton** was referred to as 'Northhamtun', to distinguish it from 'Southhamtun', to which it was linked by an old route way. 'Hamtun' means homestead.

Northampton was built up on the shoe industry. Leather was important and available, with the Nene Valley providing rich cattle grazing and oak forests for tanning as well as the availability of water in the Nene itself. In 1213 there is the first written record of the footwear industry, a pair of boots being made for King John. By the middle of the 16th century, shoemaking was the largest craft. Between 1800 and 1900 the population increased from 7,000 to 87,000 and by the end of the 19th century, 40% of the adult population was employed in the shoe industry, a figure later reduced due to the availability of imports.

In the middle of the now pedestrianised Abington Street, there is a bronze sculpture of two young children skipping across the tools of the shoemaker's trade.

Following extensive expansion and refurbishment, **Northampton Central Museum and Art Gallery**, on Guildhall Road ☏ 01604 838111 is expected to reopen during 2020 – if you are planning a visit check opening date and times. The museum contains the world's biggest boot and shoe collection. The local football team, Northampton Town, are also nicknamed 'The Cobblers', in a reflection of the town's historic industry. Aside from the boot and shoe trade, the town contains several historic buildings, mixed with the modern. The gothic guildhall has several friezes depicting events from the town's history. The castle that once defended Northampton is however, long gone.

**All Saints Church**, although badly damaged by fire and rebuilt, with the help of a donation from Charles II, still retains its 13th-century crypt, while St Peter, Mayfair has been described as the most interesting Norman Church in the county, with several unusual features. It was constructed in 1170 and replaced an earlier Saxon church. Nearby, the remains of an early Saxon settlement have been discovered.

The 17th-century **Sessions House** still retains its splendid plaster ceiling by Edward Goudge and on London Road, stands an Eleanor Cross, one of three surviving crosses by John of Battle, with the stations being designed by William of Ireland.

The poet **John Clare** (1793–1864) spent the last two decades of his life in Northampton. Known as the peasant poet, he wrote verse from the age of 13, inspired by his rural surroundings.

**Great Houghton Parish Church** St Mary the Blessed Virgin dates from 1753.

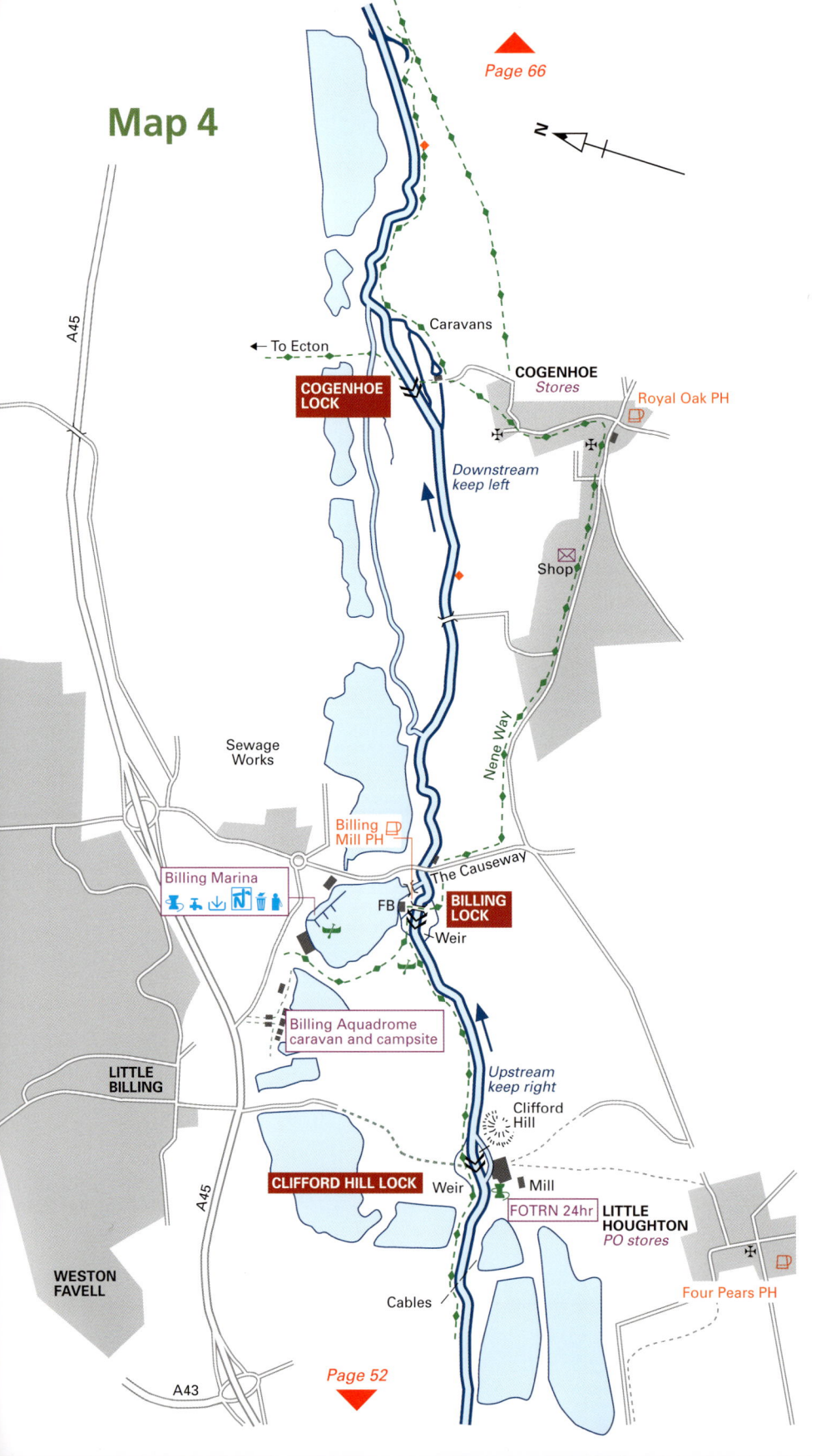

# Map 4

# Northampton Boat Club to Whiston Lock Entrance

| Map 4 Northampton Boat Club (GR SP 793606) to Whiston Lock Weir Entrance (GR SP 844617) | | | | | | | | | | | | | | | | | |
|---|---|---|---|---|---|---|---|---|---|---|---|---|---|---|---|---|---|
| Location | Miles | Locks | Lock type | Est time hours | Bridge < 2.7m | Moorings and facilities | | | | | | | Victualling | | | | Canoe |
| | | | | | | 48hr | Long stay | Water point | CDP | Pumpout | Refuse | Diesel | Shops | Pub | Café | PO or Bank | Portage | Park & access |
| Clifford Hill Lock 5 | 0.6 | 1 | ☐ | 0.5 | 2.65 | 🛟 | | | | | | In Little Houghton | 🧺 | 🍺 | 🍴 | £ | ▲▼ | |
| Billing Lock 6 | 0.6 | 1 | ☐ | 0.5 | | | | | | | | | | | | | ▲▼ | |
| Billing Marina | 0.2 | 0 | | 0.1 | | 🛟 | 🛟 | ⚓ | ⬇ | 🚽 | 🗑 | ⛽ | 🧺 | 🍺 | 🍴 | | | 🛶 |
| The Causeway Bridge (Billing) | 0.0 | 0 | | 0.0 | 2.40 | | | | | | | | | 🍺 | 🍴 | £ | | 🛶 |
| Glebe Way Field Bridge | 0.6 | 0 | | 0.2 | 2.60 | | | | | | | | | | | | | |
| Cogenhoe Lock 7 | 0.6 | 1 | ☐ | 0.5 | | | | | | | | | 🧺 | 🍺 | 🍴 | | ▲▼ | |
| Whiston Lock Weir Entrance | 1.0 | 0 | | 0.3 | | | | | | | | | | | | | | |
| Map 4 totals | 3.6 | 3 | | 2.2 | | | | | | | | | | | | | | |

THE RIVER NENE 61

## Navigation notes

After the **Northampton Boat Club** moorings, the three channels rejoin. Here there is a sign warning those travelling upstream to keep right. Another set of lakes are passed on the right bank, while the Nene Way footpath crosses Weston Favell Lock to transfer to the left bank. A power line crosses the river and lakes are to be seen on the left side too, as the river approaches Clifford Hill Lock, 0.9 miles from Weston Favell Lock and passing the caravan park on the left bank.

The river then divides again, with the southern channel being the Mill Race. At the mill is the Clifford Hill Fortification on the south bank. Here the pleasant backwater has private moorings. There is a sign warning those travelling upstream to keep right. A footpath crosses the lock from Little Billing to the west to Little Houghton to the east. Views of Northampton are still possible looking upstream.

**Clifford Hill Lock** is a vertical gate, electrically powered structure. Little Houghton's village post office/stores are a good half mile walk from the lock. After Clifford Hill Lock, the river continues in an easterly direction past Billing Aquadrome camping and caravan site. At the Aquadrome frontage, Hardingstone Dyke joins on the right bank and the river then turns northeast to **Billing Lock**, 0.6 miles from Clifford Hill Lock. Billing Lock has an electrically-powered vertical gate. Nearby also are the villages of Great and Little Billing.

After passing through Billing lock and immediately before the next bridge is the marina entrance channel to the left, at first glance it looks like a dead end but have courage and you will find the channel turns sharp left into the marina.

The road from Little Houghton and Cogenhoe to the A45 crosses the river downstream of Billing Lock. Two power lines in quick succession cross here, downstream of the Mill. The river flows past a gravel pit on the left, before dividing again into two. The minor northern channel rejoins downstream of

Swans on the River Nene

## Moorings and facilities

**FOTRN Clifford Hill** 24hr members mooring has been established immediately upstream of the lock on the southern bank. For overnight stays please contact the owner ☏ 07887 808551
GR: SP 804606

**Billing Marina** provides a full range of facilities, including visitor moorings, electricity, water, long term moorings and a slipway as well as toilets, chemical toilet disposal point, showers, a cash point, pump-out facilities and fuel.

**Billing Mill** used to provide moorings for patrons – these don't currently appear to be suitable.

Mooring is no longer allowed along the private meadow as you approach Cogenhoe lock. Neither are there any overnight visitor moorings or access to any of the Cogenhoe Caravan Park facilities.

**Little Houghton** (0·8 miles along footpath from Clifford Hill lock)
**Village stores and Post Office**
Bedford Road ☏ 01604 890555

**The Four Pears PH**
Bedford Road ☏ 01604 890900
Drinks and meals

**Billing Aquadrome**
☏ 01604 408181
Boasts several cafés, and restaurant, together with a visitor centre. Nearby is a Garden Village and Retail Shopping Outlet and a Premier Inn

**Great Billing** hosts The Elwes Inn (16th century coaching inn) ☏ 01604 407521 providing good food and drink. The Post Office, on the High Street, is situated in a building dating from 1703 ☏ 01604 401307.

**Cogenhoe** provides a post-box on the road up to village and a small Post Office/Londis store ☏ 0345 611 2970. Close by, over the level crossing, going up the hill is the Royal Oak ☏ 01604 890922 closed Mondays. Bus service number 43 runs to five times per day and a separate service runs to Tesco, in Weston Favell on Tuesdays and Wednesdays. The stop is near the pub.

Cogenhoe Lock passing by two gravel pits en route. This channel may have formed part of the old course of the Nene.

The main channel turns southeast and then east and is crossed first by another power line and then by a footbridge carrying a farm track, before turning northeast towards **Cogenhoe Lock**, where the guillotine gate is electrical, 1.4 miles from Billing Lock, where there is a sign advising those travelling downstream to keep left. Here the river divides again. The backwater mill stream turns south and then southeast past gravel workings to the village of Cogenhoe, (pronounced Cook-no).

A footpath to the village leads off from the mill stream backwater, and this then rejoins the main channel downstream of the lock. A second backwater, a little further north joins the first. At Cogenhoe the right bank feels as if it is converging on you, but the feeling passes as the river moves on to Whiston Lock around several drunken meanders.

The Nene Way footpath rejoins the bank side of the more southerly channel after the Cogenhoe road and then runs alongside the right bank of the main channel, which continues to flow east and then northeast, past lakes on the left bank towards **Whiston Lock** one mile further on.

Cogenhoe Lock

## Nature reserves and features

### Billing Aquadrome

Billing Aquadrome is helping to preserve the natural environment winning the David Bellamy Conservation Award and the Green Apple Award.

Downstream of Billing the river breathes a sigh of relief as it leaves behind the fun and frolics of Billing Aquadrome and becomes more sedate, peaceful and subsumed by meadows and copses along the banks.

## Walking and exploring

At **Billing Mill** is a footbridge over the adjoining mill stream, which leads to the roads to Weston Favell and Little Billing.

**The Nene Way** footpath changes to the right bank downstream of Billing lock and then moves away from the river bank to follow a brief detour through Cogenhoe, returning to the river at Cogenhoe Mill.

## Canoeing

**Billing Aquadrome caravan and campsite** allows customers to launch small boats and canoes into the river.

**Billing Marina** provides car parking and launching for a modest fee.

**Billing Mill** and car park adjacent to the marina provides scope for an awkward launching down a stony, tree lined bank, but far from impossible. The car park has a 2·4m height barrier.

## Local history

**Clifford Hill Fortification** is one of the largest mottes in the country but there does not appear to be any historical record of a former castle and no bailey is apparent. It is instead a circular defensive mound probably built in the 11th or 12th centuries to control the crossing of a ford near a cliff (hence the name). The soil is however unstable and landslips on the south side may have led to its abandonment. The present flat top is said to be due to the construction of a bowling green there in the 17th century.

**Little Houghton** has a pair of stocks to be seen in the village, southeast of the Parish Church St Mary the Virgin dating from 1225, on the Bedford Road.

**Billing Aquadrome** comprises of 95 hectares and was constructed after the meadows in this area were excavated for gravel, in the early 20th century. It was landscaped as 'a restful place for the public' and as a holiday venue and it contains a funfair and miniature railway. More recent developments on the site have included the creation of a caravan village and touring park and special events for instance, vintage car rallies.

**Billing Mill** is mentioned in the Domesday Book and the Mill Museum is now part of the Aquadrome complex. The present mill was built in the 19th century and worked commercially until the 1940s. It is now a Greene King Fayre and Square public house/restaurant ☎ 01604 415059.

**Great Billing Church of St Andrew** dates from 1165 and boasts a Norman nave.

The name Cogenhoe originates from the hoe (hill) of Cugga, the Anglo-Saxon owner of the manor. Here the 12th-century church of St Peter has an effigy of Nicholas de Cogenhoe who died in 1280, in the south aisle.

# Map 5

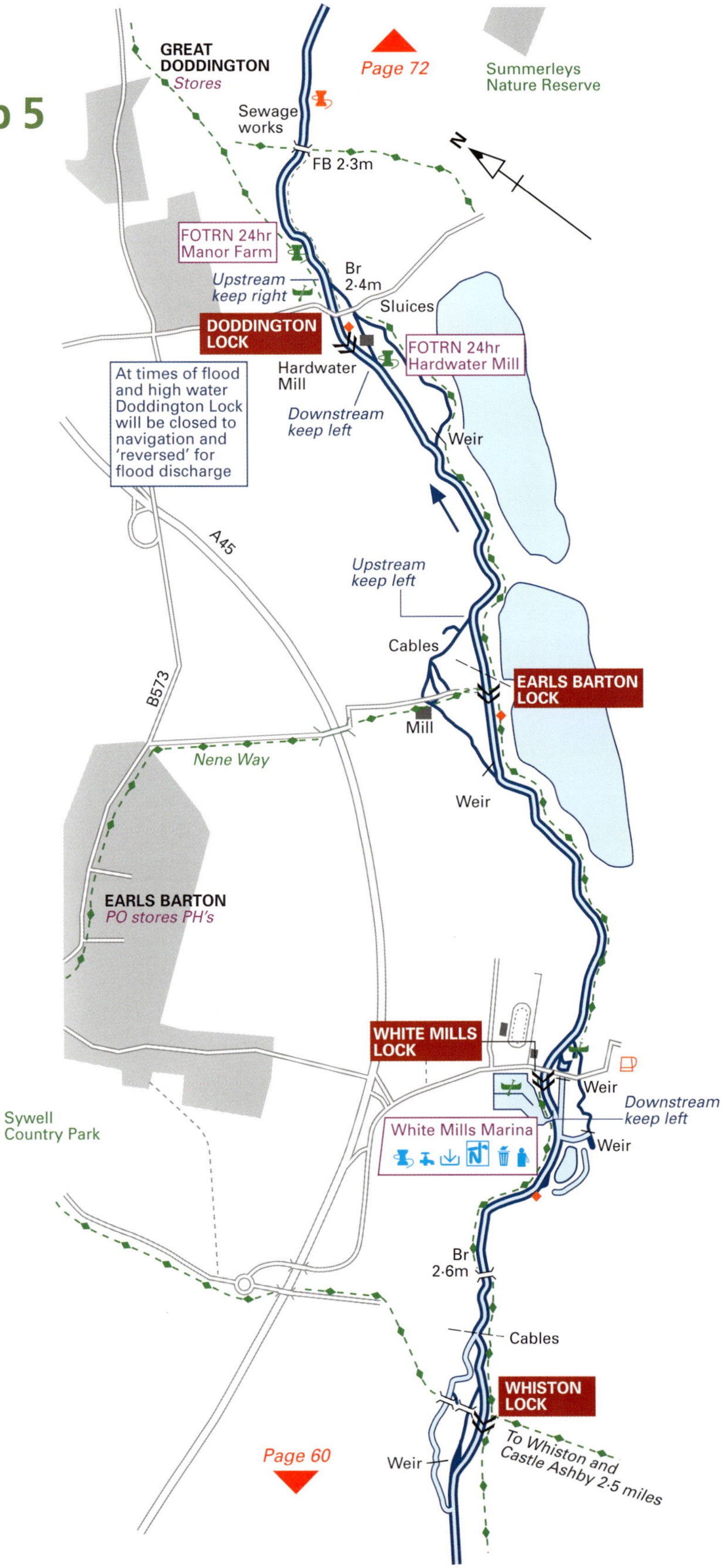

**GREAT DODDINGTON**
*Stores*

Page 72

Summerleys Nature Reserve

Sewage works

FB 2·3m

N

FOTRN 24hr Manor Farm

Br 2·4m

*Upstream keep right*

Sluices

**DODDINGTON LOCK**

Hardwater Mill

FOTRN 24hr Hardwater Mill

At times of flood and high water Doddington Lock will be closed to navigation and 'reversed' for flood discharge

*Downstream keep left*

Weir

A45

*Upstream keep left*

B573

Cables

**EARLS BARTON LOCK**

Mill

*Nene Way*

Weir

**EARLS BARTON**
*PO stores PH's*

**WHITE MILLS LOCK**

Weir

White Mills Marina

*Downstream keep left*

Weir

Sywell Country Park

Br 2·6m

Cables

**WHISTON LOCK**

Page 60

Weir

To Whiston and Castle Ashby 2·5 miles

# Map 5

## Whiston Lock Weir Entrance to Doddington Field Bridge

| Map 5 Whiston Lock Weir Entrance (GR SP 844617) to Doddington Field Bridge (GR SP 880641) | | | | | | | | | | | | | | | | | | |
|---|---|---|---|---|---|---|---|---|---|---|---|---|---|---|---|---|---|---|
| Location | Miles | Locks | Lock type | Est time hours | Bridge < 2.7m | Moorings and facilities | | | | | | | Victualling | | | | Canoe | |
| | | | | | | 48hr | Long stay | Water point | CDP | Pumpout | Refuse | Diesel | Shops | Pub | Café | PO or Bank | Portage | Park & access |
| Whiston Lock 8 | 0.0 | 1 | ☐ | 0.3 | | | | | | | | | | | | | ▲ | |
| Whiston Farm Bridge | 0.3 | 0 | | 0.1 | 2.6 | | | | | | | | in Earls Barton | | | | | |
| White Mills Marina | 0.4 | 0 | | 0.1 | | ⚓ | ⚓ | 🚰 | ⬇ | 🚽 | 🗑 | ⛽ | 🛒 | 🍺 | 🍴 | £ | | 🛶 |
| White Mills Lock 9 | 0.1 | 1 | ☐ | 0.4 | | | | | | | | | | | | | ▲▼ | 🛶 |
| Earls Barton Lock 10 | 0.9 | 1 | ☐ | 0.6 | | | | | | | | | | | | | ▲▼ | |
| Doddington Lock 11 | 0.8 | 1 | ☐ | 0.6 | 2.5 | | | | | | | | | | | | | ▲▼ | |
| Hardwater Road Bridge FOTRN | 0.1 | 0 | | 0.0 | 2.4 | ⚓ | | | | | | | | | | | | | 🛶 |
| Doddington Field Bridge FOTRN | 0.5 | 0 | | 0.2 | 2.3 | ⚓ | | | | | | | in Gt Doddington | 🛒 | 🍺 | 🍴 | | | |
| Map 5 totals | 3.1 | 4 | | 2.4 | | | | | | | | | | | | | | | |

THE RIVER NENE

## Navigation notes

Upstream of Whiston Lock, the river divides again, the backwater flowing around the lock to the north, over a weir, to rejoin the main channel downstream of the lock. A second more minor backwater branches off further downstream, just before the lock. The scenery both up and downstream of **Whiston Lock**, which has an electrically powered vertical gate, is very pleasant and it has been described as 'standing in splendid isolation at the centre of the Nene Valley'. This and White Mills Lock, 0·8 miles downstream are seemingly close to, but in fact isolated from, the village and stately home of Castle Ashby, the home of the Marquis of Northampton, which lie just under two miles away.

Downstream of Whiston Lock and in the next stretch to White Mills Lock, weed can be a nuisance at certain times during the year. The river is crossed by power lines and then by a farm bridge, at which point the footpath crosses to the left bank before turning back east on its approach to White Mills Lock. There are two small backwaters and a larger backwater channel that runs southeast, bypassing the lock. This has a weir at its entrance. Signs warn that it is advisable to keep to the left on the main channel when travelling downstream.

White Mills Marina entrance is just before the lock travelling downstream. The marina is relatively new and provides a useful spot for overnight mooring in the marina or on the river bank. White Mills Lock is electrically powered. Just downstream of the lock, the river and side channels are crossed by Station Road, leading from Earls Barton. After White Mills lock there is a short distance where there is no footpath adjacent to the bank before one joins from Station Road to run along the south bank.

The river now turns southeast past a wooded area on the north bank and gravel workings and pits on the southern bank before meandering northeast and then straightening at the junction with the Barton Mill Race to flow in a straight northeastern channel to **Earls Barton Lock**, which is 0·9 miles from White Mills lock. The large gravel pit remains on the south east bank and there are places for informal moorings, just before the lock. Because of the turns of the river, Earls Barton with its facilities remains relatively close, about one and a half miles away, but without easy access from this point.

Moving downstream, the valley becomes wider and the scenery more interesting. A track from the northwest, past the mill, carries the **Nene Way** from Earls Barton to cross the river at the lock and run along the south east bank. The Nene then runs underneath overhead power lines. The river continues to flow north-easterly past a further succession of gravel pits on its south east bank. There is a weir at the junction with a backwater which joins the south east bank at this point and a **sign advising boaters travelling downstream to keep left**. The mill race from Hardwater Mill joins on the south east bank, just upstream of Doddington Lock, which has an electrically operated guillotine gate.

Doddington Lock is 0·5 miles from the main road and 0·9 miles from Earls Barton Lock and, once the iron bridge behind the mooring is crossed, a right turn at the crossroads along the B573

## Moorings and facilities

**White Mills Marina** ☎ 01604 812057 is one of the river's newest, full facility marinas. It is well established and provides 141 berths for narrow boats and cruisers some are suitable for wide beam boats. A full range of facilities are provided, including visitor moorings in the marina or on the river bank, a small chandlery, showers and laundry facilities. **The Boathouse** is well worth a visit, providing freshly prepared homemade food and drinks 1000 to 1600 every day except Tuesday. There is also a caravan and camping site next to the marina.

**FOTRN Hardwater Mill 48-hour mooring** for members on the right before Doddington lock.
GR SP 875636

**FOTRN Manor Farm 48-hour mooring** for members downstream of Hardwater Road and Doddington lock.
GR SP 877638

**Earls Barton** is a sizeable settlement with a full range of facilities, approximately 1 mile from White Mills Lock. **The Stags Head** ☎ 01604 812267, on the High Street and **The Old Swan** ☎ 01604 810044 on The Square provide traditional meals.

**Regular buses** from Earls Barton to Wellingborough.

**Whiston** village has no shops or services.

**Hardwater Mill** offers accommodation for short breaks and has its own hydropower facility ☎ 01933 276870.

**Great Doddington** stands high on a hill, overlooking the valley, from which the broad reach of the Nene can be appreciated. There is a **Village Store** on Chapel Lane ☎ 01933 223902 and **The Stags Head** pub providing food and drinks ☎ 01933 222316. The houses here reflect the local architecture of this part of the Nene Valley with grey limestone walls and red-tiled roofs.

**Regular buses** from Great Doddington to Wellingborough.

leads to **Great Doddington** village, which can also be accessed from the Nene Way. The river then curls east and is crossed by a footbridge.

A further backwater joins the river at a weir and two minor backwaters flow downstream from the weir and rejoin the main Nene downstream of Wollaston Lock, 1·2 miles from Doddington Lock.

Approaching Earls Barton

## Nature reserves and features

**Sywell Country Park** is located 1·5 miles north-north west of Earls Barton on the Mears Ashby road. This 68-acre site is a former reservoir, previously used to supply water to Rushden and Higham Ferrers and now comprises meadow land with several lakeside walks and Edwardian buildings. It is open daily.
☏ 01604 810970
GR: SP 835651

**Castle Ashby House** has 35 acres of extensive gardens including the romantic Italian Gardens, the unique Orangery and impressive Arboretum.
GR: SP 860594

**Summer Leys Nature Reserve** is an important wetland area with a network of paths and is home to large numbers of birds particularly tree sparrows and of dragonflies. Within this reserve, there is a circular walk and bird watching hides with wheelchair access.
GR: SP 886634

## Walking and exploring

**The Nene Way** crosses Whiston Lock and continues alongside the B573 to Earls Barton following the road through the village and turning to the south to rejoin the Nene after the eastern edge of Earls Barton, at Earls Barton Lock. A footpath, however, continues along the right bank.

**Hardwater Road** crosses the Nene downstream of Doddington lock at which point the Nene Way crosses the river to move away on the left bank in the direction of Great Doddington. A minor footpath continues for a little way along the left bank as the mill race/backwater joins the main channel downstream of the lock.

## Canoeing

**White Mills Marina** welcomes canoeists, providing parking, launching, campsite and the Boathouse café.
GR: SP 856622

**Station Road** parking and picnic site provides easy launching and retrieval just downstream of White Mills lock.
GR: SP 859619

**Hardwater Road,** Great Doddington close to the FOTRN Doddington and Hardwater moorings. Access via a public footpath but limited parking.
GR: SP 875637

Earls Barton Lock

## Local history

**Castle Ashby House** is an Elizabethan mansion with parkland designed by Capability Brown, as well as Victorian gardens. It can be reached beyond Whiston by a footpath through the grounds.

**Whiston Church of St Mary** stands on its own on a hill overlooking the settlement. It contains a 16th-century monument to its builder, Antony Catesby.

**Earls Barton** All Saints Church is decorated with raised vertical stripes. This tower is regarded by many as the finest Saxon tower in England and is believed to have been once used as a lookout. The church was enlarged by the Normans and in 1972, it featured on a postage stamp. To the north of the churchyard is the motte of the Norman castle.

Earls Barton was once an important leather tanning location and the Barker's Shoe Factory, which began here in 1880, still produces about 250,000 pairs of shoes each year and has an outlet shop. **The Museum of Local Life**, in the Square, ☎01604 810289, has a collection of industrial and domestic memorabilia depicting the lifestyle of a traditional shoe worker, how they lived, worked and shopped.

**Hardwater Mill** was probably the hiding place for Thomas à Becket after fleeing Northampton.

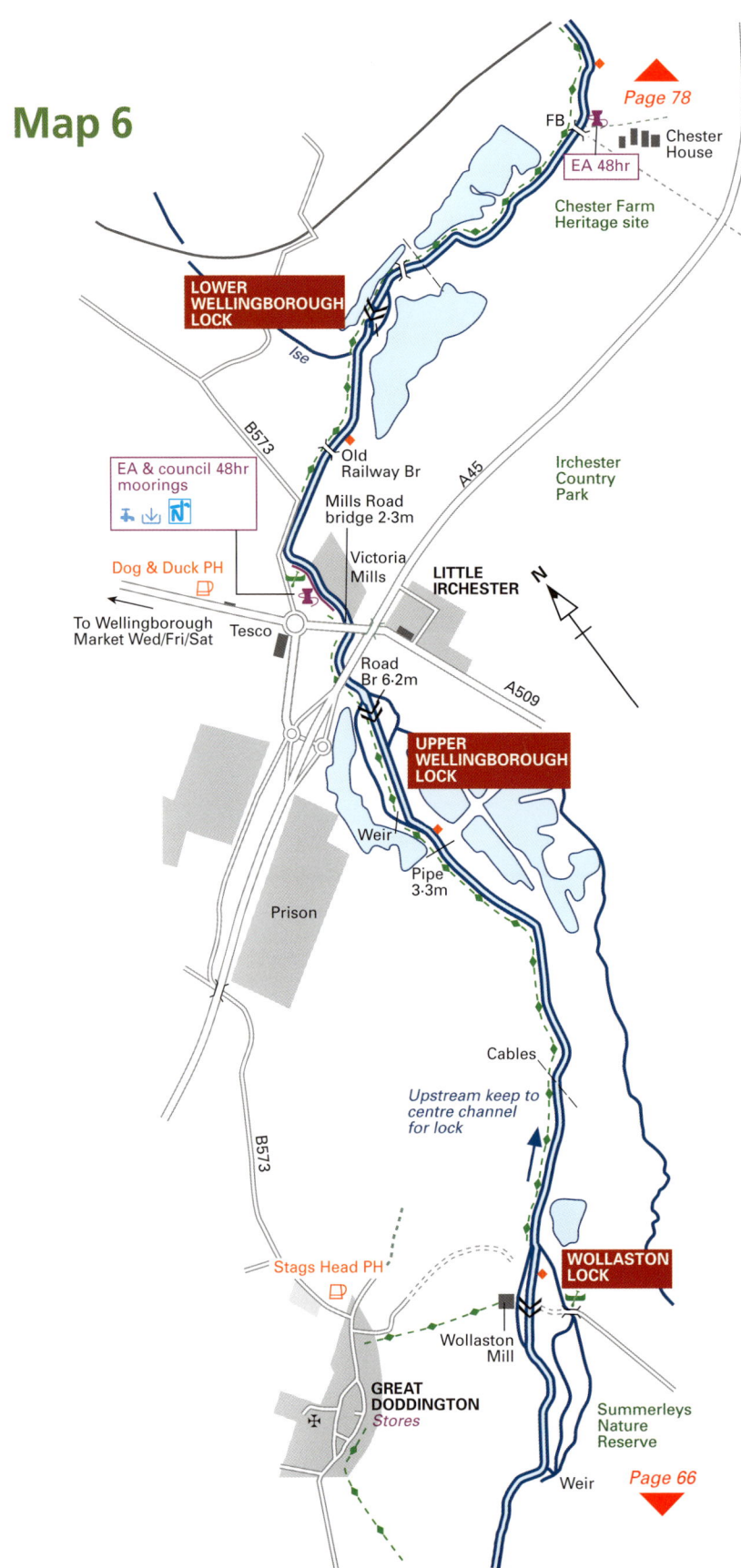

# Map 6

# Doddington Field Bridge to Chester Farm footbridge

| Map 6 Doddington Field Bridge (GR: SP 880641) to Chester Farm footbridge (GR: SP 918670) | | | | | | | | | | | | | | | | | | |
|---|---|---|---|---|---|---|---|---|---|---|---|---|---|---|---|---|---|---|
| Location | Miles | Locks | Lock type | Est time hours | Bridge < 2·7m | Moorings and facilities | | | | | | | Victualling | | | | Canoe | |
| | | | | | | 48hr | Long stay | Water point | CDP | Pumpout | Refuse | Diesel | Shops | Pub | Café | PO or Bank | Portage | Park & access |
| Wollaston Lock 12 | 0·7 | 1 | | 0·5 | | | | | | | | | | | | | ▲▼ | 🛶 |
| Upper Wellingborough Lock 13 | 1·3 | 1 | ◁◁ | 0·7 | | | | | | | | | | | | | ▲▼ | |
| Wellingborough Bridge | 0·2 | 0 | | 0·1 | 2·3 | | | | | | | | | | | | | |
| Wellingborough Embankment | 0·2 | 0 | | 0·1 | | 🧷 | | 🚰 ⚓ ⛽ | | | 🗑 | | 🧺 | 🍺 | 🍴 | £ | | 🛶 |
| Lower Wellingborough Lock 14 | 0·6 | 1 | ◁◁ | 0·5 | | | | | | | | | | | | | ▲ | |
| Chester House Foot Bridge | 0·6 | 0 | | 0·2 | | 🧷 | | | | | | | | | | | | |
| Map 6 Totals | 3·6 | 3 | | 2·1 | | | | | | | | | | | | | | |

THE RIVER NENE  73

## Navigation notes

Wollaston Lock has an electrically powered vertical gate. The two Wellingborough locks have mitre gates at both ends. A footpath crosses the lock to run to Great Doddington via Wollaston Mill on the left bank. This area forms a charming little islet amidst crowding willows and soft meadows. The right-hand channel should be taken by the mill.

From Wollaston Lock downstream, the **Nene** winds a sinuous and leisurely course, through beautiful countryside. The contours do not fall so obviously now as the change in gradient is slower than in the upper reaches. Just before the backwaters rejoin the main channel, the Nene Way, which has diverted via Great Doddington, returns to run along the north west bank. Two sets of power cables in quick succession cross the Nene, which then turns northeast past grazing meadows. There are again pits on both sides of the River here and a pipe crossing, before a weired backwater.

The buildings of **HMP Wellingborough** prison appear to the west, eerily quiet today as the prison is currently mothballed. The adjacent field is also eerily quiet as it has been abandoned by sheep to be replaced by a field of solar panels. The river flows past water-filled old gravel workings on the west bank as it approaches **Upper Wellingborough Lock**, which lies approximately half a mile upstream of Wellingborough Bridge and 1·4 miles from Wollaston Lock. After the lock, the river crosses quickly under two road bridges carrying respectively the A45 and the A509. After the first of these is the **Whitworth's Victorian Mill** built in 1866, swiftly followed by a cable crossing. Downstream of Whitworth's Mill, the east bank becomes more natural while the embankment on the west bank is popular with families, boaters, walkers and anglers, providing peaceful respite from the nearby road network.

Little Irchester is on the right bank at the junction of the A45 and the A509, (Mills Road bridge). The B573 also runs close to the left bank here as the river turns north and then east to cross the old railway bridge and pass a large lake to the south.

Here on the outskirts of Wellingborough, by Little Irchester, the Nene's largest tributary, the Ise, joins the main channel. This tributary rises near Naseby and although often small in summer, can become a real torrent in winter. At this point too, close to the B570 and on the right bank, is **Irchester Country Park**.

Between Upper and Lower Wellingborough Locks, the Nene is crossed by the route of the disused railway and, immediately afterwards, by a set of power lines. There is a weired backwater on the south east bank, just upstream of Lower Wellingborough Lock. Upper and Lower Wellingborough Locks are 1 mile apart.

Whitworth's Mill, Wellingborough Chris Howes

## Moorings and facilities

Approximately 150m of **48-hour Visitor Moorings** and canoe access are provided by the Environment Agency and Wellingborough Council along Wellingborough Embankment. Some may find the constant background noise from Whitworths mill intrusive as the machinery works a night shift!

There is a toilet block on the Wellingborough Embankment set back from the river and an **Environment Agency water point, chemical toilet disposal and pump out** on the river side which again can be accessed by the standard EA *Abloy* key. These services are closed during the winter.

Wellingborough town centre is about a mile from the river and has a full range of facilities.

Refreshments are available at several pubs and cafes. **The Hind Hotel** Sheep Street ☎ 01933 222827 17th-century coaching inn, or the **Coach and Horses** Oxford Street ☎ 01933 441848, another fine coaching inn, are both worth a visit.

There is a **Tesco** superstore and a **Homebase** at Victoria Retail Park, just across the road from the moorings on Turnell Mills Lane.

Castlefields Retail Park is 0·5 miles from the Embankment on London Road towards the town centre – M&S, Dunelm, Lidl and B&Q reside in the retail park. Opposite the entrance is the **Dog and Duck** Beefeater pub and restaurant ☎ 01933 278606. There is also a **Premier Travel Inn** on the site.

There is also a bus stop for buses into Wellingborough, the centre of which is about 25 minutes on foot from the moorings.

After Lower Wellingborough Lock, the river meanders gently as it passes the edge of yet more former gravel pits. More power lines and the footbridge leading to Chester House and the former Railway Inn on the right bank cross the river shortly after the lock.

## Nature reserves and features

**Irchester Country Park** is a County Council reserve in Northamptonshire consisting of 83 hectares of old ironstone workings, woodland areas and nature trails as well as scrub, grassland, dry slopes and wet dales.

In the 1930s and 40s the area was planted with many trees and it is particularly well known for conifers and limestone plants. It attracts sparrow hawks and woodpeckers and the grounds also contain a railway museum. ☎ 0300 126 5934

## Walking and exploring

**Wellingborough Town Heritage Trail** leaflet and map available for download: www.wellingborough.gov.uk/history or

**Walk 16–Wellingborough Heritage Trail** download from:
https://northamptonshirewalks.co.uk/about/walk-16/

THE RIVER NENE

**The Nene Way** which had followed the left bank of the river to Little Irchester, then crosses the river at the A509 bridge before moving away east into Irchester Country Park, although footpaths remain on both banks at this point. The first part of the Nene Way through the park follows the route of the old iron ore railway line.

## Cycling

**Irchester Country Park** offers several walking and cycling trails around the park and woods.

**Wellingborough** is well served by cycle trails in the town and further afield. Map and routes can be downloaded from https://cycle.travel/city/wellingborough/days_out

## Canoeing

**Wollaston lock** accessible by car along a byway, limited parking before the bridge in area shared with walkers and anglers. Launching is possible into the backwater from the field accessed by public footpath.
GR: SP 889644

**Wellingborough Embankment** free public car park with 2·05m height restriction. Short carry across the grass to the river.
GR: SP 900667

## Local history

Due to the extensive gravel extraction in this area, some significant archaeological discoveries have been made. At nearby **Wollaston**, evidence of a Roman vineyard has been uncovered and a Roman road led out of the vineyard which itself contained an Anglo-Saxon grave. The grave contained an iron sword and a bronze hanging bowl with hanging rings and decorated with round glass discs. The most significant discovery, however, was an iron helmet with a boar's crest, indicative of the high status of the wearer.

The name '**Wellingborough**' has various possible derivations, 'Wendel's burg' being favoured by some but a more likely source is from the wells or springs for which the area was previously famous – and particularly the 'red well' and the 'white well', the former name due to the ironstone content of the water.

The Embankment, named 'the Walks' is very attractive and is especially famous for the semi-tame mute swans, as well as flower beds, lawns and pathways.

In the 1600s Wellingborough became famous for its waters which it was said had healing properties and the wells are still indicated on the town's coat of arms.

By the early 18th century, lace making was the main industry, but this in turn was overtaken by boot and shoe making. The town grew with the coming of the railway and nearby iron ore extraction.

In 1886, JB Whitworth built a mill on the riverside and the canal and river were used to bring imported grain from Canada via Brentford, London. This continued until 1969, when it became no longer economic. The mill still makes flour from mainly British wheat.

In the early 20th century, **Little Irchester** was economically active, standing at the junction of two main roads and being near to the iron ore quarry and river wharf. However, the closure of the quarry and the wharf turned it into a quiet backwater. **The All Hallows** 14th-century Church, formerly occupied by monks, is however of interest. The weather vane on the Church of St Catherine, depicts the Catherine Wheel, the torture instrument on which the saint met her death.

# 3
# RIVER NENE WELLINGBOROUGH TO WADENHOE

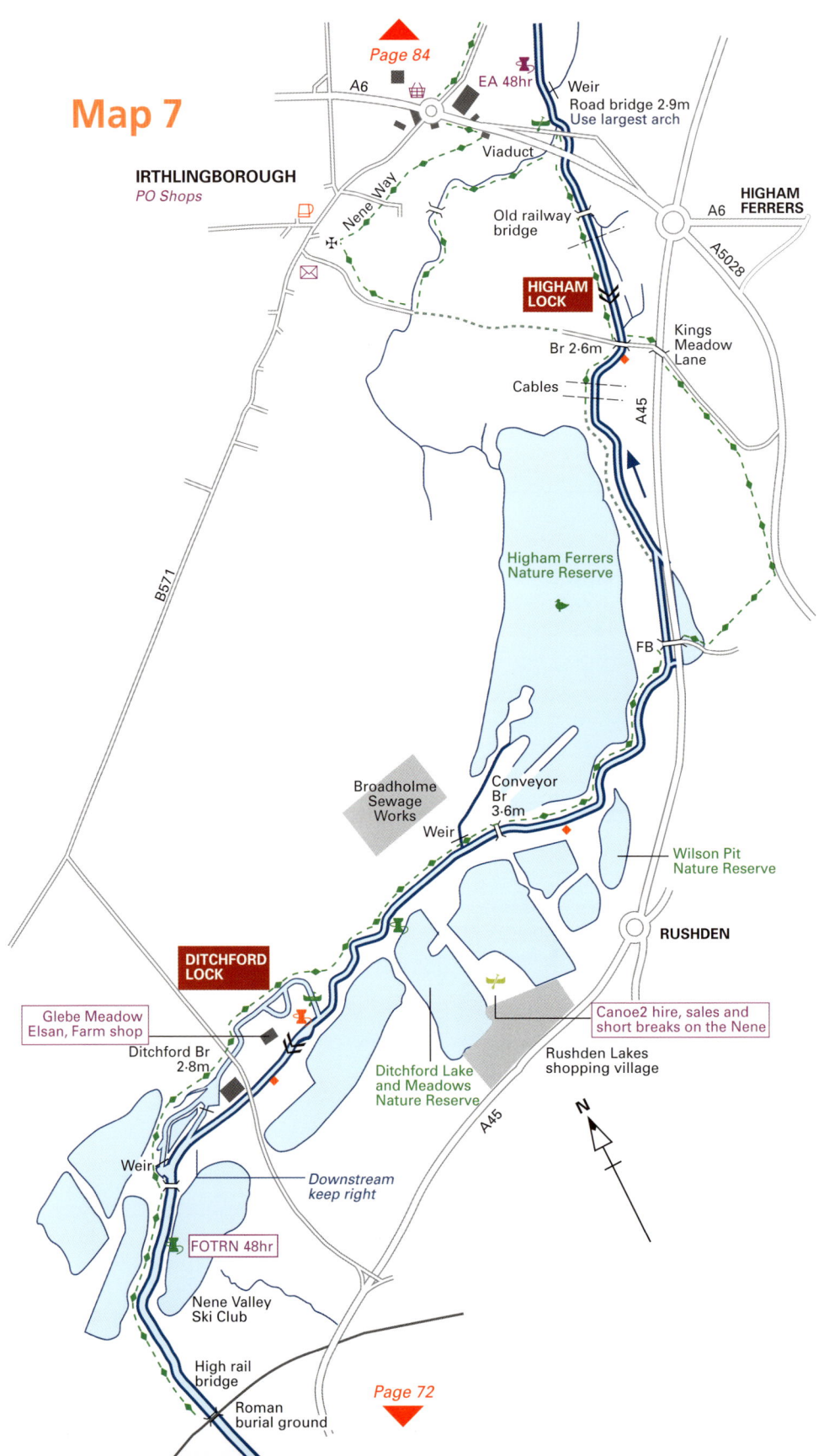

# Map 7

## Chester Farm footbridge to Irthlingborough EA 48-hour moorings

*Wellingborough to Wadenhoe*

### Map 7  Chester Farm footbridge (GR SP 918670) to Irthlingborough EA 48-hour moorings (GR SP958710)

| Location | Miles | Locks | Lock type | Est time hours | Bridge < 2.7m | Moorings and facilities | | | | | | | Victualling | | | | Canoe | |
|---|---|---|---|---|---|---|---|---|---|---|---|---|---|---|---|---|---|---|
| | | | | | | 48hr | Long stay | Water point | CDP | Pumpout | Refuse | Diesel | Shops | Pub | Café | PO or Bank | Portage | Park & access |
| Wellingborough Rail Bridges | 0.2 | 0 | | 0.1 | | | | | | | | | | | | | | |
| Ditchford FOTRN mooring | 0.6 | 0 | | 0.2 | | 48hr | | | | | | | | | | | | |
| Glebe Meadow moorings | 0.5 | 0 | | 0.1 | | 48hr | | ✓ | ✓ | permission required for use of facilities | | | | | | | | 🛶 |
| Ditchford Lock 15 (radial gate) | 0.1 | 1 | □ | 0.4 | 2.5 | | | | | | | | | | | | ▲▼ | |
| Rushden Lakes FOTRN (opening to be confirmed) | 0.8 | 0 | | 0.2 | | 48hr | | | | | | | 🛒 | | 🍴 | | | 🛶 |
| Kings Meadow Lane Bridge | 1.1 | 0 | | 0.4 | 2.6 | | | | | | | | | | | | | |
| Higham Ferrers Lock 16 | 0.1 | 1 | ◁◁ | 0.3 | | | | | | | | in Highham town | 🛒 | 🍺 | 🍴 | £ | ▲ | |
| Irthlingborough Bridge | 0.4 | 0 | | 0.1 | | | | | | | | | | | | | | 🛶 |
| Irthlingborough EA mooring | 0.4 | 0 | | 0.1 | | 48hr | | | | | | Aldi near moorings others in town | 🛒 | 🍺 | 🍴 | £ | | |
| **Map 7 Totals** | **4.2** | **2** | | **1.9** | | | | | | | | | | | | | | |

THE RIVER NENE

## Navigation notes

The Nene is shallower in the 1·9 mile stretch between **Lower Wellingborough Lock** and **Ditchford Lock**.

The railway line crosses the river at the imposing twin Wellingborough viaducts. The river then turns northeast and east flowing past lakes again formed by former gravel pits on both banks. Just before Ditchford Road Bridge, the Nene divides again with the navigation following the southern section which, between the road bridge and the lock, is a straight canalised length. A weir leads into the more meandering northern channel. The fast-flowing backwater close to the old factory is good for roach and bream. **Ditchford Lock** which has an electrified downstream radial gate is quite unusual and the only one on the River Nene.

On the right bank here is the **Skew Bridge Lake** and, on the north bank Broadholme Sewage Treatment Works is reached, after which the river turns southeast, with a small weired side channel on the north bank leading to further gravel pits.

The Nene is then crossed by a footbridge, on the site of the former mineral workings' conveyor belt. The channel meanders generally southeast running close to the A45, and then parallel to that road for a short distance, via an artificial cut. A footbridge crosses here, allowing the Nene Way, which branches off here from the river through a small former gravel pit, to proceed along the north east bank, to Higham Ferrers.

To the south, behind the river bank scrub and trees, hides Rushden Lakes Shopping Outlet. This facility, for keen shoppers, attracts visitors from a wide area.

**Friends of the River Nene** have recently established new member moorings to enable boaters to enjoy this lavish and extensive shopping experience.

The Nene turns away from Higham Ferrers and then flows generally northeast, meandering past yet another nature reserve, formed out of the former mineral workings. Just after the reserve, two power lines cross the river. The Nene continues its meandering before being crossed at Kings Meadow Lane by the previously 'notorious' **Kings Bridge**, constructed of steel and concrete with two angle irons. While the approach to this bridge should be slow, work to raise the headroom has been undertaken.

Here the **Nene Way** crosses the bridge and turns northwest to Irthlingborough, although a footpath branches off from this to return to the left bank of the river just downstream of **Higham Lock** which is 2·2 miles, by river, from Ditchford Lock. Higham Lock has mitre gates at both ends.

Downstream of Higham Lock the channel is narrow and twisting and weed can be prolific, probably due increased nutrients flowing downstream from Broadholme sewage works! At the top of a hill to the right is the ruined shell of an inn, guarding the site of a long disused ford, from which a lane leads up to the town. A minor backwater curls back to rejoin the Nene on the east bank close to this point just after the river crosses the site of the former railway line. The channel continues northeast and is crossed by the Irthlingborough Viaduct and A6 (High Road bridge). Navigators are advised to use the largest arch and prepare for a sharp turn left when travelling downstream under the old Irthlingborough Station Road bridge which next crosses the river.

## Moorings and facilities

Adjacent to Ditchford lock is **Glebe Meadow**, which has a chemical toilet disposal point and overnight visitor moorings. There is also a farm shop and a camping and caravan site.
☏ 07941 257090

**FOTRN Ditchford 48-hour members mooring** is located on the right bank upstream of Ditchford Bridge near the Nene Valley Ski Club.
GR: SP 927680

**FOTRN Rushden lakes 48hr members mooring** is located downstream of Ditchford lock on the southern bank after a couple bends. Access to Rushden Lakes shopping complex, including Canoe2, approximately 0·5 miles by signed footpath.
GR: SP 941678

Approximately 200m of **Environment Agency 48-hour visitor mooring** is available alongside, what used to be Rushden Diamonds football ground, access through the site is still available. These moorings are very popular during the summer months.

**The Environment Agency** have ambitions to open a marina here, subject to available funding.

There are plans to provide visitor moorings near to the footbridge adjacent to **Chester Farm**. From Ditchford FOTRN mooring it is 1 mile to Chester farm.

There is an **Aldi** supermarket a short walk from the EA visitor moorings at the A6 roundabout.

**Irthlingborough town centre**
**The British Arms** 400-year-old coaching inn
☏ 01933 650911

**The Oliver Twist** pub ☏ 01933 650353

**Post Office** on the High Street ☏ 0345 611 2970, a **Tesco** and several other shops and cafes.

Bus number 45 runs every 30 minutes (except Sundays) between **Irthlingborough** and **Wellingborough**.

**Higham Ferrers** is an interesting market town which provides a range of traditional shops, pubs and services.

**The Queens Head** ☏ 01933 38925
**The Griffin Inn** ☏ 01933 312612
**The Old Swan** ☏ 01933 353054

A minor channel from the gravel pits joins from the west side. Shortly after this, on the east side, there is a weired backwater. The minor channel itself subdivides into two, one of which rejoins the main channel immediately downstream of Irthlingborough Lock. The other sweeps round to the south, circling and being bordered by gravel pit lakes before turning north to rejoin the main channel, 0·5 mile further downstream.

## Nature reserves and features

**The Nene Wetlands** includes the Upper Nene Valley Gravel Pits Site of Special Scientific Interest and Special Protection Area. Four Wildlife Trust nature reserves - Irthlingborough Lakes and Meadows, Ditchford Lakes and Meadows, Higham Ferrers Pits and Wilson's Pits are now linked up with Skew Bridge Lake, Delta

Pit and Higham Lake - flooded gravel pits, wet meadow, wet woodland and reedbed at the heart of the Wildlife Trust's Nene Valley Living Landscape. This extensive series of shallow and deep open waters are surrounded with a wide range of marginal features, such as sparsely vegetated islands, gravel bars and shorelines, and habitats including reed swamp, marsh, wet ditches, rush pasture, rough grassland and scattered scrub. This range of habitat and the varied topography of the lagoons provide valuable nesting, resting and feeding conditions to sustain nationally important numbers and assemblages of breeding and wintering birds. Twenty thousand waterbirds use the wetlands every year, for breeding, for their winter quarters or as vital stopping points on their long migration routes, from as far away as Arctic Russia and southern Africa. Access available from several places, particularly Rushden Lakes.

**Ditchford Lakes and Meadows Nature Reserve** is part of the upper Nene valley floodplain, this complex 31ha site of gravel pits, grassland and scrub is important for breeding and wintering birds. In spring and summer, the meadows have a rich collection of wet meadow plants. on the right bank downstream of Ditchford Road Bridge and Lock.
☏ 01604 405285   GR: S930678

This reserve adjoins the Wilson's Pits Reserve, another 32ha site important for overwintering and breeding birds and for invertebrates.

**Higham Ferrers Pits Nature Reserve** is a 10ha reserve consisting of grassland, willow, reedbeds and open water. Like those reserves already mentioned, it is important for over wintering and breeding birds. In addition, in summer, it is home to a large variety of dragonflies and damselflies.
☏ 01604 405285   GR: SP950698

**Irthlingborough Lakes and Meadows Reserve** is a stretch of rare grazing marsh and flooded gravel pits of 117 hectares, now a hugely valuable wetland for birds and other wildlife. The site is home to wintering golden plover, wigeon and gadwall. In summer a huge variety of birds come here to breed, including many declining species such as grasshopper warblers and cuckoos. The reserve can be accessed from the old Station Road.
GR: SP 953699

## Walking and exploring

At **Chester House**, the site of a Roman settlement and Claudius Way Heritage Centre, the Nene Way returns from its diversion through Irchester to cross and follow the left bank of the river.

**The Nene Way** follows the bank of the northern channel until the Ditchford bridge. The route continues to follow the river before diverting briefly into Higham Ferrers and, after crossing the river again, visits Irthlingborough town on its way back to the river.

**Higham Ferrers Heritage Trail** is well worth exploring, a map and description of key sites is available from www.highamferrers-tc.gov.uk

**Rushden and Raunds** both have excellent heritage trails, map/leaflets available from www.nenevalley.net

## Cycling

**The East Northamptonshire Cycle Map** is a useful addition to your map box. It provides detailed maps of Rushden, Higham Ferrers and Irthlingborough with added information about cycle routes. The map is widely available from visitor centres and can be downloaded in sections from
www3.northamptonshire.gov.uk/councilservices

**AJ Cycles** provide cycle hire from their main base at **Rushden Lakes**. All types of bikes are available to suit families with maps showing suggested routes.

## Canoeing

**Glebe Meadows** campsite permits parking and launching above and below Ditchford lock.

**Rushden Lakes** is the home of Canoe2 where, from a purpose-built building adjacent to the lake, canoes can be hired and purchased. Canoe2 also provide suggested routes and organized itineraries for short breaks on the Nene.

**Station Road, Irthlingborough** has free parking with access to the river by lowering craft over the railings or from the field, through a gate, further along. GR: SP 957705

## Local history

The **Chester Farm** site was a Roman walled town with evidence of Iron Age and medieval settlement and farm buildings. The site is open to the public and further exploration and interpretation work continues with support from the Heritage Lottery Fund. There are proposals to provide short term visitor moorings near the footbridge to facilitate visits to the Chester Farm site.

**Wellingborough viaducts**, known as 'Fourteen Arches viaduct' have a span of 350 feet over the Nene and were opened in 1857. One line was built with an easier gradient for goods traffic.

Ditchford was once very popular with local people who used to come here to swim and fish. The area was known as 'Ditchford on Sea' and had its own railway station on the Northampton to Peterborough Line.

**Higham Ferrers** was in the 11th century known as Hecham from the Saxon 'heah' meaning 'high' and 'ham' 'homestead'. In the 12th century, the manor passed to the Count de Ferariis and, by 1279, the name Higham Ferrers was in common use. Henry Chichele, Archbishop of Canterbury from 1414–43 was born at Higham Ferrers in 1362. He founded the town's grammar school in 1422, Chichele College, an evocative mediaeval building still standing in the High Street. Higham Ferrers market place has a 14th-century market cross and ditches near the north side of St Mary's church are the remains of the moat of the old castle, built in the 12th century by William Peverel. St Mary's church is a grand building, with two naves and a superb spire which can be seen from some distance away, particularly if navigating upstream.

The old **Irthlingborough Bridge** and attached causeway date from mid 13th-century/14th-century, with subsequent widening in 1754 and 1922. The bridge has 10 double and triple chamfered arches. Carved into its stonework are the crossed keys of Peterborough Abbey. High Bridge was built in 1936 as the old 13th-century bridge foundations could not cope with the weight of increasing traffic.

**Irthlingborough** town dates from at least AD780 and the name is said to be derived from 'Yirtlingaburg' (the fortified place of a ploughman). John Pyel, a native of Irthlingborough and Lord Mayor of London in 1473, founded a college in the town and arranged for the building of the tower of St Peter's Church in the 13th century but was taken down and rebuilt at the end of the 19th century as it was found to be leaning. The tower stands forty feet from the nave and belongs to the College. The belfry tower was one of the College buildings and is connected to the church by a vestry.

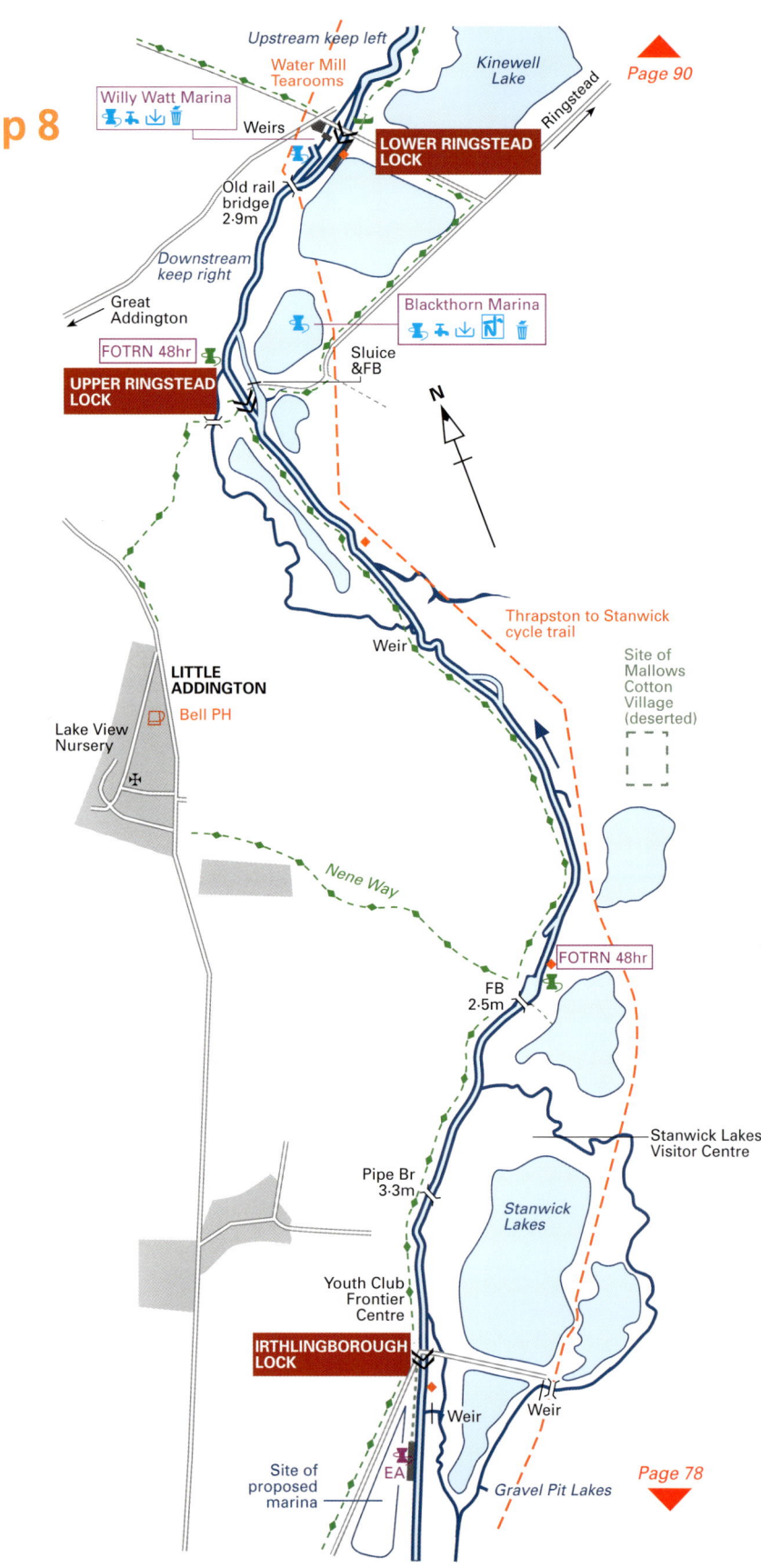

# Map 8

# Irthlingborough EA 48-hour moorings to Lower Ringstead Lock

**Map 8** Irthlingborough EA 48-hour moorings (GR: SP 958710) to Lower Ringstead Lock (GR: SP 973752)

| Location | Miles | Locks | Lock type | Est time hours | Bridge < 2·7m | Moorings and facilities | | | | | | | Victualing | | | | | Canoe | |
|---|---|---|---|---|---|---|---|---|---|---|---|---|---|---|---|---|---|---|---|
| | | | | | | 48hr | Long stay | Water point | CDP | Pumpout | Refuse | Diesel | Shops | Pub | Café | PO or Bank | Portage | Park & access |
| Irthlingborough Lock 17 | 0·2 | 1 | ☐ | 0·3 | | | | | | | | | | | | | ▲ | |
| Stanwick Footbridge | 0·8 | 0 | | 0·2 | 2·5 | | | | | | | | | | | | | |
| Stanwick Lakes FOTRN | 0·0 | 0 | | 0·0 | | 🛥 | | | | | | | | | ✕ | | ▲▼ | |
| Upper Ringstead Lock 18 | 1·5 | 1 | ☐ | 0·7 | | | | | | | | | | | | | ▲▼ | |
| Little Addington FOTRN | 0·0 | 0 | | 0·0 | | 🛥 | | | | | | | | ☕ | ✕ | | | |
| Blackthorn Lake Marina | 0·0 | 0 | | 0·0 | | 🛥 | 🛥 | 🚰 | ⬇ | | | Ringstead village | 🧺 | ☕ | ✕ | £ | | |
| Willy Watt Marina | 0·5 | 0 | | 0·1 | | 🛥 | 🛥 | 🚰 | ⬇ | ⛽ | 🗑 | | | | ✕ | | | |
| Lower Ringstead Lock 19 | 0·0 | 1 | ☐ | 0·3 | | | | | | | | | | | | | ▲▼🛶 | |
| **Map 8 Totals** | **3·1** | **3** | | **1·7** | | | | | | | | | | | | | | |

THE RIVER NENE

## Navigation notes

Leaving the moorings, the main channel continues north to **Irthlingborough Lock**, 0·9 miles from Higham Lock. The Nene here is flanked on the right bank by a further series of old flooded gravel workings which form the Stanwick Lakes.

After Irthlingborough Lock, the Nene generally curves anti-clockwise, round the spur of the hills, to Upper and Lower Ringstead locks. Downstream of the lock is the *Rock UK Frontier Centre* on the west bank. Boaters are advised to go slow and be aware of excitable youngsters in, often, uncontrollable canoes and DIY rafts. After the *Frontier Centre*, there is a track leading to the Irthlingborough–Little Addington Road.

The river channel gently curves northeast, being crossed by a pipe bridge and then by a footbridge, and flanked on the right bank by **Stanwick Lakes**, once again left as a result of former gravel workings, and the settlements of Stanwick, where a Roman villa, one of a number built along the Nene Valley, once stood and Raunds, the 'home' of the British army boot. At Stanwick footbridge on the right bank is the site of the now deserted Mallows Cotton village. There are side channels with weirs on both sides of the river. After passing a lake on the left bank, the Nene's course is straighter, towards the north as it approaches **Upper Ringstead Lock**, 2·3 miles from Irthlingborough Lock. Upper Ringstead lock provides the opportunity to perfect your spinning technique as the vertical gate is unpowered.

Here the Nene Way, leading from Little Addington, crosses the river in its track towards Ringstead village and a footpath leads across the field to Great Addington. There is a sluice and footbridge here at the lock, which has a manual winding wheel, just before this, a further side channel to the east. Just after Upper Ringstead Lock, both the minor channels on the left and right banks rejoin the main channel.

The Nene meanders to the northeast, passing the last in the series of lakes on

Stanwick Lakes

## Moorings and facilities

**FOTRN Stanwick Lakes 48-hour moorings** are available for members just downstream of the Farm bridge on the eastern bank GR: SP 968723

**FOTRN Little Addington 48-hour moorings** are available for members on the west bank just before Blackthorn Lake Marina GR: SP 968743

**Blackthorn Lake Marina** with provision for 120 narrowboat and river cruiser moorings. The marina provides a full range of facilities, but not diesel sales ☎ 07985 181358

**Willy Watt Marina** is located next to Lower Ringstead lock and provides long and short-term moorings and provides the usual facilities, but not diesel or pump-out. Narrowboat day hire is available ☎ 01933 622038

both banks which have shadowed the Nene since Wellingborough. **Blackthorn Lake Marina** is located here with the entrance cut on the right, requiring a tight turn as it is easy to miss the entrance when travelling downstream.

A further backwater is present on the left bank, leading to a mill, adjacent to the old railway viaduct crossing. There was once a second mill at this location, but it was demolished when the railway was built. Shortly after the junction with the mill channel and 0·6 miles from its neighbour is **Lower Ringstead Lock**, where the road from the mill to Ringstead crosses the river. Roads lead to Great Addington 1·1 miles and to Ringstead 1·4 miles from the lock.

**Little Addington**
**The Bell public house** (closed Mondays) is one mile away. During World War II, many Italian prisoners of war were lodged here.
☎ 01933 651700

**Ringstead**
**Post Office** ☎ 0345 611 2970
**Joe's Traditional Fish and Chips**
☎ 01933 633355
**The Axe and Compass**
Carlow Road ☎ 01933 622227
Drinks and meals

**Ringstead Grange Trout Fishery**, opened in 1975, offers 36 acres of water in which to fish for trout and salmon. It can be accessed from the track between Ringstead village and Blackthorn Lake Marina.
☎ 07584 241078

**Water Mill Tearooms** are based in the mill cross the road from lower Ringstead lock.
☎ 01933 770630. Sadly no moorings nearby.

## Nature reserves and features

**Stanwick Lakes** is a unique 304-hectare countryside attraction and nature reserve located in the heart of Northamptonshire's Nene Valley. There are extensive activity and play areas, open spaces and paths that families, walkers, cyclists and nature lovers can explore. The Heritage Trail allows visitors to trace the history of the site from Iron Age to medieval times. The visitor centre, with café, shop and function space, hosts events, throughout the year.
☎ 01933 625522
GR: SP 967 714

**Kinewell Lake** is owned by the village of Ringstead and managed by the Kinewell Lake Trust. It was named after an ancient spring and is now a pocket park nature reserve, consisting of 86 acres of

flooded former gravel pits and adjoining meadows of international importance for birds. There is good wheelchair access. The pits are connected to the Nene, which enables fish to migrate between the two water bodies. Insect life is particularly abundant here and the reserve is a haven for migratory birds.
☏ 01933 461432
GR: SP 982750

Lower Ringstead Lock

## Walking and exploring

There is a good, well-marked footpath from the moorings, over Irthlingborough lock, that goes southeast to **Stanwick Lakes** and takes about 18 min to get to the visitor centre.

**The Nene Way** follows the river from Irthlingborough lock as far as Stanwick footbridge. From here the route diverts north west away from the river to enjoy Little Addington village, before returning to cross the river at Upper Ringstead lock. From here it follows Station Road before turning left to go northwest to cross the river again at Woodford Mill and Lower Ringstead lock.

## Cycling

**AJ Cycles** provide cycle hire from their base at **Stanwick Lakes** from March to November. All types of bikes are available to suit families with maps showing suggested routes.
☏ 01933 353238

**Stanwick Lakes** provide several shorter cycle routes as well as links to Rushden Lakes, the developing *Greenway route* and north to join the *Thrapston2Rushden Boots and Bikes route*. www.nenevalley.net/see-and-do/discover/cycling/

## Canoeing

**Lower Ringstead Lock** has a downstream portage platform, On the opposite side of the road there is a set-back gateway where craft can be unloaded. There is parking across the bridge, but this can be busy, and signs restrict parking to two hours. Enquiries at the Mill Tearoom might be worthwhile.
GR: SP 973751

## Local history

**Mallows Cotton village**, together with its neighbours at West and Mill Cotton, was abandoned following the Black Death and changes in agricultural practices. The remains of the villages are visible as undulations in the ground to the east of the river. GR: SP 976733

**Little Addington** is a picturesque village with several stone and thatched cottages. St Mary the Virgin church dates from the 13th century.

**Ringstead** lies one mile to the northeast of the lock and its name means circular place. The shape of the parish suggests that it was once part of the parish of Raunds. St Mary's village church has a 13th-century west tower.

Gravel extraction at **Kinewell Lake** to the west of the village, revealed an Iron Age hut circle 11 yards in diameter. The remains of a Roman villa were also found, and excavations uncovered a tessellated floor as well as many Roman and Iron Age artefacts.

**Woodford Mill**, near Lower Ringstead lock, is known locally as **Willy Watt Mill**. It was mentioned in the Domesday Book and, over the years, has been used for cloth processing, corn grinding, paper-making and grinding bones for use as phosphates in agriculture. The water wheels remain today. There was apparently no person named 'Willy Watt' after whom the site was named but instead the name seems to be a corruption of 'Willow Islands', the name by which this location was known in the 15th century.

Willy Watt Marina, Ringstead

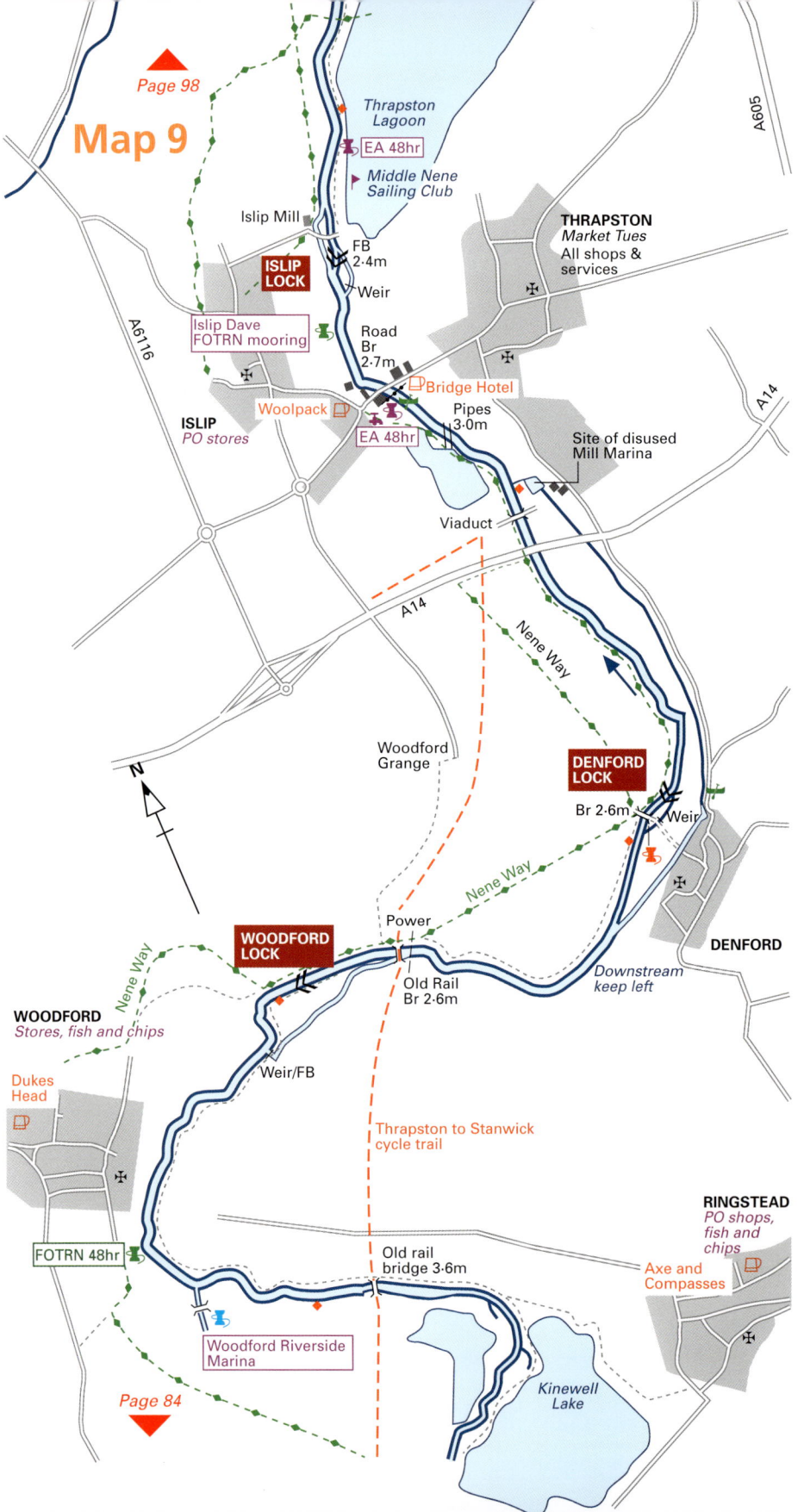

# Map 9

## Lower Ringstead Lock to Middle Nene Sailing Club EA visitor moorings

*Wellingborough to Wadenhoe*

| Map 9 Lower Ringstead Lock (GR SP 973752) to Middle Nene Sailing Club EA visitor moorings (GR SP 992793) | | | | | | | | | | | | | | | | | | |
|---|---|---|---|---|---|---|---|---|---|---|---|---|---|---|---|---|---|---|
| Location | Miles | Locks | Lock type | Est time hours | Bridge < 2·7m | Moorings and facilities | | | | | | Victualling | | | | | Canoe | |
| | | | | | | 48hr | Long stay | Water point | CDP | Pumpout | Refuse | Diesel | Shops | Pub | Café | PO or Bank | Portage | Park & access |
| Woodford Riverside Marina | 1·2 | 0 | | 0·4 | | | 🛟 | 🚰 | ⬇ | | 🗑 | permission required for use of facilities | | | | | | |
| Woodford FOTRN mooring | 0·1 | 0 | | 0·0 | | 🛟 | | | | | | | 🧺 | 🍺 | 🍴 | £ | | |
| Woodford Lock 20 | 1·0 | 1 | ☐ | 0·6 | 2·65 | | | | | | | | | | | | | |
| Woodford Old Railway Bridge | 0·0 | 0 | | 0·0 | 2·60 | | | | | | | | | | | | | |
| Denford Farm Bridge | 0·8 | 0 | | 0·2 | 2·60 | | | | | | | | | 🍺 | in village | | | |
| Denford Lock No.21 | 0·1 | 1 | ☐ | 0·3 | | | | | | | | | | by the war memorial on backwater | | | | 🛶 |
| Thrapston EA mooring | 1·1 | 0 | | 0·3 | | 🛟 | | 🚰 | | | | | | 🍺 | | | | 🛶 |
| Thrapston Bridge | 0·0 | 0 | | 0·0 | | | | | | | | | 🧺 | 🍺 | 🍴 | £ | | |
| Islip Dave FOTRN mooring | 0·2 | 0 | | 0·0 | | 🛟 | | | | | | | | | | | | |
| Islip Lock No 22 | 0·2 | 1 | ☐ | 0·4 | | | | | | | | | | | | | ▲ | |
| Islip Mill EA Mooring | 0·2 | 0 | | 0·1 | | 🛟 | | | | | | | | | | | | |
| **Map 9 Totals** | **4·9** | **3** | | **2·4** | | | | | | | | | | | | | | |

THE RIVER NENE

## Navigation notes

Although the Nene Way has moved away from the river a footpath continues along the southern bank of the river as it passes **Kinewell Lake** on the right bank and smaller lakes on the left bank, before bending to the west. Boaters proceeding upstream are warned here to keep to the left. This spot is known locally as Ringstead shallows but more widely as the Mid Northants fishery where record carp have been caught.

The Nene then spends the next 2·5 miles winding around its valley, through a broad expanse of meadows and the very pleasant scenery may be taken slowly and enjoyed. At the point of the first bend, the footpath on the south bank moves away to Ringstead and the Nene passes under the old railway bridge, just after which a minor tributary joins on the left before passing **Woodford Riverside Marina**. To the west on the skyline is the Three Hills Barrow, originally built by the Saxons as a burial ground. The name has now been borrowed by Three Hills Brewing based in Woodford. Their mission is to produce high quality, innovative and experimental small-batch beers for those who love to explore new taste sensations. Sounds good to me!

The Nene continues east, past a weired side channel on the right bank, which rejoins the main channel by the old railway bridge downstream of **Woodford Lock**. The river then turns to the north and back east as it approaches Woodford lock, another unpowered vertical gate to test the stamina. After passing through Woodford Lock, power lines cross the channel just by the old railway bridge and the navigator enters a spacious broad reach, for the next mile to Denford. Shortly after the lock, a footpath moves away on the north bank towards Woodford Grange and the road to Islip.

A minor footpath continues to follow the left bank as the river curls south, east and then northeast back over the former railway line (with a warning sign to keep left when travelling downstream) before splitting into two upstream of Denford Lock. The minor channel moves towards the village of Denford and often contains Aylesbury ducks, hoping for titbits from passers-by. In summer the channel can be a mass of water lilies and the adjacent pollarded willows are also a feature. The backwater passes the outskirts of this charming village and then curls north to flow parallel to the main channel and run between it and the Denford to Thrapston road, rejoining the main channel just downstream of the A14 road bridge.

The main Nene continues northeast. There are potential spots to moor between the weir stream and the footbridge, subject to permission from the landowner. A farm bridge crosses the channel on the approach to **Denford Lock**, which again is unpowered, but at least you get more time to admire the meadows and village. At this bridge, the Nene Way turns away from the Nene to head north towards the A14, which crosses the Nene at its new bridge.

The stretch from here to Thrapston sees the river loop past pleasant marshy meadows, with several small streams crossing the flood meadows to join with the Nene as the boater approaches Thrapston. Close by is the viaduct for the now dismantled railway at which use of the higher arch is recommended. On the east bank lies the disused and unkempt Mill marina and caravan site.

## Moorings and facilities

**Woodford Riverside Marina** provides residential and leisure moorings with the usual range of facilities available.
GR: SP 970762
www.woodfordriversidemarina.co.uk

**FOTRN Woodford 48-hour moorings** for members 300m after Woodford Riverside marina on the west bank. In places the bank can be unstable, so care needs to taken when mooring and putting the plank out. From these moorings it is a short walk to Woodford.
GR: SP 969 765

**Environment Agency 48-hour visitor moorings** and a water point are available at Thrapston Bridge. Entry and exit from these very pleasant moorings can be a challenge for skippers. There is only room for a couple of narrowboats, and it is difficult to see if there is space until past the point where you need to turn! Being adjacent to the bridge it leaves little space to manoeuver, particularly in strong winds and current – but don't be put off as it is worth the struggle to be near services.
GR: SP 990786

**FOTRN Islip Dave 48-hour members** mooring on the west bank after **Thrapston Bridge**, named after Dave Sands, whose kind donation made the construction possible. While camping and barbecues are currently permitted, the mooring itself is presently land locked, and there is therefore no access to Thrapston from the site.
GR: SP 990788

Thrapston Lagoon is the home of the **Middle Nene Sailing Club** ☎ 01832 732871. Adjacent are approximately 70 metres of **Environment Agency 48-hour visitor moorings** downstream of Islip lock on the right bank, adjacent to the sailing club. A haven for boats and boaters when Strong Stream Advice is in force.
GR: SP 992793

Woodford village boasts **stores and a Post Office** on the High Street ☎ 01832 732315 **a fish and chip shop** ☎ 01832 732422 and nearby, also on the High Street, is the **Dukes Arms** ☎ 01832 732224. There is also a **medical centre** ☎ 01832 732494.

The **number 16 bus service** runs from **Woodford** to **Raunds** and **Kettering**.

**The Cock Inn**, High Street **Denford** serves food and drink ☎ 01832 358735.

**The Woolpack at Islip** provides meals and drinks and is close to the EA Thrapston Bridge moorings.
☎ 01832 732578

**Thrapston** has a full range of facilities and a market on Tuesday, although many of the shops still close early on Thursdays.

On the Thrapston side, the **Bridge Hotel** offers food and accommodation.
☎ 01832 732128

There are several other pubs in the town, some serving food.

Islip Mill bridge under construction

There is a lake, formed from yet more former mineral workings on the west bank and two sets of power lines cross just before the Thrapston-Islip road bridge. **Nine Arches Bridge** is offset and small and the current can be tricky. Care should be taken when navigating. There are power lines and a pipe crossing, just upstream of the road bridge and the Nene Way follows the road through Islip, moving away from the river at this point.

In the 19th century barges came frequently to **Thrapston** and the old wharves stand as a memory. An attractive housing development has taken place on the Thrapston side of the bridge with grassed areas between the river and the houses.

**Thrapston Bridge** also marks the approximate location where the pronunciation of the river changes. From its source, it has so far been the 'Nen'.

Now, downstream to its outfall, it is the 'Neen'. Just downstream of the bridge is a broad reach, where in summer water lilies proliferate, as do the private moorings for the riverside properties.

There is a weired side channel on the east bank, with the mill race on the west bank, while the main channel continues as the middle channel to **Islip lock** where the vertical gate is electrically powered. A track leads from Islip to Islip Mill and Lock. The mill in former times stood close to wharfs and warehouses and, until 1960, corn was ground there.

For many years' boaters have been frustrated by the low headroom of **Islip Mill footbridge**, at times of just a modest rise in level boats would have difficulty passing under without dismantling cratch covers and clearing poles and planks off the roof. A joint venture between Northamptonshire County Council, The Environment Agency and Association of Nene River Clubs in 2017 enabled a new bridge to be installed – now providing 3 metres of headroom and ramp access for pedestrians.

Below the new footbridge is **Thrapston Lagoon**, one of the biggest gravel pits in the country, adjoining the high ridge along the road from Aldwincle to Lowick. It contains an old wildfowl decoy and is just the largest example of the proliferation of gravel workings in this area. Here the Nene Way rejoins the east bank of the river and a track continues for a little way along the right bank. Downstream, the mill race rejoins the main channel.

## Nature reserves and features

East of the village is **Woodford Shrubbery** (also known as Stone Pit Common), an area rich in wild flowers, insects and butterflies. The Shrubbery is reputedly the place where, in former times, limestone workers gathered for illicit drinking sessions. There are several footpaths from the village and the Nene Way that pass through the common.

**Denford churchyard** contains a 0·4-hectare nature reserve, of grasslands, ponds and springs, with mossy lichened walls. The reserve is home to caterpillars, butterflies, ash, hawthorn, willow, wild flowers and abundant birdlife.

## Walking and exploring

**The Nene Way** leaves the river at Mill Road in order to explore the village of Woodford, returning to the river just before Woodford lock. The Nene Way does not follow the serpentine windings of the Nene here but continues to pursue a straight course due east to Denford Lock. From the lock the trail keeps a modest distance from the river in order to negotiate the underpass under the A14 it then heads directly to the Woolpack pub in Islip. Once through Islip village the Nene Way strikes north across the meadows.

**Thrapston Heritage Trail**, produced by and available from East Northamptonshire Council, is well worth discovering, if you have time.

## Cycling

**The Thrapston to Stanwick cycle way** (National Cycle route 71) can be joined via the Nene Way from Mill Road at Lower Ringstead lock. The cycle/walking route heads almost directly to Thrapston along the track bed of the Northampton to Peterborough railway, crossing the river on two old railway bridges.

## Canoeing

**Denford war memorial** stands by the river on the northern edge of the village. There is a convenient layby next to the river with easy access into to the backwater where you have the choice of continuing north along the backwater to Thrapston, negotiating a low bridge and plenty of nettles around the old Mill marina site, or going left along the backwater to pick up the main channel upstream of Denford lock.
GR: SP 993768

**Thrapston Bridge EA moorings** provide access for launching, unloading in the set-back gateway, before parking across the road near the Woolpack.
GR: SP 990786

## Local history

**Woodford** is a large village, inhabited since Saxon times; it appears in the Domesday Book as Wodeford, meaning ford by a wood. In 1867 a mummified human heart was found in the church of St Mary the Virgin. Many believe this to be the heart of Sir Walter Trailly, the lord of the manor, who died on Crusade in 1290. Like many churches on this reach, the spire of St Mary the Virgin overlooks the valley from its proud position on the hill. The church is now on the edge of the village but there is evidence that this was not always so. The grassy bumps, in a nearby field, reveal the outlines of houses.

Woodford also contains **Woodford House**, owned in the first half of the 19th century by a friend of the Duke of Wellington and often frequented by the Duke himself. Later, General Charles Arbuthnot, when living in the house in the late 1850s, started the Woodford Iron Ore Company, mining from an adit in the grounds of the house. The enterprise was considerably helped by the opening of the Kettering to Cambridge railway link in 1865.

Near to the Shrubbery are the terraced remains of Lord St John's Dower House, demolished in the early 19th century. In addition, from the vantage point of the old post mill site to the north of the village, ten church spires may be viewed.

'**Denford**' could mean settlement on a hill slope but was recorded in Domesday as 'Deneford', with the more likely meaning of 'ford in a valley'. The parish contains evidence of the former ridge and furrow agriculture, while a mound at the south of the village is all that remains of a former windmill. Denford Church of The Holy Trinity, which dates mainly from the 13th century, rises majestically above the trees. The War memorial stands on the bank of the River Nene, on the edge of the village. It taller than most other memorials and was erected in 1921. A small layby and seat overlooking the backwater is a tranquil place to rest for a while.

**Thrapston** has been a market town since King John granted it a charter in 1205 and once boasted two railway stations, neither of which now survives. It lies on the edge of the historic and once much larger Rockingham Forest, an area itself of much historical and nature interest. On the west wall of the 13th-century St James' church is a tablet, depicting the stars and stripes, the crest of Sir John Washington, a former lord of the manor of Thrapston. This Washington died in 1668 but was the ancestor of the more famous Washington – George. The family crest formed the basis for the flag of the United States of America, a century later.

Grazing on flood meadows

**Thrapston Nine Arches Bridge** spans the River Nene between **Islip** and **Thrapston**. 15th-century records describe a seven-arch bridge on the present site, five arches of the bridge were rebuilt, following the serious flood of 1795. Later the bridge was extended to 24 arches but when the railway was built in the 19th century, the length was reduced to form the present nine arch bridge.

Islip's name derives from an old English word meaning 'slippery place', referring to the hill leading down to the Nene banks. Islip House was once the home of Thomas Squire, one of the leaders of the bid to make the Nene navigable between Thrapston and Peterborough in 1737. It is alleged that a secret passage leads from the house to the Woolpack Inn.

The Washington connection can also be seen in Islip Church, St Nicholas, which contains a memorial tablet to Mary Washington. Near here was the factory of the Loveday family, of which eight generations harvested bulrushes, to be made into mats, baskets, horse collars and chair seats. The factory closed in 1960.

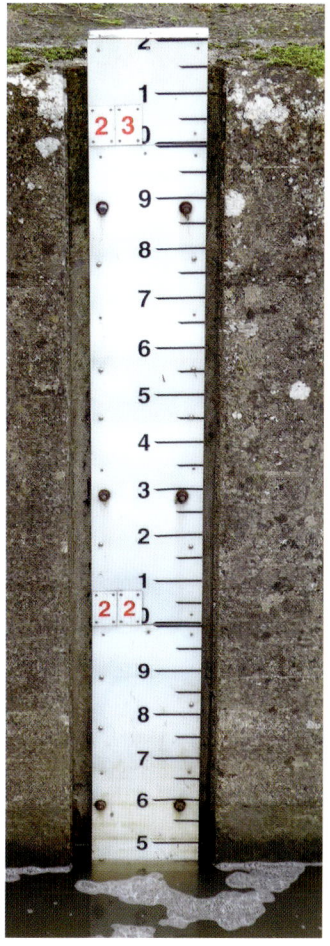

Inverted height gauges (depth gauges) are used at locks to provide an indication of the depth of water above the lock cill

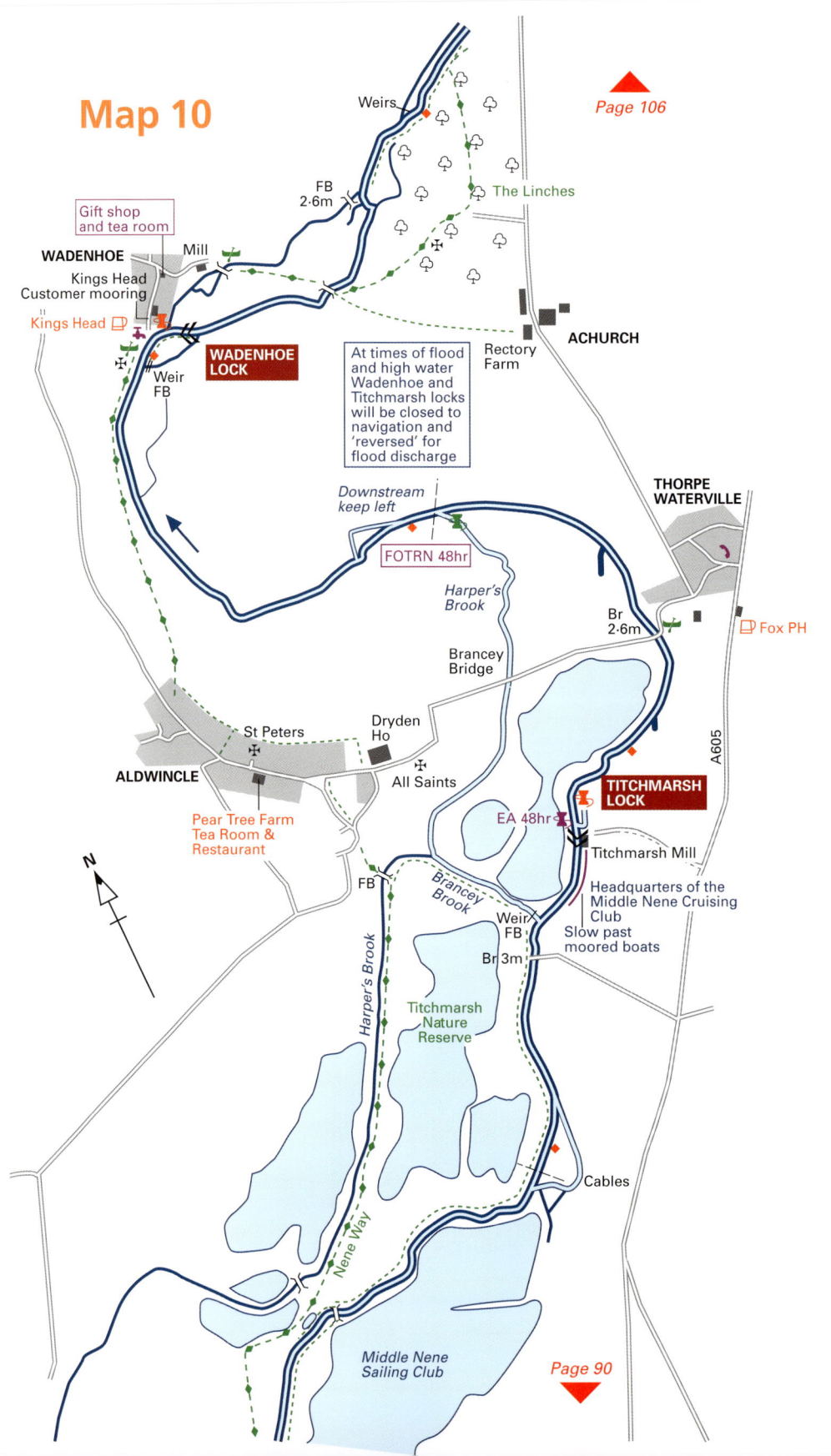

# Map 10

# Middle Nene Sailing Club EA moorings to Lilford Lock upstream weir exit

Wellingborough to Wadenhoe

## Map 10  Middle Nene Sailing Club EA moorings (GR SP 993793) to Lilford Lock upstream weir exit (GR TL 0023835)

| Location | Miles | Locks | Lock type | Est time hours | Bridge < 2·7m | Moorings and facilities | | | | | | | Victualling | | | | Canoe | |
|---|---|---|---|---|---|---|---|---|---|---|---|---|---|---|---|---|---|---|
| | | | | | | 48hr | Long stay | Water point | CDP | Pumpout | Refuse | Diesel | Shops | Pub | Café | PO or Bank | Portage | Park & access |
| Mill Lakes Footbridge | 0·5 | 0 | | 0·1 | 2·40 | | | | | | | | | | | | | |
| Titchmarsh Lock 23 | 1·5 | 1 | ☐ | 0·7 | | | | | | | | | | | | | ▲▼ | |
| Middle Nene Cruising Club | 0·0 | 0 | | 0·0 | | 🛥 | | 🚰 | permission required for use of facilities | | | | | | | | | |
| Titchmarsh EA moorings | 0·0 | 0 | | 0·0 | | 🛥 | | | | | | | | | | | | |
| Thorpe Road Bridge | 0·5 | 0 | | 0·1 | 2·60 | | | | | | | | | The Fox Thorpe Waterville 🍺 | 🍴 | | | 🛶 |
| Peartree Farm FOTRN mooring | 0·6 | 0 | | 0·2 | | 🛥 | | | | | | | | | | | | |
| Kings Head, Wadenhoe | 1·3 | 0 | | 0·4 | | 🛥 | | 🚰 | | | | | | 🍺 | 🍴 | | | 🛶 |
| Wadenhoe Lock 24 | 0·1 | 1 | ☐ | 0·3 | | | | | | | | | | | | | ▲ | |
| Achurch footbridge | 0·3 | 0 | | 0·1 | 2·60 | | | | | | | | | | | | | |
| Lilford Lock Weir entrance | 0·5 | 0 | | 0·1 | | | | | | | | | | | | | | |
| Map 10 totals | 5·3 | 2 | | 2·1 | | | | | | | | | | | | | | |

THE RIVER NENE

## Navigation notes

After leaving **Islip**, the scenery changes to a succession of flat meadows, forming the flood plain of the river, interspersed with scrub and woodland. The Nene curls under a low footbridge and care should be taken. The river then moves to the northeast. Harper's Brook, which rises close to Market Harborough, flows through Titchmarsh reserve before joining forces with Brancey Brook further north.

An overhead power line crosses the river at this point and the succession of lakes continues until **Brancey Bridge** on the Aldwincle -Thorpe Waterville road is reached. Brancey Brook also provides a fluvial border to the reserve. Immediately by the reserve, there is a minor backwater to the right as the main Nene turns north. After a further half mile, **Titchmarsh Bridge** crosses, carrying a track to meet the A605 and the road to Titchmarsh and Brancey Brook moves off from the north bank to join Harpers Brook, just before one of the latter's two junctions with the Nene. The old bridge previously at this location has been removed and the Environment Agency have constructed a new bridge to give a 3m air draught at normal water level. Adjacent to **Titchmarsh Lock** is Titchmarsh Mill, the headquarters and moorings of **Middle Nene Cruising Club**.

The Nene meanders in a generally north-easterly direction passing the end of the Nature Reserve, before meeting the bridge crossing of the Thorpe Waterville-Aldwincle road. The Nene passes close to **Thorpe Waterville** at this point and its character is narrow and winding as it approaches the early 14th-century bridge in the village.

Having passed Thorpe Waterville, the Nene loops west and after a further half mile, meets the second outfall of Harper's Brook/Brancey Brook on the southern bank. There are alder woods on the bank here and the river departs from its previous narrow sinuous course to become broad and deep, dividing round a small wooded island. **The navigation channel is to the left**, but the backwater is popular with fishermen and crammed with tench. Overhead lines cross the channel at this point. Beyond the small island, on the right bank is **Achurch (Wadenhoe) Meadow**.

Having passed **Aldwincle** on the south west bank, the Nene curls back north again and the Nene Way joins the from its diversion through Aldwincle, close to a wooded area just upstream of Wadenhoe. There is a weired backwater on the right bank, while the main channel passes the isolated church of St Michael and All Angels, Wadenhoe, on the north west bank.

After the moorings at the **King's Head**, the mill channel leads off the north bank to the mill just upstream of a sharp turn into **Wadenhoe lock** cut. The lock at Wadenhoe, which has an electrically powered guillotine gate, leads from a deep wide pool and the village, the lock and their settings still convey something of the feel of a settlement in the wilderness.

After Wadenhoe Lock, the next stretch to Lilford takes the voyager past a channel now flanked with water meadows, in contrast to the previous accompaniment of the former mineral workings. After the lock, the back channel from the right re-joins the main channel. This section is a delight to cruise as you will almost certainly be treated to an aerobatic display performed by red kites circling on thermals high in the sky. At a lower level there are often kestrels in a frenzied

## Moorings and facilities

**Middle Nene Cruising Club**
There is a slipway here for members' use and overnight visitor moorings for affiliated members. Club Secretary ✆ 07733 0815581
GR: TL 015810

**Environment Agency 48-hour visitor moorings** are available on the left bank just downstream of Titchmarsh lock. Boaters need be aware that these moorings are also currently being used as a temporary downstream lock landing. An alternative nearby location is being sought to reinstate the mooring.

**FOTRN Peartree Farm 48-hour members mooring** where Brancey Brook enters the river from the south, between Thorpe Bridge and Wadenhoe.
GR: TL 016822

An **EA water point** is situated adjacent to the Kings Head and the village hall at Wadenhoe.

**Overnight moorings** for customers can be found on the banks of the Kings Head (one of the only food-serving pubs with moorings outside).

Accommodation is available at **Pear Tree Farm, Aldwincle** ✆ 01832 720055

Meals and refreshments are available at **The Fox** public house, Thorpe Waterville ✆ 01832 720274

**Wadenhoe** can present a very pleasant picture, particularly in the summer months, when cream teas are served at the village hall. The village also has a gift shop and tea room at **The Old Barn,** Mill Lane ✆ 01832 721129

The village has a conference and training centre in **Wadenhoe House** ✆ 01832 720777

**The King's Head** pub Church Street ✆ 01832 720024

## Nature reserves and features

**Titchmarsh Nature Reserve,**
Close to the A605 and Aldwincle village, provides superb bird watching facilities and consists of 72 hectares of former gravel pits, wetland meadows and a large heronry, comprising the Titchmarsh Duck Decoy (now known as the Heronry Lake), built by Lord Lilford in 1885. It is now managed by the Beds, Cambs and Northants Wildlife Trust and is particularly important for ducks, including, goosander, wigeon and gadwall. At present it also has a breeding colony of herons. The reserve is also well known for great-crested grebe, mallard and sand martins and incorporates a right of way along the adjacent former railway line.
✆ 01604 405285
GR: TL 006812

**Achurch Meadow SSSI,** is a flower meadow, containing over 100 different species of flowering plant and the former course of the Nene can be seen across the meadows, which also provide suitable breeding and feeding grounds

hover looking for their next meal. Towards Lilford, Kingfishers can often be spotted flitting briefly between the branches.

The Nene turns to the northwest and the left side channel rejoins a quarter of a mile further downstream. A weired side channel joins on the left, just upstream of **Lilford Lock** and runs parallel to the main channel for a short distance, before rejoining it.

for birds, such as redshank, snipe and lapwing. On the west bank, **Wadenhoe Marshes**, where a ridge of limestone descends to the river, is covered by old alder and willow trees making it a habitat frequented by woodpeckers. Several brooks arise within the meadows.

Downstream of the village, **The Linches escarpment** of the backwater is thick with trees, while to the west is a wild wooded track, once part of Rockingham Forest. It is the remains of a once great wood named 'Bareshanks', said itself to be named after the dilapidated appearance of Black Watch deserters, caught there in 1743.

## Walking and exploring

**The Nene Way** continues to move away from the river to follow the right bank of Harper's Brook, passing several lakes on its way through Titchmarsh nature reserve. The trail diverts north to visit Aldwincle village and then strikes off across the fields to rejoin the river bank, via Wadenhoe marshes, near the church.

**The Nene Way** follows the road through this delightful village, turning to the west down Mill lane to cross the left-hand side channel and the main channel at a bridge 0.3 miles after the lock, before dividing into two just to the west of Achurch. The Nene Way moves off to the north through the very pleasant wooded Linches. It tracks northeast towards Lilford Bridge, adjoining Lilford Park.

Northamptonshire County Council have produced a leaflet and map which suggests several **Riverside Walks around Aldwincle and Wadenhoe**. The leaflet also includes information about key buildings and areas of interest.

## Cycling

If you avoid the busy A605 there are several possibilities for exploring the villages and local area on relatively quiet roads and tracks by cycle.

## Canoeing

**Aldwincle/Thorpe Bridge at Thorpe Waterville** provides easy access to the river on the downstream side of the bridge. Parking is possible on the grass off the narrow road.
GR: TL 021815

**Wadenhoe, Church Street** car park next to the Village Hall and Kings Head provides access to the river – a fence and fairly high bank can make this a bit tricky.
GR: TL 011833

**Wadenhoe, Mill Lane** provides a pretty place to start a trip. Free parking and launch into the mill pond.
GR: TL 013833

## Local history

The name '**Aldwincle**' probably originates from a bend in the river. In the Domesday Book, it is shown as 'Eldewincle' from the Saxon 'wincel' meaning 'bend or corner'. The village has a church at either end and John Dryden, the poet and playwright, was born in the rectory of All Saints Church in 1631. The church is now disused, but the rectory stands opposite. St Peter's church is however, still in use and is interesting for the remains of 14th-century glass figures of St George and St Christopher in the south windows.

Gravel extraction in the Brancey Brook area, in 1968, revealed the wooden remains of a Roman bridge and

Wadenhoe Mill

causeway across the river. This was part of the old Gartree road, linking Leicester and Godmanchester.

**Thorpe Waterville** has the remains of a Norman castle which was fortified by the Bishop of Lichfield in 1301. On the left of these remains, across a meadow, stands a farmhouse - all that now remains of the mansion house of the Waterville family, although signs of the moat are still present.

The name '**Wadenhoe**' is probably derived from the Saxon for 'Wada's spur of land'. It has a bridge dating from 1760, with three round arches and an attractive long village street. The remains of a Neolithic mortuary enclosure and two Bronze Age round barrows have been found. The church of St Michael and All Angels is situated on a high hill slightly removed from the village. The bells here are said to produce the most musical peal in the county. The church also contains a memorial tablet to the former squire, Thomas Hunt and his bride Caroline, who were robbed and killed by bandits near Salerno in Italy, while on honeymoon in 1824. The estate was afterwards inherited by George Ward Hunt, who became Chancellor of the Exchequer in the Disraeli government, with the result that Wadenhoe was the first village to have a postal telegraph office to help him keep in touch.

The old mill, over the hill from the Church on the northeast side of the village, has a roof tiled in Collyweston tiles. Near the mill is a circular dovecote, built in 1650, which is a county heritage site and the interior of which is well worth viewing. The Nene Way passes the mill.

**Achurch** has been settled since the Iron Age and is named after the Saxon 'Aas-Kirk', 'the church by the water'. In Achurch is a well, a memorial to Thomas Powys, whose grandson became the first Lord Lilford. William Peake, born in Achurch in 1603 became Lord Mayor of London while Alfred Leete, born there in 1882, was the artist responsible for the famous 'Your Country needs you' recruiting poster of the First World War.

A footpath incorporating the Nene Way leads from the Church, St John the Baptist, built in 1218, to the river, flanked by grazing meadows on both sides. About 1830, the village was however, rebuilt by Lord Lilford, who demolished the former houses and replaced them with estate houses; lumps and bumps in the field on the other side of the road are all that remain of the former village. The church has Saxon origins but was rebuilt at the end of the 13th century in the shape of a cross, by Sir Asceline de Waterville, in gratitude for a safe delivery from the crusades. Sir Asceline's tomb is in the church.

Upper Barnwell lock near Oundle

# 4

# RIVER NENE WADENHOE TO STIBBINGTON

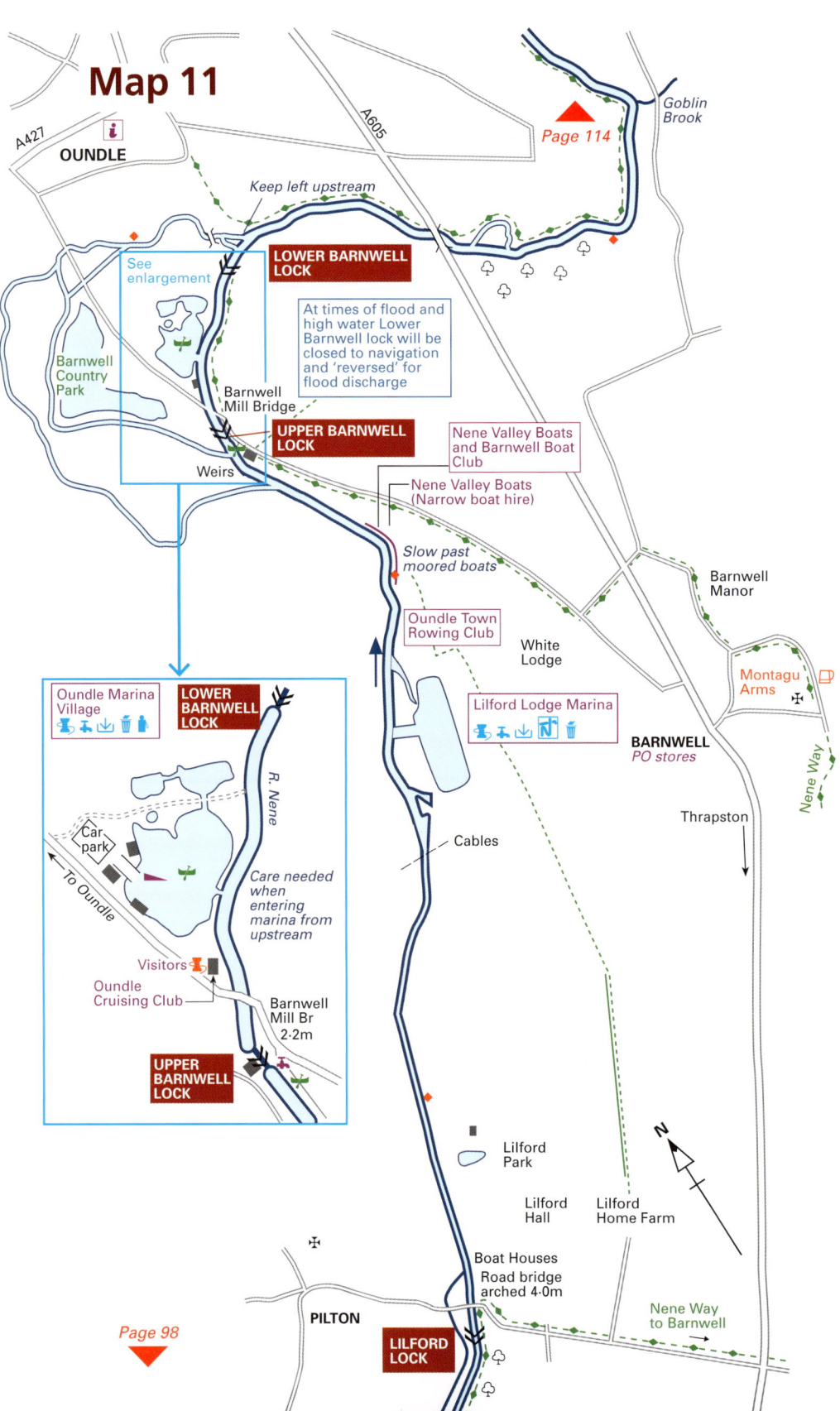

# Map 11

# Lilford Lock upstream weir exit to Goblin Brook, Polebrook

Wadenhoe to Stibbington

| Map 11 Lilford Lock upstream weir exit (GR TL 0023835) to Goblin Brook, Polebrook (GR TL 058869) ||||||||||||||||||
|---|---|---|---|---|---|---|---|---|---|---|---|---|---|---|---|---|
| Location | Miles | Locks | Lock type | Est time hours | Bridge < 2.7m | Moorings and facilities |||||| Victualling |||| Canoe ||
| | | | | | | 48hr | Long stay | Water point | CDP | Pumpout | Refuse | Diesel | Shops | Pub | Café | PO or Bank | Portage | Park & access |
| Lilford Lock 25 | 0.5 | 1 | ☐ | 0.4 | | | | | | | | | | | | | | |
| Lilford Bridge | 0.1 | 0 | | 0.0 | | | | | | | | | | | | | | |
| Lilford Lodge Marina | 2.2 | 0 | | 0.6 | | | ⚓ | 🚰 | | | | | | | | | | |
| Barnwell Boat Club | 0.1 | 0 | | 0.0 | | ☕ | | 🚰 | ⬇ | permission required for use | | | | | | | | |
| Upper Barnwell Lock 26 | 0.0 | 1 | ☐ | 0.3 | | | | 🚰 | | | | | | | | | ▲▼ | 🛶 |
| Barnwell Road Bridge | 0.0 | 0 | | 0.0 | 2.20 | | | Barnwell village | | | | | 🛒 | 🍺 | | £ | | |
| Oundle Cruising Club | 0.1 | 0 | | 0.0 | | ☕ | | 🚰 | | | 🗑 | permission required for use of facilities | | | | | | |
| Oundle Marina Village | 0.0 | 0 | | 0.0 | | ☕ | ⚓ | 🚰 | ⬇ | | 🗑 | | 🛒 | 🍺 | 🍴 | £ | | 🛶 |
| Lower Barnwell Lock 27 | 0.2 | 1 | ☐ | 0.3 | | | | | | | | | Oundle town | | | | ▲▼ | |
| Goblin Brook entrance | 1.3 | 0 | | 0.4 | | | | | | | | | | | | | | |
| Map 11 totals | 4.5 | 3 | | 2.1 | | | | | | | | | | | | | | |

THE RIVER NENE

## Navigation Notes

**Lilford Lock**, with its 'fairytale look', is 1·1 miles from Wadenhoe Lock and one of the most beautiful spots along the navigation. It seems to suddenly emerge from the background of trees and vegetation as a reminder that we are here to stretch our muscles. Downstream of the lock is Lilford Bridge, a structure that adds the final touch of magic to this part of the river. The Nene continues past **Lilford Hall boat house** on the east bank and past **Lilford Hall and Park** which is not, unfortunately, open to the public. After one mile **Lilford Lodge Marina** entrance is passed on the east bank.

Pilton vicarage and church, St Mary and All Saints appear on the west bank which form a fine group with the old manor house. Between Pilton and Barnwell, the Nene travels sinuously through an almost unspoilt valley setting with high ground either side typified by water meadows with cattle grazing. A backwater from Stoke Doyle village joins on the north west bank. As the river moves northwest, more overhead lines cross and a footpath leading from Lilford joins the right bank and meets the Oundle to Barnwell road along which the Nene Way has travelled on its journey back towards the Nene. The entrance to Lilford Lodge marina is passed to the north east.

**Oundle Town Rowing Club** headquarters and launching platform appear just downstream of the marina on a bend in the river. The river between the club and Lilford bridge is frequently used for training. Boaters need to be vigilant and recognise that coxless boats will have their backs to you as they approach, sometimes at a fair speed!

After a further 0·3 miles, the river reaches a weired side channel on the left on the approach to Upper Barnwell Lock 2·3 miles from Lilford. A second side channel leaves on the left immediately upstream of the lock, skirts round the south, west and north of the lakes in **Barnwell Country Park** and joins the first side channel at two points either side of the Barnwell–Oundle road. The main channel continues to **Upper Barnwell Lock** where there is a water point set back from the upstream lock landing. Upper Barnwell Lock has an electrically powered guillotine gate. Adjacent to the lock on the left bank is Barnwell Mill.

Height gauge
Oundle Mill

## Moorings and facilities

**Lilford Lodge Marina** is now open and provides long term moorings. Pump-out and diesel are available on a Saturday morning at present. The site will be developed further with a full range of facilities and services.

**Barnwell Moorings and Nene Valley Boats** provide long term moorings. Nene Valley Boats provide narrowboat hire, RYA courses ☎ 01832 272585

Downstream of Barnwell Road bridge are the headquarters of the **Oundle Cruising Club** on the left bank, which are open at weekends in season. Short stay moorings may be available at the Club. FOTRN have a rubbish skip located at the club for members use. ☎ 01832 278297

**Oundle Marina Village** is a secure site at night, with gates locked at 6.00pm for visitors and public. It has a car park, chandlery, slipway, water point, refuse disposal, workshop facilities, craneage, fuel (diesel and petrol), toilets, chemical toilet disposal, a launderette and showers. It offers both overnight and long stay moorings. St Peter's church spire, a prominent Oundle landmark, is clearly visible from the marina. From here, it is about 20 minutes, on foot, to the centre of Oundle.
☎ 01832 272762

**Barnwell village** to the southeast has a **Post Office/stores** on Church Lane ☎ 0345 611 2970 and the **Montagu Arms** pub ☎ 01832 273726

**Oundle** has a full range of facilities, shops, chemists, doctors, dentists, hotels, pubs, cafés, restaurants etc. There is an information centre in West Street and a market is held on Thursdays.

There are plenty of bus services linking Oundle to local villages, Northampton and Peterborough.

Just after the Upper Barnwell lock, is Barnwell Country Park accessed from the road opposite Oundle Marina entrance. Immediately after the lock, the Oundle to Barnwell road crosses the Nene at Barnwell Mill Bridge The bridge is low and askew and care should be taken in navigating it. There are numerous house martin nests under the bridge and the residents fly in and out regardless of the proximity of passing boats.

After the bridge on the west side of the river are the premises of **Oundle Cruising Club**. Immediately downstream of the club is the entrance to **Oundle Marina Village**, care is required when entering, particularly from upstream, in view of the narrow, stone lined below the waterline, entrance. Opposite the entrance is a favourite spot for anglers, making a wide turn into or out of the marina difficult if you want to remain on good terms with them!

Downstream of Oundle Marina and 0·4 miles from its neighbour, stands **Lower Barnwell Lock** where the guillotine gate is electrically powered. The Nene at this

Oundle Marina

point seems unsure of its passage towards Oundle, first approaching the town, and then veering away through flood meadows and old flooded gravel pits – before looping onwards to Polebrook and Ashton.

After the lock the two side channels rejoin the main Nene which flows again as one. A footpath leads over these backwaters and across the meadows up Basset Farm Road to Oundle, emerging at the Market Place. The Nene turns southeast, with poplars prominent on the south bank and the silver spire of Achurch church can still be seen beyond Lilford Woods.

The river then turns south and after 0·25 miles is crossed by the A605. A power line crosses here with a semi-circular backwater then joining immediately downstream. The Nene Way diverts round this, then returns to follow the left bank. There is a densely wooded area on the right bank leading up from the Barnwell–Armston road and, after this area, the river turns northeast and, passes the entry of Goblin Brook before turning north. For the last two miles The Nene has skirted the town of Oundle ending up encircling it, but this is an unfair course, for Oundle is well worth a visit.

### Nature reserves and features

**Barnwell Country Park** has 15 hectares of tranquil lakes, ponds, meadows and riverbank, a network of accessible surfaced trails, wildlife observation hides, picnic meadows, waymarked trails, waterside walks, nature trail and children's activity trail leaflets, children's adventure play area. Day permit coarse fishing. Award winning visitor centre with activities, souvenirs, countryside information and The Kingfisher Café (℡ 01832 273435). If you are moored at Oundle Cruising Club or marina the country park is just across the road.

## Walking and exploring

At Lilford Bridge **the Nene Way** diverts 'inland' for approximately 5·5 miles to follow the B662 southeast, crossing the A605, then turning north-north-east towards Wigsthorpe and Barnwell village.

From here the trail follows Barnwell Road towards Oundle, where it is reunited with the river at Upper Barnwell lock. It then moves to the east, to cross the Nene at Lower Barnwell Lock and the side channel, as it rejoins the main channel just downstream of the lock and continues along the north bank.

**Oundle**, like most of the other Nene Valley towns, has a **Heritage Trail** leaflet which provides interesting snippets of history about the many buildings of key interest. Copies are available from www.east-northamptonshire.gov.uk/tourism

**Oundle Riverside Walks** is another leaflet and map worth acquiring. It provides information about places of interest and several suggested walking routes covering a town and river circuit with extensions to Cotterstock and Ashton. Available from visitor centres and Oundle Customer Service Centre ℡ 01832 274333.

## Cycling

**The Oundle Rural cycle route** is a 26-mile route around the villages near Oundle, mostly of quiet country roads. Route details are available from www.nenevalley.net/adventure/cycling/

Lilford Bridge Chris Howes

## Canoeing

It is possible to launch near **Lilford Bridge** but probably best used for an emergency pick up. Verge parking is possible with access into the field on the right via a public footpath but directly to the river bank.
GR: TL 025839

**Upper Barnwell lock** has a large area of off-road parking for launching upstream and downstream of the lock. Access to the back waters and Barnwell Country park is by launching upstream, crossing the river and portaging into the inner backwater at a portage platform.
GR: TL 037869

**Oundle Marina** provides parking and launching for a modest fee, including use of the marina facilities.
GR: TL 038873

Oundle Wharf

## Local history

The graceful humpbacked balustraded stone **Lilford Bridge**, 160 metres downstream of Lilford Lock, carrying the road to Pilton, has few equals in the country. It is set amongst the linch escarpments, subsumed within the Nene valley, amidst woods and spinneys. The Nene flows directly by Lilford Hall, a Jacobean mansion built around 1635 of Ketton stone and noted for its unique double chimney stacks and superb façade. It is not open to the public but may be seen through the trees. Lilford was previously a Saxon village, but the first Lord Lilford demolished this in 1755 when the hall grounds were landscaped to create a 240-acre parkland estate, centred on the house.

**Barnwell village** was home to the Earls of Sandwich (Montagu's) and many are commemorated in the ruined All Saints church, which was partly demolished in 1825, leaving only the chancel. Today, only the 13th-century St Andrews church remains for worship. The chancel of this church was remodelled by Sir Gilbert Scott in 1851 but the 15th-century stained glass windows have been retained. To the southeast of the church, are the Lathams Alms-houses, built in 1601.

The gardens of Barnwell Manor, which can be reached via a beech lined footpath over the stone bridge from the church, include the ruins of a 13th-century castle, said to be haunted by the ghost of a monk with a whip. At the time of the dissolution of the monasteries, the castle was bought from Peterborough Abbey by Sir Edward Montagu, who built a new house in the outer courtyard.

**Oundle** has been a settlement since the Iron Age and the name comes from 'Un dalum', a 'dal' being a share of land and 'undals' either people dispossessed of land or who took over land not given to others. There was once a monastery here dedicated to St Wilfred, who died in AD709.

The north bridge of the town was destroyed in a flood in 1570 but was rebuilt the following year and widened just prior to the First World War, to accommodate the increase in traffic. It now looks out, on the western side, over its stone parapet on Oundle Wharf, a short canal, about 400 yards long, dug from the Nene just downstream of what is now the A427 road bridge.

The town contains many fine 17th and 18th-century buildings and has been greatly helped by the A605 bypass, which follows the course of the old railway line. Perhaps the finest of the buildings of Oundle is the Talbot Hotel whose 400-year old grey stone front was constructed in the early 17th century by William Whitwell, whose initials, with the date 1626, appear in the gable of a nearby house. Whitwell used materials from Fotheringhay Castle in this construction and the staircase within the hotel is said to be the one walked down by Mary, Queen of Scots, on the way to her execution. Around the market place, are several fine old buildings, including Bramston House, which dates from the 18th century, the former White Horse Inn from 1641 and Lathams Hospital which is 30 years older still. St Peter's Church spire, at 64 metres high, is a landmark of elegance for many miles around.

Oundle is home to the famous Oundle public school, which had its origins, in the 14th century, as a small grammar school, attached to the Guild of Our Lady of Oundle. After the dissolution of the monasteries, a famous former pupil, Sir William Laxton, rescued the school. His foundation, in 1556 of the Old Laxton School, which was rebuilt in 1852, is sandwiched between the market place and the graveyard of St Peter's Church. However, it was the later buildings that made the school most famous, particularly under the guidance of Frederick Sanderson, a famous headmaster of the school in the late 19th century. The school is now scattered throughout the town and is Oundle's biggest employer. Sir Peter Scott was amongst its former pupils.

There is also **Oundle Museum** ☎ 01832 272735 open from March to October, at the town end of Barnwell Road, with exhibits tracing the history of the settlement over the past 2,000 years.

North Bridge, Oundle

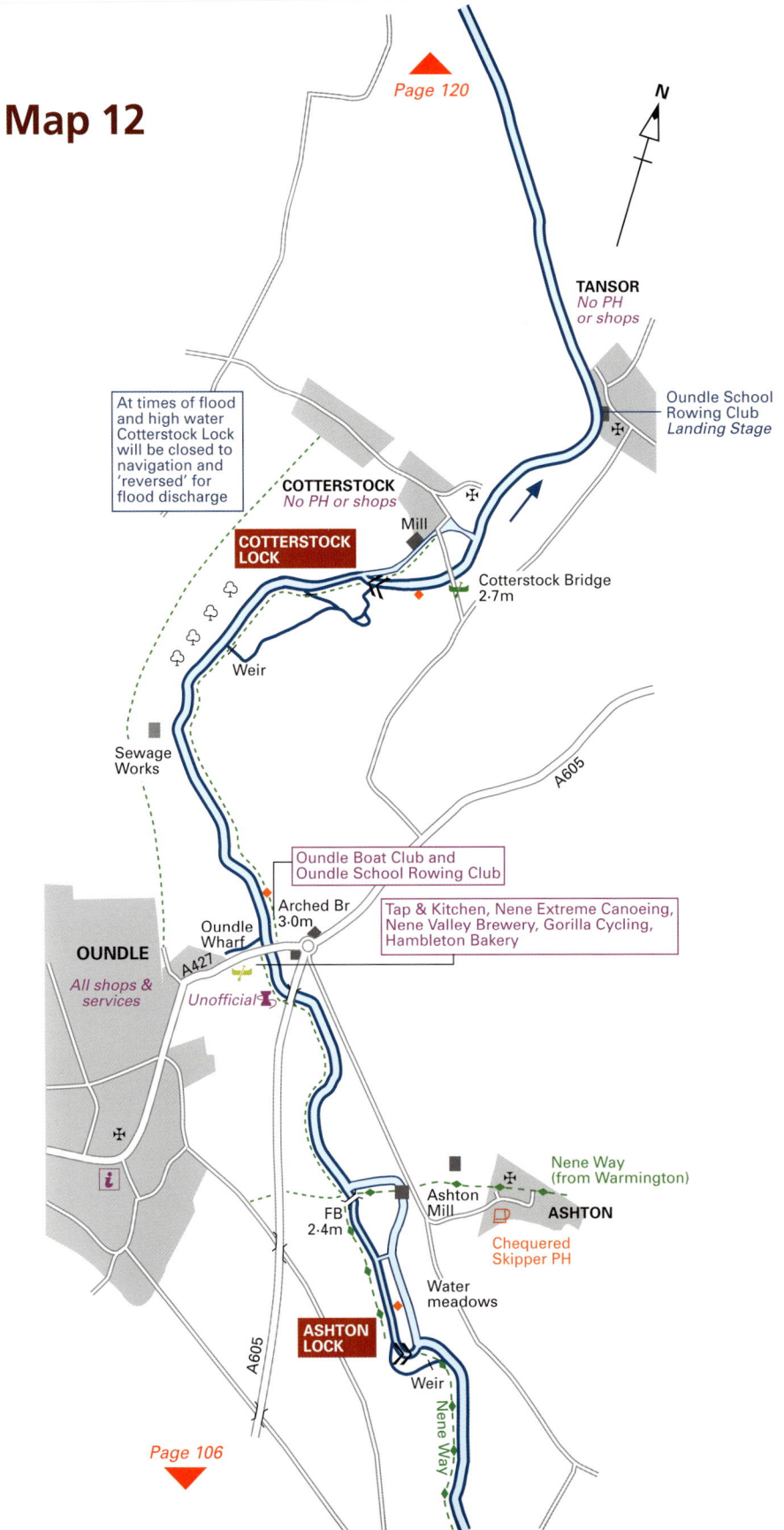

# Map 12

# Goblin Brook, Polebrook to Perio Lock Weir Footbridge

*Waddenhoe to Stibbington*

### Map 12  Goblin Brook, Polebrook (GR TL 058869) to Perio Lock Weir Footbridge (GR TL 044922)

| Location | Miles | Locks | Lock type | Est time hours | Bridge < 2·7m | Moorings and facilities | | | | | | | | Victualling | | | | Canoe | |
|---|---|---|---|---|---|---|---|---|---|---|---|---|---|---|---|---|---|---|---|
| | | | | | | 48hr | Long stay | Water point | CDP | Pumpout | Refuse | Diesel | Shops | Pub | Café | PO or Bank | | Portage | Park & access |
| Ashton Carr FOTRN mooring | 0·7 | 0 | | 0·2 | | ⚓ | | | | | | | Oundle town | | | | | | |
| Ashton Lock 28 | 0·0 | 1 | ☐ | 0·3 | 2·60 | | | | | | | | Chequered Skipper in village | 🍺 | 🍴 | | ▲▼ | | |
| Ashton Footbridge | 0·1 | 0 | | 0·0 | 2·50 | | | | | | | | | | | | | | |
| Oundle Bridge | 1·5 | 0 | | 0·4 | | | ⚓ unofficial | | | | | | Oundle Wharf | 🛒 🍺 | 🍴 | | | | 🪰 |
| Cotterstock Lock 29 | 1·1 | 1 | ☐ | 0·6 | 2·65 | | | | | | | | | | | | ▲▼ | | 🪰 |
| Perio Lock weir bridge | 1·7 | 0 | | 0·5 | | | | | | | | | | | | | | | |
| **Map 12 totals** | **5·2** | **2** | | **2·0** | | | | | | | | | | | | | | | |

THE RIVER NENE

## Navigation notes

The river below Oundle is generally broader and, downstream of the town, is flanked to a large extent with rich flood meadows. It is also deeper now, from here up to the tidal sluice at Dog-in-a-Doublet.

**Ashton Lock** is 0·9 miles from Oundle Bridge, and stands secluded in beautiful meadow surroundings, with a tree lined south bank. The downstream guillotine gate is manually operated and requires stamina. Upstream of the lock is a small weired backwater on the south bank, which curves around the lock. Immediately upstream of the lock a side channel turns north to Ashton Mill and rejoins the main channel by a small cut 200 yards further on. After Ashton Lock, from which the spire of Oundle Church is clearly visible, the millstream rejoins the main channel on the right bank after Ashton Mill, as it continues north past the east side of Oundle. The privately-owned water meadow before the New Road bridge is sometimes used for mooring. A footpath continues along the left bank as the river turns briefly northwest, northeast, north and then northwest again, before the New Road Bridge of the A605 crosses. Immediately afterwards, the A427 running from the A605 then crosses the Nene at the North Bridge and the footpath follows this, crossing to run along the right bank.

Immediately downstream of North Bridge to the east is **Oundle Boat Club** and **Oundle School Rowing Club** premises and launching stages. On the west, town side, opposite is a cut dug to create Oundle Wharf, built primarily to serve the needs of several breweries in the town. It is good to see that a local brewery has premises at Oundle Wharf today.

The Nene continues in a general north-westerly direction, past the Oundle sewage treatment works on the west bank and overhead lines before turning northeast, by a very pleasant heavily wooded area of countryside on the north west side. A weired side channel on the east bank leads downstream of Cotterstock Lock, this side channel is followed 200 yards further downstream by a second side channel, which joins with the first to meet at **Cotterstock Lock**, 2·1 miles downstream of Ashton Lock.

Cotterstock lock is exposed to southwesterly winds and the upstream lock landing is short, close to the lock exit and on a fairly tight bend. When exiting the lock upstream, on a windy day, take care that you don't end up pinned to the far bank, from experience this embarrassing situation is not uncommon! Immediately upstream of the lock, Cotterstock Mill stream leaves on the left, leading to the mill, which has now been converted into a private house.

Leaving Oundle

The mill race exits on the left bank of the Nene, close to Cotterstock Church. The Nene vista remains essentially rural, passing through meadows where sheep graze and lambs frolic in the spring. The river then turns northeast and is crossed after a short distance by Cotterstock Bridge carrying the road leading to the A605 and Tansor village where the footpath moves away from the river. The Nene's next meander is to the northwest and then due north as it passes Tansor.

Because it is relatively straight, the stretch of the Nene adjoining Tansor is used by the senior rowers of Oundle School and their boathouse and landing stage is situated here on the east bank. Caution should be exercised here, due to the possible presence of the school racers who may not know that a steel hull is creeping up on them. Overhead lines cross the river just before the school stages. After skirting Tansor, the Nene flows straight and north-west on the next stretch to Perio Lock footbridge. The fields begin to change with evidence that the rich soil encourages market gardening and the north bank is for a while very much more tree lined than has been the case upstream.

## Moorings and facilities

**Unofficial mooring** spots can be found alongside the private water meadow before North Bridge. A footbridge and footpath across the meadow leads to Ashton Village. There is also a footpath into Oundle town across the meadow. GR: TL 053877

**The Chequered Skipper** ① 01832 273494 on the village green in **Ashton** is widely known. It is a pleasant thatched structure. The green in front of it is frequented by peacocks, originally introduced to the estate by the Rothschilds. The pub takes its name from a rare butterfly, Ashton being the last place at which it was recorded, before becoming extinct in England.

After North Bridge a weed and reedy 400 metre channel heads up to **Oundle Wharf** where several outlets may be of interest to the boater.

**The Tap Kitchen Restaurant**
① 01832 238558

**The Nene Valley Brewery**
① 01832 272776

**Gorilla Firm Cycling**
Cycle hire ① 01832 273783

**Nene Extreme Canoe Hire** ① 01832 27205.

From here it is only a short walk to **Waitrose** and the town.

Canada goose

## Nature reserves and features

**Ashton** is famous for its private 54-hectare nature reserve, **Ashton Wold**, which contains many old oaks, 250-years old or more and a lake planted with both marginal and emergent vegetation to attract dragonflies. The Wold was created by Charles Rothschild (1877–1923) a keen conservationist, who created the society for the Protection of Nature Reserves (now the Royal Society for Wildlife Trusts) in 1912 and set aside part of his Ashton Estate as a nature reserve. The Wold is designated in the Register of Historic Parks and Gardens as an important and unusually intact and coherent model Edwardian Estate. There is a public right of way that passes the Wold – access north from the Polebrook/Lutton Road. GR: TL872089

## Walking and exploring

**The Nene Way** continues to run parallel to the river, bordered by water meadows. The trail crosses the footbridge carrying the footpath running from Oundle to Ashton, and the millstream at the mill to go through Ashton in a north-easterly direction to the village of Warmington.

To reach **Ashton village** cross the main Nene at the footbridge and then the mill side channel at its bridge, head straight to the road then turn right and cross the road to pick up the field path to the village.

## Cycling

**Gorilla Firm Cycling** at Oundle Wharf is a specialist cycle sales shop providing cycle builds, servicing and repairs ☎ 01832 273783.

## Canoeing

**Nene Extreme** based at Oundle Wharf provides canoe and kayak hire at weekends May to September and 7 days a week during school summer holidays - 0900 - 1700. Canoe-camping trips can also be arranged ☎ 01832 272050.

At **Cotterstock Bridge** there is parking either side of the bridge and access for launching down a steep-ish slope into the backwater. GR: TL 049093.

## Local history

**Ashton Mill** was originally a water powered corn mill. It was adapted in 1900 to form an electricity generating and water pumping station serving the Ashton estate. In recent years Historic England have provided small grants to enable the mill and machinery to be preserved and mothballed.

**Ashton** village is owned by the Rothschild family and contains a village green, horse chestnut trees and thatched cottages. It has a chapel and school dated 1705. In 1860, Baron Rothschild bought the parish and around 1900, his son Charles rebuilt the village in local stone and thatch. He also converted the mill to supply the village with piped water and electricity. Ashton's main claim to fame was, however, the World Conker Championships, which had been held in the village every year since 1965. In recent years, though, Southwick has hosted the annual event.

**Cotterstock** was once a Roman settlement and, over a thousand years later, the poet John Dryden often stayed at the Jacobean Cotterstock Hall, where he enjoyed the views of the church and river. St Andrews Church is of interest, a small but spacious building with ancient drawings of deer on the left-hand side of the porch. This is not that surprising. The present building dates from the 12th century and is built on the site of an earlier structure. In the year 1100 it would have been situated deep in the ancient Rockingham Forest now much reduced in size.

**St Mary's church** at Tansor has a quaint square shape with its churchyard going right down to the river, where it is framed by a tree-lined left bank. The carved choir stalls at St Mary's came from the east end of Fotheringhay church, when the latter was demolished.

Ashton Watermill Chris Allen geograph.org.uk

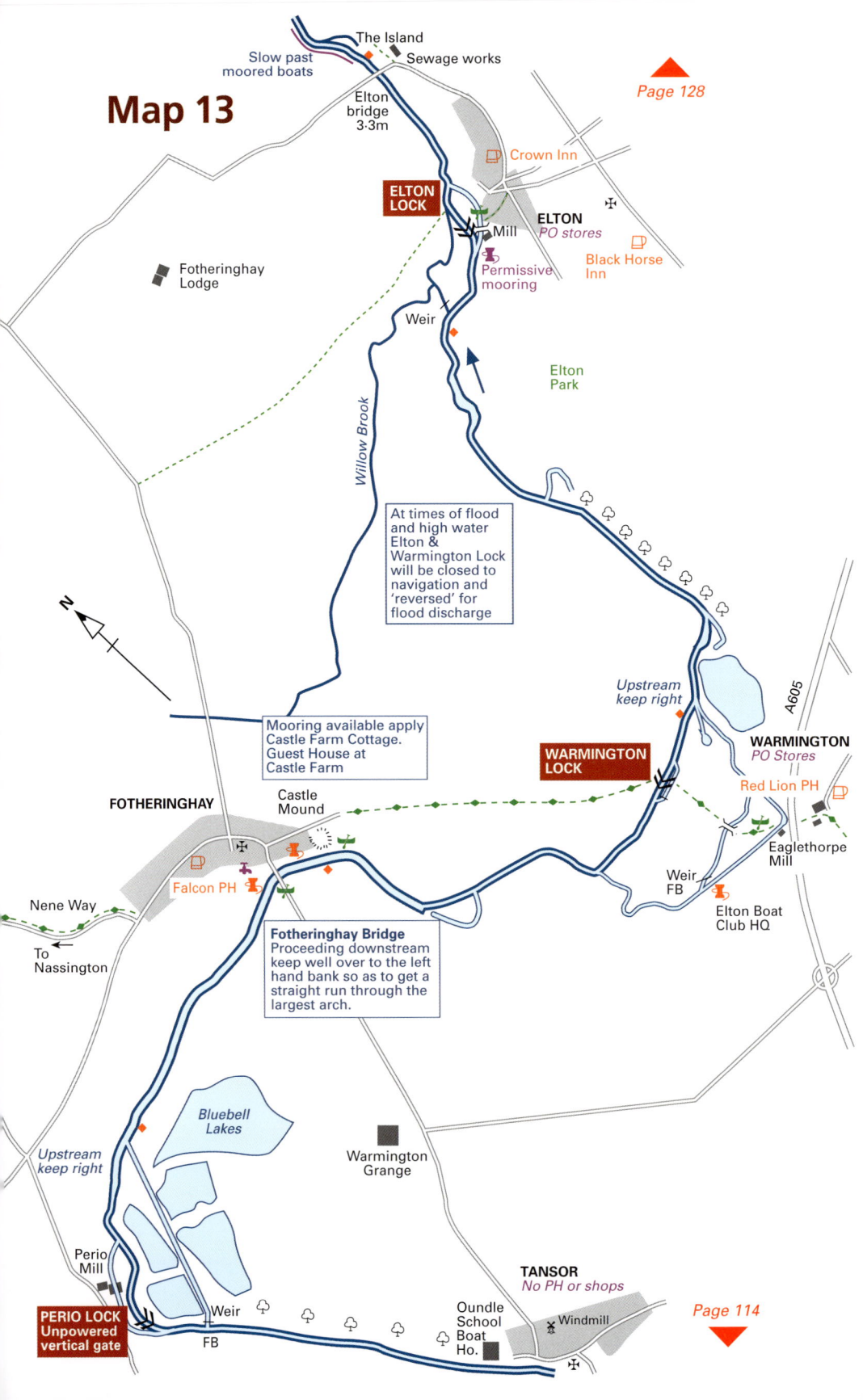

# Map 13

# Perio Lock Weir Footbridge to Elton Road Bridge

| Map 13 Piero Lock Weir Footbridge (GR: TL 044922) to Elton Road Bridge (GR: TL 085945) | | | | | | | | | | | | | | | | | | |
|---|---|---|---|---|---|---|---|---|---|---|---|---|---|---|---|---|---|---|
| Location | Miles | Locks | Lock type | Est time hours | Bridge < 2·7m | Moorings and facilities | | | | | | Victualling | | | | Canoe | |
| | | | | | | 48hr | Long stay | Water point | CDP | Pumpout | Refuse | Diesel | Shops | Pub | Café | PO or Bank | Portage | Park & access |
| Perio Lock 30 | 0·0 | 1 | ☐ | 0·3 | | | | | | | | | | | | | ▲▼ | |
| Fotheringhay Bridge | 1·2 | 0 | | 0·3 | 2·10 | 🍺 | | 🚰 | | | | | | 🍺 | 🍴 | | | 🛶 |
| Castle Farm Mooring | 0·8 | 0 | | 0·2 | | 🍺 | | | | | | | | | | | | 🛶 |
| Warmington Lock 31 | 0·3 | 1 | ☐ | 0·4 | 2·45 | | | | | | | | 🛒 | 🍺 | 🍴 | | ▲▼ | |
| Elton Boat Club | 0·2 | 0 | | 0·1 | | 🍺 | | 🚰 | permission required for use of facilities | | | | | | | | | 🛶 |
| Elton Permissive mooring | 1·3 | 0 | | 0·4 | | 🍺 | | | | | | | 🛒 | 🍺 | 🍴 | | | |
| Elton Lock 32 | 0·1 | 1 | ☐ | 0·3 | | | | | | | | | | | | | ▲ | 🛶 |
| Elton Bridge | 0·5 | 0 | | 0·1 | | | | | | | | | | | | | | |
| Map 13 totals | 4·4 | 3 | | 2·1 | | | | | | | | | | | | | | |

THE RIVER NENE   121

## Navigation notes

On approach to **Perio Lock** a backwater, leaving from the north east bank, runs between two of the lakes that make up Bluebell Fishery, parallel to the main course of the Nene, as the river continues north west to Perio Lock, 1·9 miles from the lock at Cotterstock. Perio Lock has an unpowered vertical gate just to keep you in trim! A second, minor channel, then divides from the main river and continues to Perio Mill, now converted to a private residence, and then curls northeast, matching the direction of the main Nene here, which flows past the north western side of the last lake. A footbridge crosses the river just prior to the point where the downstream end of Perio Mill channel rejoins the Nene after a short distance on the west bank. When proceeding upstream at this point, you are advised to 'keep right'.

Two minor tributaries, from the west then meet the north bank in quick succession before the backwater from the weir rejoins the main channel from the south. The main Nene continues to flow east past the northern side of the Bluebell Lakes to approach the village of **Fotheringhay** with the splendid and rather majestic St Mary and All Saints church overlooking and dominating the water meadow and river. The stunning lantern tower is visible for miles and it is difficult to pass by without a short stop at the moorings to take in the atmosphere or a at least a photo while passing. Despite having to pay a modest fee for mooring at Fotheringhay it must be one of the most idyllic spots on the river to while away time exploring the church, village and castle or just sipping something suitable while listening to the ripple of the river as a background to sheep and lambs playing in the meadows. 18th century Fotheringhay bridge is of the stone humped back variety with beautifully proportioned arches. It is, however, set low and the navigable arch offset, so navigators are advised, particularly when going downstream, to keep well to the left to get a straight run through the largest left-hand arch, as the current is also a significant factor. Headroom and width can make passage difficult for wide beam craft with high superstructure.

Once Fotheringhay has been left behind, the countryside changes dramatically in character, the previous rolling nature of the banks now replaced by flat meadows and houses built from local stone. The Nene is crossed by the Fotheringhay–Tansor road, which also leads to Warmington Grange. A small tributary joins the north bank. The Nene then curves southeast, crossing the route of the now dismantled former railway line, and then turns northeast, passing a small backwater on the right bank, before splitting just upstream of Warmington village. Here, the main navigation

St Mary and All Saints Church, Fotheringhay

## Moorings and facilities

At Fotheringhay excellent, peaceful overnight or short stay moorings are available upstream and downstream of Fotheringhay Bridge on payment to the landowner, **Castle Farm Guest House** ☎ 01832 226200 current rates £5 for 24hrs and £2.50 for a short stop to explore.

Close to and just upstream of the bridge is an **EA Water point**.

Chemical toilet disposal may be available, subject to permission from the camp site and caravan park just downstream of the bridge next to the moorings.

For details of moorings at the **Elton Boat Club** contact the club secretary ☎ 07941 313713. The Club may have visitor moorings but can only accommodate boats up to 36 feet. A water point is also available at the Club.

Just upstream of Elton Lock on the right bank are the permissive overnight moorings made available by the Elton Estate. These moorings are well situated for exploring the local shop and excellent pubs.

**The Falcon** at **Fotheringhay** at the east end of Main Street is a popular hostelry serving food and drinks. ☎ 01832 226254

An hourly **bus service** runs from Fotheringhay to Peterborough (just over 30 minutes). **Warmington** village is adjacent to Eaglethorpe and the A605. A footpath from the lock takes you into this settlement via Chapel Street, where the first turn right leads to the **Post Office Stores** on Hautboy Lane. ☎ 01832 226254

**The Red Lion** public house Peterborough Road. ☎ 01832 280362

**Warmington Garage**, on the A605 roundabout, provides basic provisions and a cash point. ☎ 01832 226417

**Elton** is well served for those with a discerning appetite. For those who enjoy a fish meal, the **Old Dairy** in Elton has been converted into the **Loch Fyne Seafood Restaurant** . ☎ 01832 280298
**The Black Horse Inn** on Main Street ☎ 01832 281222 and **The Crown Inn and Restaurant** on the village green ☎ 01832 280232 provide good ales and meals.

The footpath from the lock leads to the village green and Middle Street and a well provisioned **village stores**. ☎ 01832 281545

**Daily bus service** from the centre of the village to Peterborough.

---

channel turns east and northeast to **Warmington Lock**, 2·3 miles from Perio Lock and, like its neighbour, Warmington Lock has an unpowered vertical gate, I'm afraid!

The minor channel turns south then, after a loop, northeast where it itself splits in two. On the southernmost of these channels, which runs close to the adjacent A605 at this point, is Eaglethorpe Mill, with the moorings and headquarters of **Elton Boat Club**, just upstream within the millstream. There is a weir at the junction of the minor split which carries a footbridge. The two side channels rejoin the main channel as the Nene curves northwest past a heavily tree-lined right bank (Rowley's Wood),

THE RIVER NENE 123

Elton Boat Club moorings

and more minor backwaters connect with the river as it flows past Elton Park, passing **Elton Hall** on the east bank.

One of the other main tributaries of the Nene, Willow Brook, having risen near Corby, joins from the west here in two channels, one connected via a weir which carries a footpath and the other joining downstream of Elton Lock and Mill. At this point the channel again splits in two for a short distance, with Elton Lock on the northern channel. **Elton Lock** has an electrically powered guillotine gate and is 1·6 miles from Warmington Lock. The southern channel moves to the east close to Elton village. At Elton, pleasant woods almost march down to the water's edge. Aromatic poplars are prominent. The village lies up a steep hill with the main road at the top. The footpath from the lock follows the road through Elton to rejoin the Nene again at Elton Bridge close to the sewage treatment plant on the south bank by 'the island' a wooded area between the Nene and its backwater. At Elton, the Nene leaves Northamptonshire and enters Cambridgeshire and the river marks the county boundary for the next four miles. The river here is shallow and gravel bottomed. Between Elton and Wansford, there are few examples of sheltering woods as the course of the Nene travels through open spacious countryside, mainly comprising water meadows with attractive rush and tree lined banks.

## Nature reserves and features

The lakes next to **Perio lock** are known as the **Bluebell Lakes** and are now a carp fishery, created following gravel extraction.

Downstream from **Fotheringhay** the are several willow pollards in the fields, a feature throughout parts of the Nene Valley. These are willows, whose tops have been cut off above cattle grazing height. Willows produce lots of shoots, which grow into poles and were traditionally harvested on 3–15-year cycles. However, many of the traditional uses of the pollarded material, basket making, hurdle fencing etc. have declined and now grants are given by various organisations to restore and maintain these trees and their impact on the landscape.

## Walking and exploring

**The Nene Way** has been conspicuous by its absence since it left the river at Ashton footbridge to visit Warmington. At Fotheringhay we pick it again briefly while it passes through fields above the river after it has crossed the Nene and the two side channels on its way from Warmington Lock and village. From Fotheringhay the trail strikes west and then north-east towards the villages of Nassington and Yarwell.

**Fotheringhay and Wood Newton riverside walks** is another great little leaflet and map providing information about places of interest along the route of two suggested walks. Available from www.nenevalley.net/adventure/walking

**Elton Hall** is open to the public on Wednesdays and Thursdays in June and July and Sundays in August ☏ 01832 280223 www.eltonhall.com Check the website or telephone to confirm opening times. Refreshments are available in the cafe at the Bosworths Garden Centre ☏ 01832 343104.

## Cycling

There are plenty of options for exploring the surrounding villages on two wheels with quiet roads and a couple of good bridleways at Fotheringhay (Nene Way) and Elton (Greenhill Road).

## Canoeing

**Fotheringhay Bridge** can be used to access the Nene, parking might be limited.

**Castle Farm** welcomes paddlers and it is possible to park, launch and camp next to the river, downstream of Fotheringhay Bridge. GR: TL 060930

**Elton** provides parking options around the village green and a bit of a walk along a public footpath to launch at Elton Lock just after the mill.
GR: TL 084 939

There is parking and access to the backwater for canoes at **Eaglethorpe Mill** and **Elton Boat Club**. GR: 074916

Fotheringhay Bridge

## Local history

**Perio** is a mediaeval name whose origins are unclear. Its mill is small compared to Ashton and the millstream and Bluebell Fishery is artificially stocked.

The name **'Fotheringhay'** has three possible derivations. It could be from 'Frodinga', 'the island of Froda's people'; from 'forth here inga' 'the island of people following an army leader' or, most likely, from 'fodring-eg' 'foddering island'. The suffix 'hay' refers to the clearing in Rockingham Forest where deer were foddered in winter.

An earth mound is now the only reminder of **Fotheringhay Castle**, which was most famously the execution site of Mary, Queen of Scots. The castle mound is covered in thistles, a poignant reminder of Mary, who was said to have planted them there during her imprisonment. She had been incarcerated at Fotheringhay following her abdication from the Scottish throne in 1567, subsequent to her marriage to Bothwell and flight to England. Eventually however, she was seen as the figurehead for English Catholics, disillusioned with the Protestant Elizabeth I and went to her fate on 8th February 1587. The castle however, had almost 500 years of history, before Mary met her end. It was built around 1100 by Simon de St Lys, the first Earl of Northampton and Huntingdon and husband of Maud, the great niece of William the Conqueror. A second castle was built in the 14th century around 1377, by Edmund de Langley, first Duke of York and fifth son of Edward I and, by the time of Henry VIII, there was a 'castle fair and meatly strong with very good lodgings in it', defended by double ditches with a very ancient and strong keep covering 10 acres. King Richard III was also born at Fotheringhay castle. Today, however, little remains. The line of the moat is still visible but otherwise only crumbling masonry and tangled bushes signify the history of the site.

Fotheringhay's famous Perpendicular style church of St Mary and All Saints is a small part of a once great Collegiate foundation dating from 1411. Striking features include the octagonal lantern tower, the two storey north porch and the pinnacles and flying buttresses along the length of the nave. The lantern tower can be seen from a distance at various places along the river, acting as a 'lighthouse' for river users.

**Eaglethorpe** was de-populated in the 16th century, when the Proby family enlarged the grounds of Elton Hall. The watermill became redundant in 1880 and was finally closed in the 1890s. Near the mill is a dovecote, made from a wooden framework covered in mortar, which is listed as a scheduled ancient monument. It has nesting boxes for 800 birds. When the adjacent A605 was being constructed, a Beaker burial, of a man buried 3,000 years ago, was discovered.

**Warmington** means 'the farm of Wyrm's people' and the village is two miles on foot from Ashton but, because of the sweeping bends of the Nene, six miles away by river. The Romans were active here and built a road between the two villages, its remnants surviving as part of the Nene Way. Warmington later belonged to the Abbey of Peterborough and was very prosperous in mediaeval times. Its church, St Mary the Virgin, finished in 1290, is noted for its broach spire.

Elton Lock with abandoned Elton Mill beyond

**Elton**, whose name means 'princes' farm' was formerly a farming village, but is now a Peterborough 'dormitory' settlement, with typical housing estates. The centre is very pleasant with several thatched cottages and there are five Roman sites with a major Roman road which can still be traced through part of the parish, confirming the important part in daily life that the river has played at least since those times. The parish boundaries were laid out by Saxon settlers and two Saxon gravestones can still be seen on the north side of the church. Stocks Green still has a set of stocks, after which the location was named and adjoining the Green is a water mill referred to in Domesday although the present building, a three storey brick structure, dates from about 1840.

All Saints 15th-century church, with some evidence of Saxon origin, has a splendid William Morris stained glass window.

**Elton Hall** was never a castle but was defended. There has been a house on this site since the Norman Conquest, with the present house completed in 1666. It contains several Old Masters and the state coach used by the owners to attend Queen Victoria's Jubilee. The library includes a prayer book, containing the writing of King Henry VIII. Elton Hall has been the home of the Proby family for 380 years. The author Kenneth Grahame, famous for The Wind in the Willows, spent many summers at Elton Hall and indeed, one of the islands in the Nene opposite Elton Hall, between the river and its side channels, is known as 'Ratty Island'.

**Elton Mill** is a long abandoned water-powered corn mill, originally constructed in the latter half of the 18th-century but closed some considerable time ago. The mill race is still visible through the lower floor of the mill, although the wheel no longer turns.

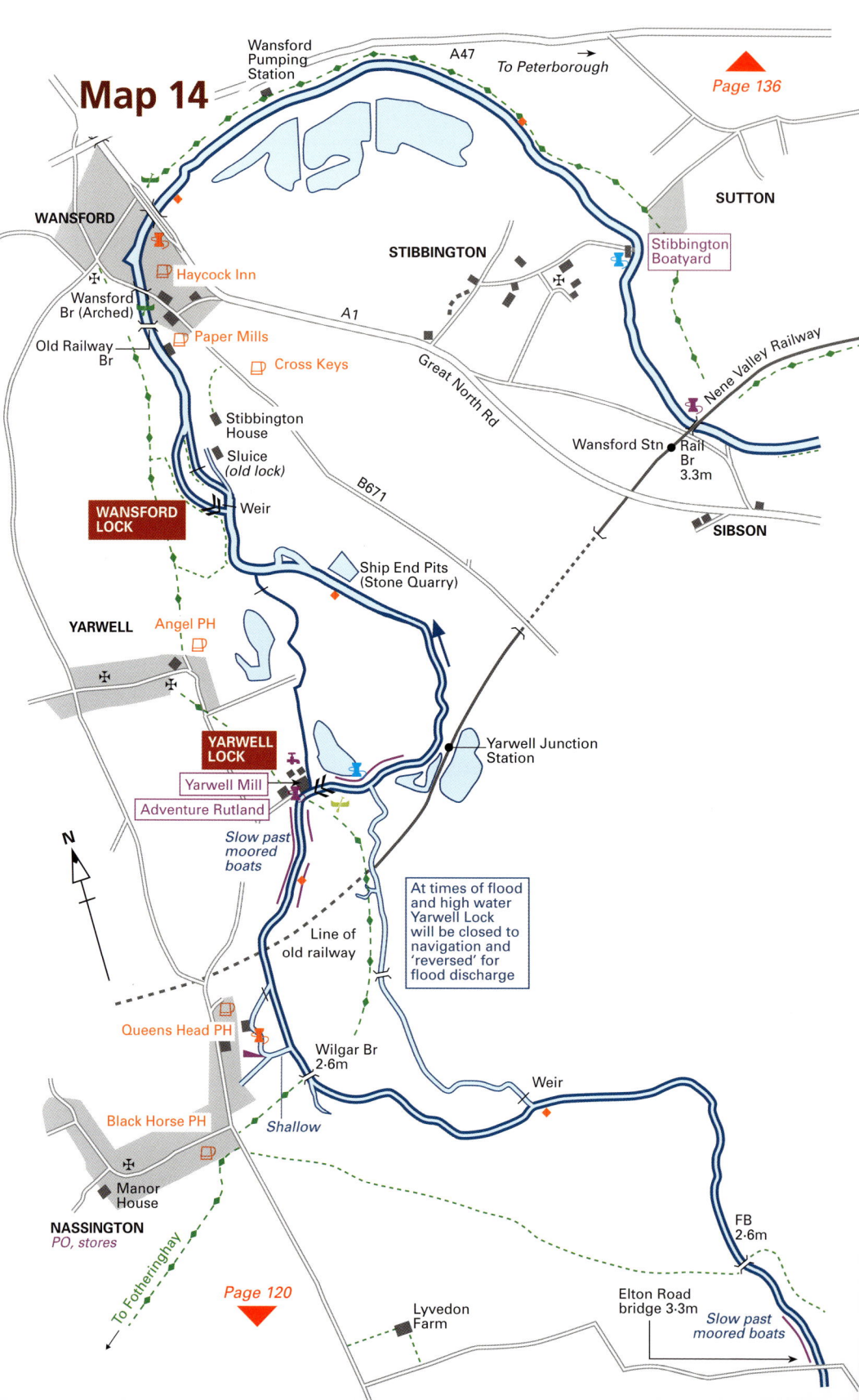

# Map 14

# Elton Road Bridge to Stibbington Boatyard

## Map 14  Elton Road Bridge (GR TL 085945) to Stibbington Boatyard (GR:TL 093987)

| Location | Miles | Locks | Lock type | Est time hours | Bridge <2.7m | Moorings and facilities | | | | | | | Victualling | | | | Canoe | |
|---|---|---|---|---|---|---|---|---|---|---|---|---|---|---|---|---|---|---|
| | | | | | | 48hr | Long stay | Water point | CDP | Pumpout | Refuse | Diesel | Shops | Pub | Café | PO or Bank | Portage | Park & access |
| Duck Street Footbridge | 0·2 | 0 | | 0·1 | 2·60 | | | | | | | | | | | | | |
| Wilgar Footbridge | 1·5 | 0 | | 0·5 | 2·60 | | | | | | | | | | | | | |
| Queens Head Arm | 0·1 | 0 | | 0·0 | | short, shallow draught only | | | | | | | | 🍺 | 🍴 | | | |
| Yarwell Mill Holiday Park | 0·6 | 0 | | 0·2 | | | 🍺 | | | | | | | | 🍴 | | | 🛶 |
| Yarwell Lock 33 | 0·0 | 1 | □ | 0·3 | 2·40 | | | 🚰 | | | | | | 🍺 | 🍴 | | | 🛶 |
| Wansford Lock 34 | 1·2 | 1 | □ | 0·7 | | | | | | | | | | | | | | |
| Wansford Bridge | 0·6 | 0 | | 0·2 | 🍺 | | | | | | | | 🛒 | 🍺 | 🍴 | £ | | 🛶 |
| Stibbington Boatyard | 0·2 | 0 | | 0·1 | 🍺 | | | check first | | | | | | | Wansford A47 picnic area | | | 🛶 |
| **Map 14 totals** | **4·4** | **2** | | **2·0** | | | | | | | | | | | | | | |

THE RIVER NENE   129

## Navigation notes

Upstream of the sewage treatment works, **Elton Road Bridge** carrying the road from Nassington crosses the Nene and the footpath continues along the west bank for 0·5 miles before splitting, after crossing the river at the next footbridge; one section continuing to Nassington, where it is joined by the Nene Way from Fotheringhay while the other tracks along the left bank, before switching to the right bank at the next minor channel junction.

After two more minor channels join, the Nene turns north and divides. The more minor stream joins at the location where the old railway bridge, which carried the route of the former railway line from Oundle, crosses the Nene, heading over a weir north to rejoin the main channel downstream of Yarwell Lock, a low structure with a guillotine gate.

**Wilgar bridge**, carrying the Nene Way, crosses the channel which then turns northeast to pass by the village of Nassington while a shallow side channel loops in the direction of the village. Whilst there are moorings for patrons of the Queens Head on the backwater, but the channel is only navigable by small shallow drafted boats and canoes. The side channel continues northeast to rejoin the main channel, which continues to **Yarwell Lock** and Yarwell Mill, 2·8 miles from Elton Lock, with the mill stream then leaving on the north bank. The water meadows here are prolific with flowers in spring/summer. Yarwell village which lies about 0·5 miles from the Nene has fine views over the river.

The Nene swings east past a further series of lakes and Yarwell Mill caravan site on the northern bank, before turning north and then northwest past Ship End Pits, a disused stone quarry, now a small group of select houses clustered around a private marina. Here the Yarwell Mill stream rejoins the main channel. The Nene then divides again on the approach to Wansford Lock 1·2 miles from Yarwell Lock. The western left-hand channel contains the lock, although remnants of the old lock, as a sluice, remain in the eastern right-hand channel.

The footpath follows the left bank of the lock channel for a short distance, before circling to join the Nene Way and move away from the immediate bank side, in the direction of Wansford village. The remnants of Old Sulehay Forest lie on the western side of the Yarwell–Wansford Road at this point. The lock is a vertical gate, electrically powered structure and navigators are advised to approach it with great care when travelling downstream, when there is a heavy flow in the river, and to beware of the side channel weir hazard.

The best access to **Wansford** village is via the footpath on the right bank by Wansford Old Bridge. Wansford in fact now boasts three road bridges, since the old bridge has now been joined by the two modern structures carrying the A1. The Great North Road used to pass through the centre of the village, across the graceful old bridge whose architecture merits favourable comparison with the modern structures. Now the old bridge takes the B671 over the Nene. There is also a railway bridge just upstream of Wansford, built in 1850. On the left bank is a footpath and the Wansford Pasture Nature Reserve.

The two separate channels of the Nene rejoin opposite Stibbington Hall and flow to Wansford. So far in our journey, the Nene has flowed generally northeast from Northampton. Now, for the final

## Moorings and facilities

There is an **EA water point** on Yarwell upstream lock landing.

**Yarwell mill** has 45 private long-term moorings both above and below the lock. There is also a slipway, which can be booked ☎ 01780 782344.
The mill complex includes a caravan and camping site and recently added park homes.

There is an informal arrangement for moorings in **Wansford**, whereby boats pull in to the steep bank on the Peterborough side of the old Wansford Bridge. This mooring facility, while close to the village centre and popular also with fishermen, is not, formally dedicated to public use, and is reported to be overgrown with nettles, but seems to be available to patrons of the Haycock ☎ 01780 782223

**Nassington, Queens Head Inn** ☎ 01780 78400) food and refreshments are also available the **Black Horse** public house, Fotheringhay Road, ☎ 01780 784835 from which a footpath leads to Wilgar Bridge and the flood meadows and there is a **Post Office Stores** ☎ 01780 782624 on Station Road. Meals and refreshments can be found in **Yarwell** at **The Angel Inn** on Main Street ☎ 01780 782582.

**Wansford** contains several pubs, one called **The Paper Mill** ☎ 01780 782328 which is also a restaurant, being the only reminder of a local bustling paper industry in the 18th and 19th centuries, with the mills being situated in the grounds of Stibbington Hall nearby.

**The Cross Keys** ☎ 01780 782266 and the **Haycock Inn**, now a MacDonald Hotel, ☎ 01780 782223, are also in the village. There is also a restaurant, **Fiddlesticks**, just down from the Haycock ☎ 01780 784111. Wansford also contains shops and a **Post Office** on Elton Road, close to the Haycock ☎ 0345 611 2970.

leg of its trip to the sea, it turns east. Once Wansford Old Bridge and its adjoining permissive mooring area have been passed, a footpath continues along the right bank, past the Haycock, under the old bridge, before opening into a tree-lined meadow area. The Nene is then crossed by the A1 bridges adjacent to which is a picnic area and toilets.

Downstream of Wansford, a footpath continues for a short distance on both banks, with that on the left bank being the Nene Way. The Nene passes Wansford Pumping Station, where much of its water is now diverted to Anglian Water's major water supply reservoir at Rutland Water. Having left Wansford behind, the Nene sweeps past a series of lakes on its southern bank and the A47 trunk road, which runs close to the northern bank at this point. The Nene then turns south as it approaches Sutton, to the east, and Stibbington to the west. The Stamford to Wansford branch line ran close to the river on its route via Sutton village to Wansford.

Nene Valley Railway map

## Nature reserves and features

**Old Sulehay Forest Reserve** is one of the last remnants of the ancient Rockingham Forest, noted for its amazing woodland flora including carpets of bluebells and wild garlic and contains limestone quarries, woodland, grassland and wetland habitats within the 85 hectares. The reserve is managed by the Wildlife Trust for Bedfordshire, Cambridgeshire and Northamptonshire. Several public footpaths traverse the reserve which is open to the public all year.
GR: TL054980

**Wansford and Standen's Pasture Nature Reserve** is primarily a limestone grassland habitat, comprising seven hectares of grassland, hedges and streams forming well-grazed pastures, rich in chalk-loving plants and invertebrates. The reserve is managed by the Wildlife Trust for Bedfordshire, Cambridgeshire and Northamptonshire and is open all year. GR: TL069994

A short detour of two miles to the west of Wansford lies **Bedford Purlieus**, a 211-hectare nature reserve comprising a fragment of the old Rockingham Forest consisting of semi-natural native woodland.

The reserve is owned and managed by the Forestry Commission. GR: TL 042995

**Sacrewell Farm and Country Centre**, 0·6 miles north east of Wansford, is open seven days a week 0930–1700, ☎01780 782254. The Centre includes **Sacrewell Mill**, a small stone estate water mill dating from 1755. It is a three-storey building and has the miller's house attached. The Centre café is open for snacks and gifts and campers and caravanners are welcome.
GR: TL080997

## Walking and exploring

**The Prebendel Manor House and Tithe Barn Museum** in Nassington, to the southwest of the church, is well worth a visit. Normally open to the public on Sunday and Wednesday and all Bank Holiday Mondays from Easter Monday to the end of September. ☎01780 782575

**Yarwell Junction NVR station** is an easy well marked 15-minute walk from Yarwell lock. As there are no visitor short stay moorings boaters may wish to moor further downstream at Wansford station and catch a train back to Yarwell Junction to explore Nassington and Yarwell.

**The Nene Way** crosses the river, following its inland excursion from Fotheringhay, at Nassington footbridge. The trail curves round, passing the current 'end of the line' for the Nene valley Railway, near Yarwell Junction Station. Shortly after it crosses the river at Yarwell Mill and proceeds north through Yarwell village and then above, but parallel to the river until it reaches Wansford. From Wansford the Nene Way passes through the picnic site off the A47 and then follows the river bank to Stibbington.

## Canoeing

**Adventure Rutland** have a base at **Yarwell Mill Country Park** where they offer paddle boarding and Kayaking River Nene trips and hire. Open weekends from April until September.
☏ 07818 226565
www.adventurerutland.com

**Yarwell Mill** can be used for access to the river for launching and retrieval. They have a small car park near reception that you may be able to use, subject to asking permission in the reception office.
☏ 01780 782344 GR: TL 074972

**Wansford Old Bridge** that carries the A6118 road into the village, almost opposite the Haycock Inn, may be a possible launching site where there is a kissing gate and footpath down to the river. Check the FOTRN website for updates on the location. GR: TL 075992

**Wansford Picnic Area**, off the A47 towards Peterborough has access to the river and may be suitable for launching. Check the FOTRN website for updates on the location. GR: TL 077995

## Local history

**Nassington**, whose name means 'farm of the headland dwellers', was founded by the Romans due to the extensive mineral workings in the locality in those days. Nassington itself supplied ironstone, while quarries at nearby Yarwell produced limestone for building, clay for bricks and gravel for road building. The Nene itself, of course, formed the means of transport.

Nassington All Saints Church has a Saxon nave and 14th-century wall paintings, with the remains of a Saxon cross in the churchyard. In 1942, a Saxon cemetery was found here, which contained 65 bodies, along with grave goods.

The Prebendel Manor House and Tithe Barn is a Grade I listed manor and is thought to be the oldest surviving dwelling in Northamptonshire, with a history going back to the Anglo-Saxon Period. It now includes lodgings dating from the 15th century and a 16th-century dovecote, together with an 18th-century tithe barn and its hall still possesses original doorways. It was the base of an official (the Prebendary) of the Diocese of Lincoln. There are also the remains of several prehistoric barrows in the vicinity.

At **Yarwell village** Church of St Mary Magdelene, parts of the 13th-century chapel remain. Between Yarwell and Wansford, at the side of the King's Cliffe Road, are Roman remains, a building, possibly a bailiff's house and a quarry. By the Nene at Yarwell are the remains of a wharf where several mills, including a paper mill, formerly operated. Paper was produced for newspapers, until an explosion in 1855 put an end to business.

**Wansford Old Bridge** was originally built of wood but was replaced with a stone structure in the mid 13th-century and later partly rebuilt, after flood damage in 1796. The bridge arches on the village side are irregular. The small round arch next to a wider one is dated 1795, the next three 1672–4 and the next seven, 1577. On the bridge is a marker, showing the county boundary between the old Huntingdonshire and Soke of Peterborough. Wansford is also known as Wansford-in-England, the name deriving from the local tale of one Barnabee, a traveller who, in the reign of Charles I, because of his fear of the plague, was afraid to sleep in local inns and so spent the night on top of a haystack in a meadow by the river. However, during the night, the river rose sharply due to a storm upstream and the haystack floated away down the Nene. Its journey was however, halted when it became wedged in the buttresses of the Old Bridge. Next morning, when Barnabee awoke, he asked where he was. On being told that he was in Wansford and being confused about just how far he had travelled, he replied 'What, Wansford in England?' The name has stuck.

The most well-known establishment in Wansford is the **Haycock Inn**, now a MacDonald Hotel, with its five bay centre and two bay wings. Parts of it dates to the 13th century and it was an inn known as 'the Swan' until the 18th century, when it was renamed to commemorate Barnabee's voyage. The inn sign now depicts Barnabee.

Wansford was a very important port with significant cargoes being unloaded even 100 years ago. The Haycock itself once adjoined a bustling wharf as, for example, quarried limestone and timber from the remnants of Rockingham Forest were loaded there, while grain and coal from up river were the main items unloaded.

**Sacrewell Mill** stream forms the boundary between the parishes of Wansford and Thornhaugh and the site contains prehistoric circles and Neolithic implements. The name 'Sacrewell' probably comes from the spring rising in one of the fields. There are the remains of several Romano-British villas on the farm and of buildings used for grain dying and malting.

# 5

# RIVER NENE STIBBINGTON TO DOG-IN-A-DOUBLET

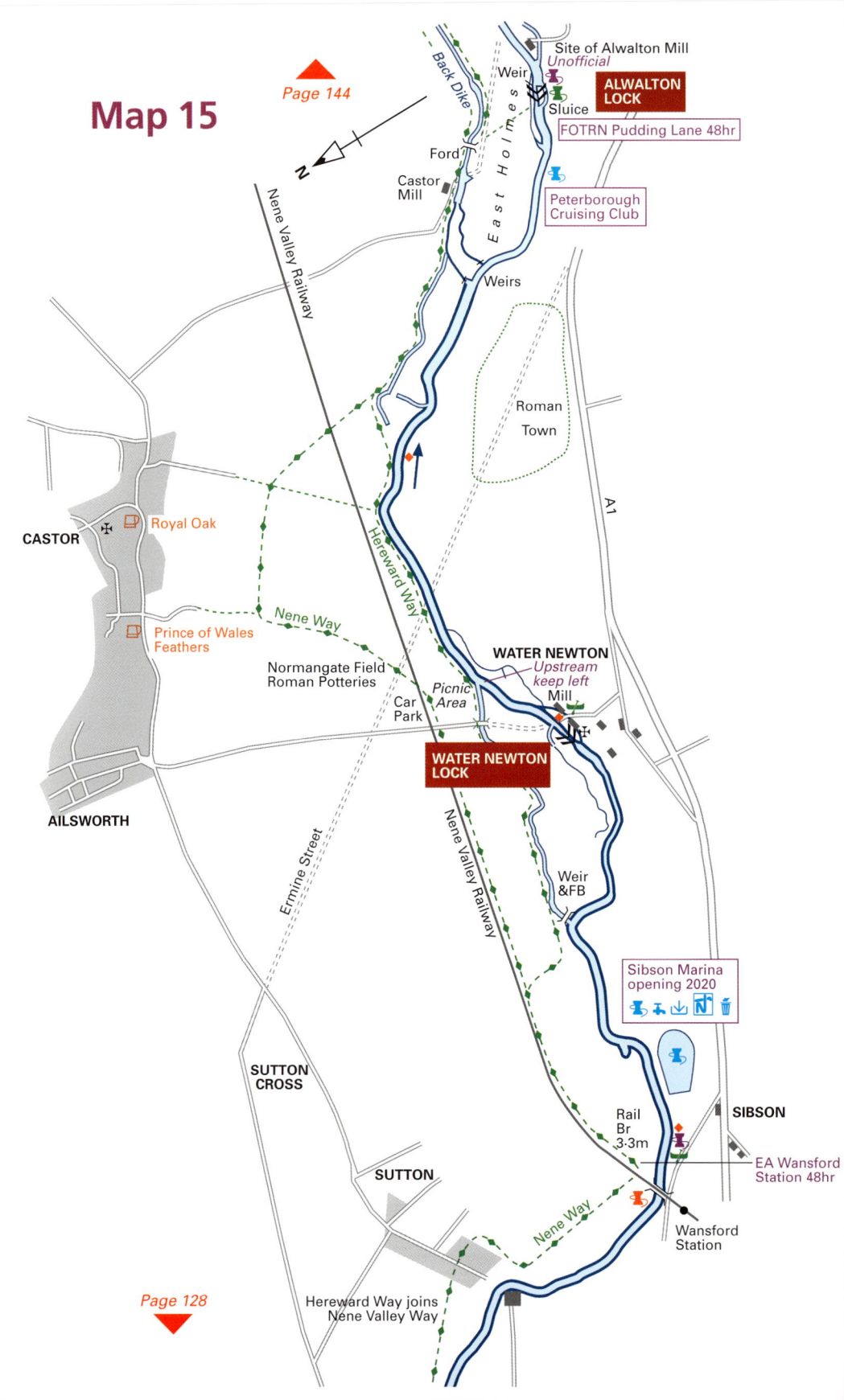

# Map 15

## Stibbington Boatyard to Alwalton Lock

| Location | Miles | Locks | Lock type | Est time hours | Bridge < 2.7m | Moorings and facilities | | | | | | | Victualling | | | | Canoe |
|---|---|---|---|---|---|---|---|---|---|---|---|---|---|---|---|---|---|
| | | | | | | 48hr | Long stay | Water point | CDP | Pumpout | Refuse | Diesel | Shops | Pub | Café | PO or Bank | Portage | Park & access |
| Wansford Station EA mooring | 0·4 | 0 | | 0·1 | 🍶 | | | | | | | | | | | | | 🛶 |
| Sibson Marina | 0·2 | 0 | | 0·1 | 🍶 | | | 🚰 | ⚓ | ⛽ | 🗑 | | | 🍺 | ☕ | | | |
| Water Newton Lock 35 | 1·0 | 1 | ☐ | 0·6 | | | | | | | | | | | | | | 🛶 |
| Peterborough Cruising Club | 1·8 | 0 | | 0·5 | 🍶 | | 🚰 | | | | | in Castor village | 🍺 | ☕ | | | | |
| Alwalton Lock 36 & FOTRN | 0·0 | 1 | ☐ | 0·3 | 🍶 | | | | | | | | 🧺 | 🍺 | ☕ | £ | | |
| **Map 15 Totals** | **3·4** | **2** | | **1·6** | | | | | | | | | | | | | | |

## Navigation notes

Leaving behind Stibbington boatyard and long-term moorings a railway bridge soon comes into view downstream. Stibbington is the home of the **Nene Valley Railway**, which crosses the Nene at this point and runs to Peterborough, even though the station at Stibbington is known as Wansford Station. Navigators are advised to use the right-hand arch of the railway bridge. Shortly after the Wansford Station moorings on the south bank is Sibson Manor House and the new **Sibson Marina**.

The Nene, while following a meandering course, continues to follow an easterly direction. The scenery has certainly changed now. From the valley bottom with its picturesque fall, the banks are now more open having left their trees behind and now flat-water meadows and pastureland border the Nene. Leaving the Nene Valley Railway on the north bank for a time, the Nene divides just upstream of Water Newton Lock. The northern channel is weired and there is a footbridge at this point. A minor footpath, which enables walks along each of the channels at this point, with the aid of footbridges, then follows the left bank of the main channel. The minor channel rejoins the Nene downstream of Water Newton Lock.

The main Nene continues to **Water Newton Lock** some 3·9 miles from Wansford Lock. At the lock, two mill streams discharge into the navigation channel immediately downstream of the structure and boaters are advised to keep to the right, when leaving the lock downstream, and use plenty of power. A footbridge and power lines cross here. The Hereward Way now turns north to cross the minor channels and join the road leading to Ailsworth. Once through Water Newton Lock, there is an upstream 'keep left' instruction adjoining Normangate Field Roman Potteries. Just upstream of this point, the Nene is 'crossed' by the route of the Roman Road of Ermine Street which ran from London to York but no bridge to take the roadway now survives. As the Nene meanders southeast, it passes the site of a Roman Garrison Town, Durobrivae, lying across the route of Ermine Street, to reach weirs at the westerly junctions of Back Dike and the Nene.

The scenery is of peaceful willow-studded meadows, and Back Dike joins the Nene here by a series of channels and leads past Castor Mill on the left bank, just downstream of which is the site of an old windmill. The Back-Dike channel is forded and from here a footpath runs the short distance south between the channels to Alwalton Lock (1·8 miles from Water Newton Lock) on the main channel. Here the Nene meets the outskirts of Peterborough, running close to the village/suburb of Alwalton and the East of England showground to the south.

At Alwalton Lock, where the vertical gate is electrically powered, there is good access for canoes and after the lock both Back Dike and the Main Channel turn to the northeast, where the Main Channel is joined via a weir to a backwater. A footpath leads across the Nene, towards the A1 to the south and Castor Mill to the north. A little way up the road from the lock, turning right at the top of this road, is Alwalton.

## Moorings and facilities

**Stibbington Boatyard** provides a long established and respected boat building service with premises and long-term moorings at the end of Church lane, Stibbington on the west bank of the river ☎ 07970 210670. Overnight mooring may be possible with permission.

**Wansford Station** - mooring is possible either side of the railway bridge on the far bank opposite Wansford station.

Better moorings are available on the **Environment Agency 48-hour visitor mooring pontoon**, downstream of the bridge and adjacent to the station although these moorings are quite small and only have room for a few vessels. (Note that these are rising flood moorings and during periods of Strong Stream restrictions the 48 hour limit is relaxed.)

**Sibson Marina**, visible downstream on the south bank, is due to open shortly (2020), and will provide moorings and the usual range of services for boaters - reservations for moorings are now being taken. ☎ 07544 636844

Upstream of Alwalton Lock is **Peterborough Cruising Club** with moorings, water point and a slipway which may be used by visiting boats subject to permission (Harbourmaster ☎ 07759034764).

**FOTRN Pudding Lane, Alwalton** 48-hour members mooring on the south bank of the lock relief channel parallel to the lock.
GR: TL 130963

There are also a couple of permissive moorings against the lock island that are sometimes available.

There is **café** on the platform at Wansford Station providing drinks and light snacks

The nearby **Sibson Hotel** on the Great North Road ☎ 07419 332414 provides meals and refreshments.

Refreshments are available in Castor at the **Prince of Wales Feathers** ☎ 01733 380222 and the **Royal Oak** ☎ 01733 380217 both on the Peterborough Road.

The neighbouring **Fratelli's Ristorante** (the former Fitzwilliam Arms), also on the Peterborough Road, has recently re-opened as a boutique restaurant.

## Nature reserves and features

**Conservation and reinstatement of grassland meadows**, instead of arable crops is taking place around the lakes to the south of the river between Wansford and Stibbington. This project is being managed by local landowners as part of the **Countryside Stewardship Scheme**. Details of a couple of walks, that can start at either Wansford or Stibbington are available on the parish Council website: stibbington.org.uk/footpaths

Water Newton Mill Chris Howes

## Walking and exploring

**The Nene Way** comes back south to meet the river at the Nene Valley Railway bridge after a brief sojourn in Sutton. It follows the railway track for 0.4 miles before hugging the backwater bank and then the main river bank to the site of the Roman pottery at Normangate. The trail then passes Castor Mill as it follows back Dike until it rejoins the Nene beyond Alwalton.

**The Hereward Way** is another long-distance footpath that links the Viking Way at Oakham with the Peddars Way at Knettishall Heath, near Thetford. The path takes its name from Hereward the Wake, the 11th-century leader who fought against William the Conqueror.

These two long distance paths join to follow the same route from Sutton to Peterborough.

## Cycling

A section of **National Cycle Route 63** provides a good ride on quiet roads from Peterborough to Stamford – the route passes through Castor and Ailsworth.

There are several cycle routes around Peterborough that include the villages to the west and most cross or join the river at strategic points.
Further suggestions and details at www.cycle.travel/city/peterborough/map

## Canoeing

**The EA visitor mooring pontoon at Wansford Station** provides a suitable spot for access and launching into the river. There is usually plenty of parking on the roadside, but you may have to lift craft over the locked gate (EA *abloy* key) to get down to the pontoon.
GR: TL 094979

**Mill Lane in Water Newton** can be used to quickly drop-off or pick-up canoes for launching/retrieval into/from the river. Parking is at a premium unless you are happy to park back in the village.
GR: TL 109973

## Local history

**The Nene Valley Railway** was previously part of the old London to Birmingham railway, which opened in 1838, with an extension to the line being opened between Blisworth and Peterborough, in 1845. Ironically, the building of the line created a huge demand for commercial traffic on the Nene, with thousands of tons of rails and sleepers being delivered by barge. This upsurge was purely temporary as the railway took over and assisted in the decline of commercial river traffic. In turn however, the growth of road traffic saw the death knell of the railway and the very last train ran in November 1972, as a result of the 'Beeching cuts'. However, enthusiasts managed to preserve the last 7·5 miles of track, which now provide a genteel reminder of a bygone age of travel. The railway runs from **Yarwell Junction** to **Peterborough**. It attracts enthusiasts and visitors alike through an ambitious programme of special events with visiting locomotives. It is the home of Thomas the Tank Engine and there is a shop, café and railway museum.
☏ 01780 784444

**Stibbington Hall** dates from 1625 and in its grounds, as well as in the area locally, have been found pottery relics of Roman times, although even more prominent finds have been uncovered just downstream.

The area around **Sutton** contains much of historical interest. The village of Sutton is itself is a conservation area and contains not only the site of the Sutton cross but also the Church of St Michael and All Angels, which was originally called St Giles. To the west of this church is a road which becomes a track leading to the Nene and formerly ran across an old ford to Stibbington. The presence of Ermine Street is the village's most interesting feature, confirming as it does the very significant Roman presence formerly in this area. The A1 follows much of the route of this road, which crossed the Nene between Water Newton and Castor.

Normangate Field Roman Potteries provides a further hint at the presence, beside Ermine Street near Alwalton, of the remains of the Roman garrison town

Wansford Station mooring
Chris Howes

of **Durobrivae** (the fort at the ford). This five-acre fort was centred around a courtyard which lay in the area of what is now the parish church, defended by a wall, bank and ditch. The boundaries of the town can still be picked out and aerial photographs show the irregular grid of streets set out slightly askew to Ermine Street. The town was rediscovered when a small Roman camp, 0·25 miles to the north along Ermine Street, was being excavated by Edmund Artis, steward to the Earl Fitzwilliam, when a new estate road was being constructed in the 19th century. It was not however, until further excavations, by OGS Crawford in the 1930s, that the full significance of the find was realised. These excavations produced finds of pottery, coins and silver, including a find of first-century Christian silver, the earliest Christian religious silver found in the Roman Empire. In Roman times, there was a huge pottery industry centred between Billing Brook and where the A1 now runs, and local clay was used to produce Castorware, which was exported throughout the Empire.

The modern settlements of **Castor** and **Ailsworth** on the left bank of the Nene are almost but not quite joined together, for, while there is no visible boundary between the villages, each has its own character, while sharing a church and school.

**Castor** is derived from the Roman word 'castra' meaning 'camp' and materials from Durobrivae were used to build the village church, which was founded in the 7th century and, uniquely in England, is dedicated to St Kyneburgha, daughter of the founder, Penda King of Mercia. The church was largely rebuilt by the Normans, and over the chancel door is the Latin inscription, 'this church was dedicated on April 17, 1124'. On the north wall are three paintings, depicting the martyrdom of St Catherine. Pevsner described Castor Church as the most important Norman Parish Church in the county of Huntingdon and Peterborough. The St Kyneburgha Building Preservation Trust is a group of dedicated trustees which has been charged with ensuring the preservation and upkeep of the historic church building and its grounds. It aims to raise awareness of the rich and varied history of this important site, and of the surrounding area.
www.castorchurchtrust.co.uk

**St Kyneburgha Church** Andy Vernum, Studio One, courtesy of St Kyneburgha Building Preservation Trust

The trust also offers guided tours to groups of visitors throughout the year, both of the beautiful church and the surrounding landscape which is steeped in history tours@castorchurchtrust.co.uk. Castor House, which stands to the east of the village, is Georgian. The Denver Causeway, which ran through the Fens left King Street, northwest of Castor at the south end of Moore Wood near Upton Church and joined, at Milton Park, another Roman road, leading back to the Nene Bridge at Castor. The route of this road can still be seen from the Peterborough Road, running through fields from the west side of Milton Park to Castor. It then passes through Peterborough, and eventually forms Low Road, Whittlesey, before moving into the fen. Large quantities of pottery were shipped from Castor in Roman times, via jetties on the Nene.

**Castor watermill** and windmill tower are worth seeing external exploration, via a short walk on a public footpath from Alwalton lock.

**Ailsworth**, on the other hand, is mainly of Saxon origin, although the site of a Roman villa, a house of the corridor type, has been found southwest of the station, beside the Nene, 0·5 miles upstream of the ford, following excavations in the 19th century.

**Water Newton's** St Remigius church is a typical 13th/14th-century country church. It is approached by a private drive leading to the rectory. The church is dedicated to St Remigius, the Roman Bishop of Rheims. The 'water' in the name of the settlement is, of course, a reference to the Nene and to the east of the church is the old watermill, a three-storeyed mansard-roofed structure, now a dwelling, dating from 1791, adjacent to which is the former lock keeper's cottage.

Castor watermill  Chris Howes

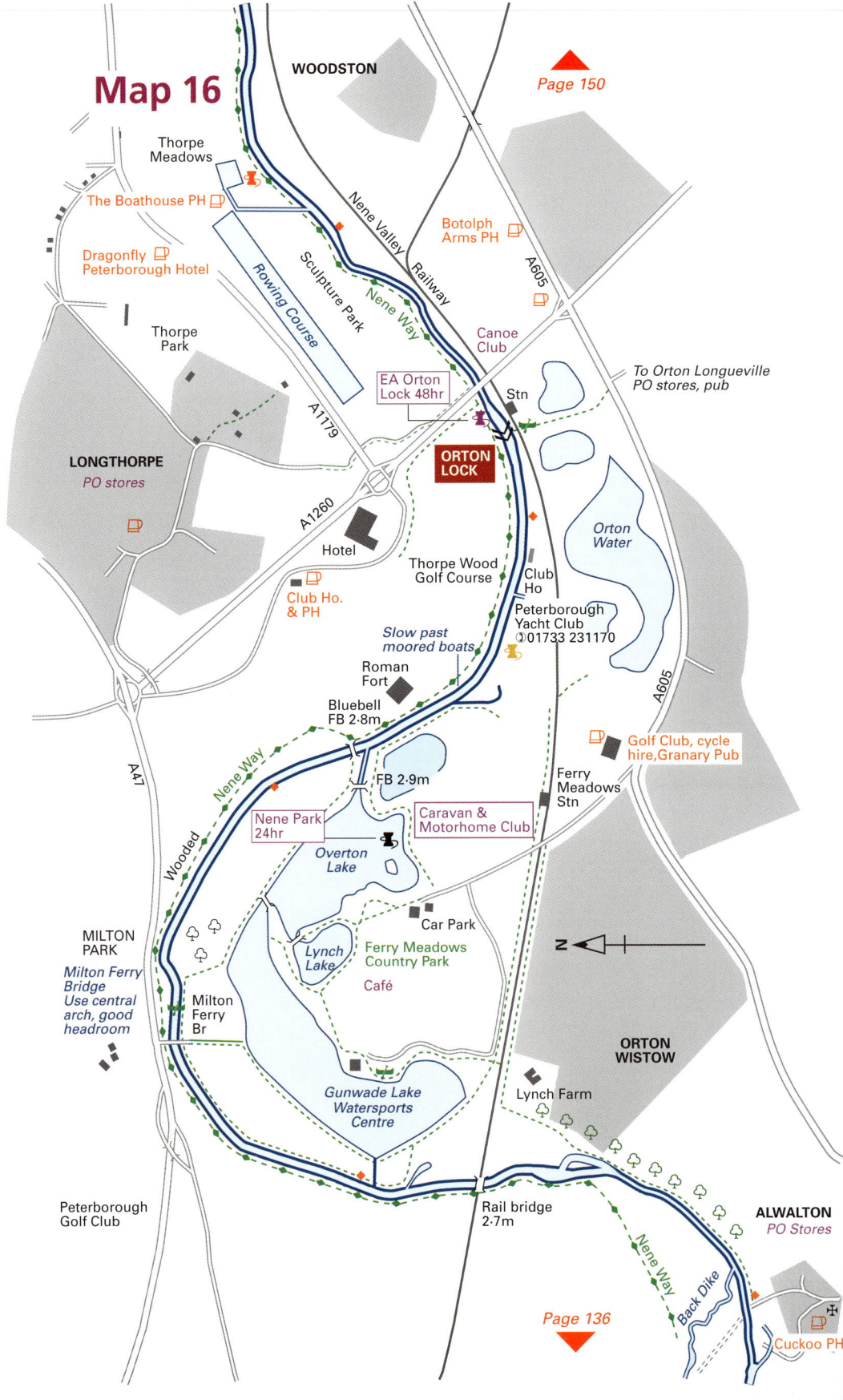

# Map 16

# Alwalton Lock Downstream landing to Thorpe Meadows boathouse

| Map 16  Alwalton Lock downstream landing (GR: TL 131962) to Thorpe Meadows boathouse cut (GR: TL 175980) | | | | | | | | | | | | | | | | |
|---|---|---|---|---|---|---|---|---|---|---|---|---|---|---|---|---|
| Location | Miles | Locks | Lock type | Est time hours | Bridge < 2.7m | Moorings and facilities | | | | | | | Victualling | | | Canoe |
| | | | | | | 48hr | Long stay | Water point | CDP | Pumpout | Refuse | Diesel | Shops | Pub | Café | PO or Bank | Portage | Park & access |
| Alwalton Lock landing | 0.1 | 0 | | 0.0 | | | | | | | | | | | | | | |
| Nene Valley Railway Bridge | 0.8 | 0 | | 0.2 | | | | | | | | | | | | | | |
| Milton Ferry Bridge | 0.8 | 0 | | 0.2 | | | | | | | | | | | | | | 🛶 |
| Overton Lake Ferry Meadow Mooring | 0.9 | 0 | | 0.3 | | 🏆 | | | | | Ham Lane/A605 | | | 🍺 | 🍴 | | | 🛶 |
| Orton Lock 37 | 0.9 | 1 | ☐ | 0.5 | | | | | | | | | | | | | ▼ | 🛶 |
| Orton Lock EA Moorings | 0.1 | 0 | | 0.0 | | 🏆 | Orton Longueville village | | | | | | 🛒 | 🍺 | 🍴 | £ | | |
| Thorpe, Boathouse Cut | 0.7 | 0 | | 0.2 | | 🏆 | | | | | | | | 🍺 | 🍴 | | | |
| **Map 16 totals** | **4.3** | **1** | | **1.5** | | | | | | | | | | | | | | |

## Navigation notes

From Alwalton to Peterborough, the Nene meanders partly through water meadows but the tree-lined banks in places hide the increasing urbanisation, particularly on the right bank, as the Alwalton Business Park and the suburbs of Orton are reached with Peterborough Cathedral appearing above the tree tops.

On the south east bank immediately after Alwalton Lock, the Fitzwilliam estate has woods down to the water's edge but, once under the arch of the bridge carrying the private road to the Fitzwilliam kennels, the river is broad and the woods cease abruptly, with the skyline of the City of Peterborough in view. Between Alwalton and Orton Lock, is a four mile stretch of interest and pleasant typical English countryside with the city views behind. The Nene turns east by Peterborough Golf Club, at Milton Park, on the left bank, to run close to the A47 trunk road, on that bank, before being crossed by Milton Ferry Bridge. This bridge, as its name suggests, marks the position of a former ferry. Boaters are advised to use the central arch of this bridge, where there is good headroom. Here, for a short while, we are back in real countryside, Milton Park to the north and Nene Park to the south.

Milton Ferry Bridge Chris Howes

On the Peterborough side of the **Milton Ferry Bridge** the Nene turns southeast to be crossed by the Bluebell footbridge. Immediately downstream is the artificial cut on the right into Overton Lake where there are excellent pontoon moorings in the southeast corner of the lake (some of the finest on the river).

The moorings and clubhouse of Peterborough Yacht Club are passed on the south bank and boaters are advised to travel slowly past the moored boats. **Orton Lock** is an electrically-powered, vertical gate with upstream mitre gates. There are three substantial sluices immediately to the right of the lock chamber going downstream, which can generate a very strong cross current. When entering or leaving the lower Peterborough end of the lock, boaters need to be prepared for a cross current pushing them towards the north bank. Above the lock there can be a pull towards the weir and boaters should keep to the north bank. In former times these sluices marked the upstream tidal limit of the Nene, until the building of the Dog-in-a-Doublet Sluice in 1938.

Downstream of Orton Lock boaters are advised to navigate with care due to the **Proteus Canoe Club,** which organises events on many weekends on this stretch of the river and on the slalom course below the sluices.

## Moorings and facilities

**Ferry Meadows, Overton Lake 48hr visitor moorings** near the visitor centre and café are floating pontoon moorings. Access channel into Overton Lake is immediately downstream of Bluebell footbridge.

**Caravan and Motorhome Club** site on Ham Lane near the entrance to Ferry Meadows, allows camping.

**Alongside Orton Meadows** Peterborough Yacht Club moorings line the southern bank. Visitors are welcome. The slipway is for members only. Harbourmaster ☎ 07787 777519

**Environment Agency 48-hour visitor moorings** are available below Orton Lock, with high rise mooring posts.

**Thorpe Wood Boathouse Cut** has moorings at the end adjacent to the pub.

From **Alwalton** there is a twice daily bus service to Peterborough. On the Oundle Road there is a **Post Office Stores and Tearoom** ☎ 01733 233555 and **The Cuckoo Inn** serving meals ☎ 01733 239638. A footpath leads from Water End adjoining the inn, to the river.

From **Ferry Meadows** a short (0·5 mile) walk from the moorings along Ham Lane leads to **Rutland Cycle Hire, Thorpe Wood golf course, Beefeater Granary, Premier Travel Inn** and **Notcutts garden centre and café**.

**Orton Longueville** 'village' has a **Post office Stores** on Oakleigh Drive ☎ 0345 611 297 and shops and a post-box at its entrance.

In the grounds of Orton hall is the **Ramblewood Inn** ☎ 01733 391111 and nearby, on Oundle Road, both the **Gordon Arms** ☎ 01733 231374 and the **Botolph Arms** ☎ 01733 234170 provide food and drink.

At Thorpe Wood **The Boathouse Chef and Brewer pub** ☎ 01733 898469 serves meals and drinks.

**The Dragonfly Hotel** ☎ 01733 564240 provides accommodation, drinks and meals.

---

The bank sides here are tree lined and manage to retain rural tranquility close to the city centre. The Nene Valley Railway runs alongside the southern bank of the Nene here to **Orton Mere station**, from where a footpath crosses the river and leads to the A605 and **Orton Longueville** 'village'.

Flowing past the lakes to the south, the A1260 dual carriageway crosses the Nene downstream of the lock. The Nene turns northeast to pass Sculpture Park, on the northern bank. Adjacent to the park is the rowing course and the headquarters of Peterborough City Rowing Club. This area is Thorpe Meadows and the Nene Valley Railway continues to run alongside the south eastern bank of the river towards its terminus at Peterborough. There is a man-made channel, near the rowing lake, that leads to the Boathouse pub and Dragonfly Hotel moorings. The channel is navigable and there is turning space at the end for narrowboats.

THE RIVER NENE

## Nature reserves and features

**Nene Park** ☏01733 234193 is a 1012 hectare regional park created along seven miles of the Nene from Peterborough city centre to the A1. Managed by the Nene Park Trust it contains meadows, havens for wild flowers, and woods, fishing lakes, two golf courses, a water sports centre and café, several children's play areas and a miniature railway ☏01933 398889. The visitor centre and café is the focal point for most of the attractions. Its centrepiece is **Ferry Meadows**, three large (49 hectares) connecting lakes formed by the extraction of sand and gravel between 1972–77.

*Gunwade Lake*, the location of the water sports centre, with a café, information point and toilets.

*Lynch Lake*, adjoining which is a car park and the Ferry Meadows station on the Nene Valley line.

*Overton Lake*, on which there are visitor moorings. Footpaths go right around the park, one running close to the right bank of the Nene.

**Nene Park Golf** includes Thorpe Wood Golf Course and Orton Meadows Golf Course both close to the river. ☏01733 267701

Adjacent is **Thorpe Wood**, a 20-acre site of ancient coppice and woodland.

## Walking and exploring

**The Nene Way** and **Hereward Way** continue alongside the right bank of Back Dike before rejoining left bank of the river as it turns to the north through a wooded section of bank between the Nene and the suburb of Orton Wistow. Both trails now follow the north bank of the river, with minor detours though Bluebell woods just after Milton Ferry Bridge, passing Gunwade and Overton lakes across the meadows to the south.

**Nene Park** and **Ferry Meadows** provide excellent flat and interesting walking with several waymarked tracks that intertwine and follow routes in all directions.

## Cycling

The paths and trails around **Ferry Meadows** and the other Nene Park sites welcome cyclists. The tracks are well surfaced and traffic free. Maps are available from the visitor centres to you plan your day.

**Rutland Cycling** cycle hire facility is based at the Watersports Centre with their main sales outlet and hire centre along Ham lane next to the Granary pub.

## Canoeing

**Milton Ferry bridge** is sometimes used for canoe launching on the downstream side on the north bank, where there is a small parking area. GR: TL 143986

**Ferry Meadows Watersports Centre** allows launching and hire of canoes and small boats, car park, toilets and café all on site. GR: TL 143977

**Orton Lock** is a good site to launch/retrieve, short walk across the sluices and the NVR with a good free car park. GR: TL 166971

Good canoe access is also available from the Environment Agency canoe portage between the visitor moorings and downstream lock landing stage. GR: TL 167973

## Local history

**Alwalton** rather straggles up the A1. Sir Henry Royce, of the Rolls Royce car fame was born here and his ashes are now buried in the parish church, St Andrews. In the 1860s Frank Perkins, who founded the engineering firm Perkins Engines, lived in Alwalton.

St Andrews Church has a 13th-century transept tower and a late 12th-century south doorway. Northeast of the church is a cottage, bearing the date 1645 and northeast of this is the porch of Chesterton Manor lived in by poet John Dryden, demolished in 1867, but with the porch later rebuilt. The Manor House, northeast of the porch, dates from 1700.

The mill which previously served Alwalton has gone but its leat remains and the high grown linches on the southern bank of the river downstream of the mill leat mark the site of an ancient quarry, from which the Romans took marble.

The manor of Alwalton was given to the Abbey of Peterborough by Leofwine, ealdorman of Mercia, in the 11th century and, in the Precentor's records at Peterborough, there are still ancient archives telling of the right to transport marble from Alwalton to Peterborough, free of boat and barge toll. This Alwalton marble was highly prized and a notable exhibit can be seen in the font bowl at Peterborough Cathedral.

Just to the west of **Milton Park** are two stones, referred to as Robin Hood and Little John. These mark the route by which Barnack stone was transported 'toll free' to Gunwade Ferry for onward shipment by river. GR: TL 139983

**Orton Longueville** village has become a 'Peterborough overspill'. The village has a Roman connection and remains were discovered there in 1907. The Church of Holy Trinity retains a bell from Plantagenet times and a 16th-century wall painting. It is also the site of Orton Hall, the ancestral home of the Gordon family, who held the titles of Marquess of Huntly and Earl of Aboyne. The doorway of Orton Hall originates from Fotheringhay Castle.

Nearby **Thorpe Hall** built in 1653 by Peter Mills for Chief Justice St John is now a Sue Ryder Home, while St Augustine church, in the nearby parish of Woodston, has Anglo Saxon masonry in the west tower. Close by at Longthorpe, St Botolphs church has an interesting leper window and Longthorpe Tower, commissioned around 1300 by Robert de Thorpe, Steward of Peterborough Abbey, has walls between six and seven feet thick and, in the vaulted first floor great chamber, remarkable mid 14th-century wall paintings on subjects taken from the bible and the contrast between worldly and spiritual life. The 'Wheel of the Five Senses' is particularly noteworthy. In the first century AD, a large Roman fort, 11 hectares in size, stood near here on the left bank of the Nene. Its site is now part of the Thorpe Wood Golf Course.

Boathouse moorings, Thorpe Wood

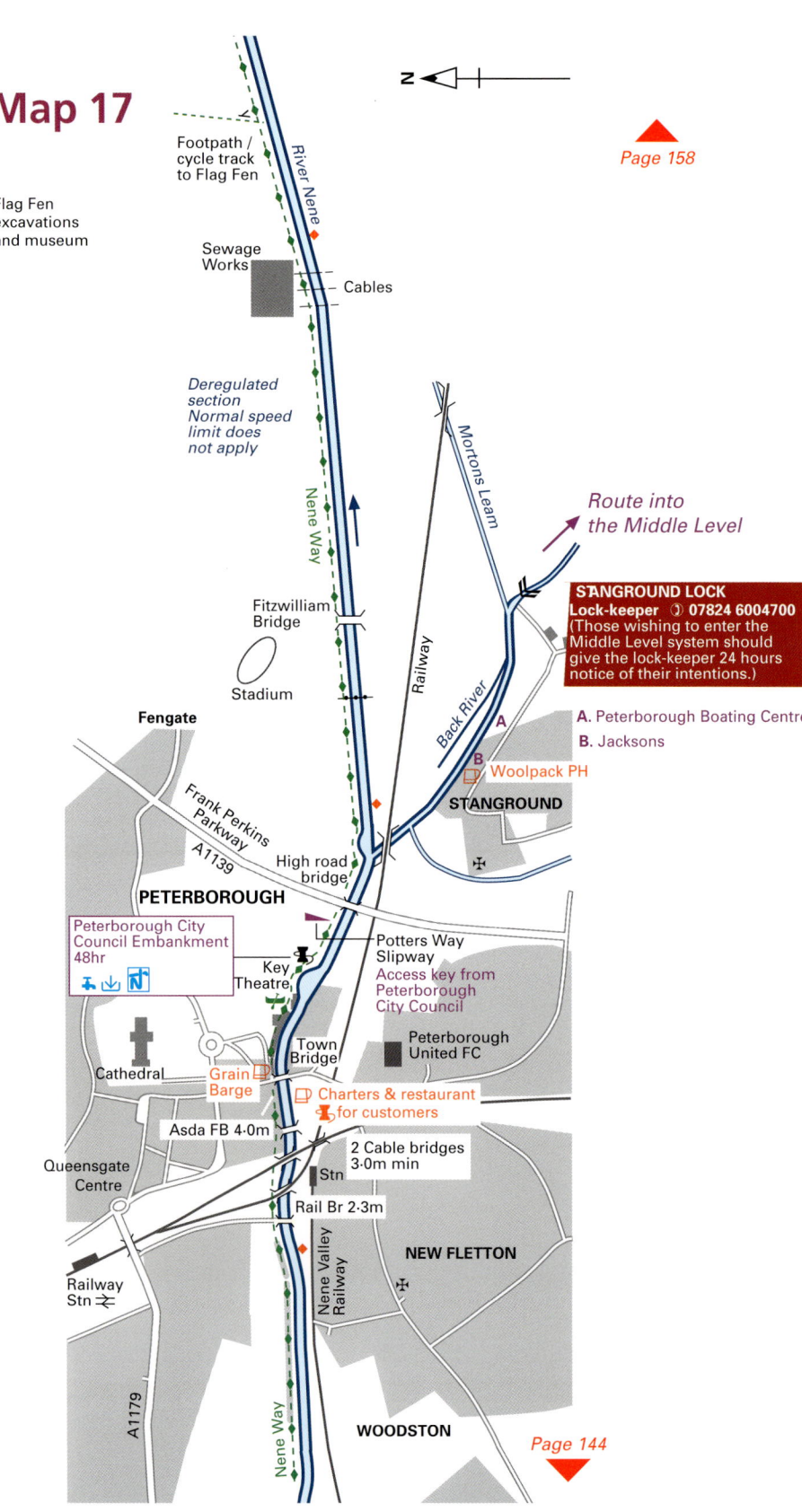

# Map 17

## Thorpe Meadows, Boathouse cut to Flag Fen

*Stibbington to Dog-in-a-Doublet*

| Location | Miles | Locks | Lock type | Est time hours | Bridge < 2·7m | Moorings and facilities | | | | | | | Victualling | | | | | Canoe | |
|---|---|---|---|---|---|---|---|---|---|---|---|---|---|---|---|---|---|---|---|
| | | | | | | 48hr | Long stay | Water point | CDP | Pumpout | Refuse | Diesel | Shops | Pub | Café | PO or Bank | | Portage | Park & access |
| Peterborough-Ely Rail Bridge | 0·8 | 0 | | 0·2 | 2·50 | | | | | | | | | | | | | | |
| GE Railway Bridge | 0·1 | 0 | | 0·0 | | | | | | | | | | | | | | | |
| Peterborough Town Bridge | 0·2 | 0 | | 0·1 | | | | | | | | | | | | | | | |
| Peterborough Embankment | 0·4 | 0 | | 0·1 | | ⚓ | | 🚰 | ⬇ | ⛽ | 🗑 | | 🛒 | 🍺 | 🍴 | £ | | 🛶 | |
| Middle Level Junction | 0·2 | 0 | | 0·1 | | | | | | | Stanground | | 🛒 | 🍺 | 🍴 | | | | |
| Fitzwilliam Field Bridge | 0·4 | 0 | | 0·1 | | | | | | | | | | | | | | | |
| Flag Fen access footpath | 1·4 | 0 | | 0·4 | | | | | | | | | | | | | | | |
| **Map 17 totals** | **3·5** | **0** | | **1·0** | | | | | | | | | | | | | | | |

THE RIVER NENE 151

## Navigation notes

The Nene passes lakes, formed by former gravel workings, past Woodston and the adjoining suburb of New Fletton. The river wends its way towards Peterborough City Centre, in partnership with the railway and Woodston path and cycle lane on the south bank and the Nene/Hereward Way on the north bank.

As the crow flies, Northampton is only 36 miles from Peterborough but with the turns and twists of the Nene, a journey by river covers 58 miles.

Upstream of **Town Bridge**, where the A15 road goes over the river, two railway bridges, the bridge leading to Railworld and power cables cross the Nene. There is also a new footbridge here built in conjunction with the new riverside development of flats and apartments. Just downstream of Town bridge, a pleasant stone arched construction, is **Town Quay and Peterborough** embankment a pleasant grassed area with walks, paved areas and shrubs. The Nene is wide here and overhung with trees on the north bank, which is piled for a short distance. From here the floodlights of the ground of Peterborough United FC on London Road are visible to the south. **Fletton Quays**, on the south bank, is a major development of apartments, offices and a hotel, in contrast to the gardens of the embankment opposite, behind which the cathedral is visible. Fishing is generally allowed from the embankment except where yellow indications sign a prohibition.

After Peterborough Embankment is left behind, the river takes on a more natural look as the A1139 High Road bridge carrying the Frank Perkins Parkway is approached, although the presence of electricity pylons is very noticeable together with the power line crossing and the bridge itself can only be described as functional. After this bridge, the spire of Stanground Church can be seen to the south. To the left is a signpost designating the **Green Wheel** and Flag Fen.

The Nene divides after the Parkway Bridge and just before the railway crossing, with **Morton's Leam** moving off to the southeast and crossing under the Nene Valley Railway line running east, while the main channel continues to the northeast. Morton's Leam rejoins the main channel of the Nene at Guyhirn and, between it and the main Nene, are the **Nene Washes**. On entering Morton's Leam care should be taken in navigating Black Bridge, the railway bridge carrying the Nene Valley railway, as three of the bridge pillars are in the waterway. Both arches are, however, navigable.

Morton's Leam provides the route to Stanground and entry via the manned **Stanground Lock** ☏ 07824 600470 to the Middle Level Commissioners' River system. The upstream landing stage just prior to Stanground Lock has been refurbished in recent years by the Environment Agency. Those wishing to enter the Middle Level system should give the lock-keeper 24 hours' notice of their intention to do so. The lock is, however, closed on Tuesdays in the months of November, December, January and February and the first week in March. Historically, prior to the 'Great Drayning' of the 17th century, the route through Stanground was the major course of the Nene.

The main Nene continues northeast from its junction with Mortons Leam, with the Nene Way still on its left bank. The Nene is now uniformly wide and deep. Peterborough Greyhound Stadium

## Mooring and facilities

**Peterborough City Council 48-hour visitor moorings** can be found along the Embankment. They also provide water, pump-out and chemical toilet disposal facilities.

**Potters Way slipway**, on the Embankment is available. An access key from the City Council is required.

**Middle Level** Navigation notes are available from the Commissioners ✆ 01354 653232
www.middlelevel.gov.uk/navigation/navigation-information

**Peterborough** contains all the facilities that can be expected of a city, with cafés, pubs, restaurants and a large variety of shops particularly in the **Queensgate** and **Rivergate Centres**. There is a large **Asda** store near to the Embankment.

**The Charters Bar** and **East Restaurant** are here, located in a converted Dutch Barn. Providing Authentic Thai cuisine with hand-pulled Real Ales by the acclaimed Peterborough based Oakham Ales open every day.
✆ 01733 315702

Just downstream on Quayside is **the Grain Barge floating restaurant** serving Chinese food ✆ 01733 311967.

The nearby **Key Theatre** (box office ✆ 01733 207239) provides an established entertainment venue for concerts and theatre productions and includes the **Riverside Bar and Café, Clarkes** ✆ 01733 892681.

**Stanground** village has a boatyard, shops and a pub, **The Woolpack** on North Street, which serves meals. ✆ 01733 753444

---

stands on the left bank, adjacent to which more power lines traverse the channel and the Nene passes this just before Fitzwilliam Bridge crosses the river, a slightly more pleasing structure than the functional High Road Bridge. Here the embankment opens out on the left bank into a wider grassy tree lined area. The right bank has a softer more natural look and opens out on to meadows. To the rear, views of Peterborough Cathedral can still be seen. The river from here to the sea is now embanked to protect its waters from spilling over into the adjoining low fen ground, most of which lies at or below sea level, in total contrast to the valley, through which the river previously passed.

Downstream of the Fitzwilliam Bridge, the normal speed limit of 11·2kph/7mph is removed for the next mile to allow water skiing to take place on a straight section of the river. The water-skiing course is clearly signed at both ends but caution is obviously required when navigating this length.

At the end of this mile, are two bends in the river before a straight two mile stretch marks the end of the unrestricted area and the river turns slightly north to pass the Flag Fen sewage works by which there is an overhead cable crossing and the Flag Fen excavations and museum. The minor road from Eye runs along the left bank for a short distance with former sand pit lakes on the landward side of it. The Northey Road bridge crosses here and boats are often moored on the downstream side.

## Nature reserves and features

**The Nene Washes** is a 1,522-hectare biological Site of Special Scientific Interest on the bank of the River Nene east of Peterborough. They were constructed in the 17th century as a flood storage reservoir for the River Nene in periods of high flow, the grassland here is frequently flooded during the winter.

This is described by Natural England as one of Britain's few remaining areas of washland which are vital for the survival of wildfowl and waders. An area of 280 hectares is managed by the RSPB. Wintering wildfowl includes hen harriers, peregrines, wigeons, teals, pintails and Bewick's swans. The rich flora in ditches include uncommon species such as frogbit, water violet and flowering rush. There is access to the RSPB reserve immediately east of the B1040 road from the Nene Way.
GR: TL318991

## Walking and exploring

**The Nene** and **Hereward Ways** continue in partnership to follow the north bank of the river Nene on their way out of the city past the site of Flag Fen.

Peterborough Embankment

**Flag Fen** is well worth a visit if you have time. There is a cycle/walking track from the river that heads north, soon after the sewage treatment works, following Cat's Water Drain for about 0·5 miles to the site.

## Cycling

**The Green Wheel** network of cycle routes provides over 45 miles of continuous sustainable routes around the city established 2000. The route threads through picturesque scenery, including woodland, lakes and rivers, nature reserves and pretty villages, where riders will find plenty of country pubs serving excellent value food and other refreshments. Information boards provide notes on the history and natural habitat of each area.

Not only does the Green Wheel contribute to a sustainable transport system, it also celebrates over 3,000 years of social, cultural and economic history through colourful interpretation boards and a series of sculptures.

The Shanks Millennium Bridge over the River Nene at Stanground Washes provides a direct, safe and fully off-road link between Peterborough and Whittlesey for commuter and leisure cyclists, horse riders and pedestrians. It is designed to minimise any disturbance to the birds that live and breed on the Nene Washes.

## Canoeing

**Peterborough Embankment** is ideal for launching canoes as the bank is very low and close to the river level. Parking is available in the public car park near the Key Theatre. GR: TL 195983

## Local history

**Peterborough** is the only Cathedral City on the Nene. Its earliest recorded name is Medeshamstede, (the meadow homestead) in AD655. A Benedictine monastery was founded here in AD650 by Paeda, King of Mercia, which subsisted until the Reformation. It was an important Saxon religious centre, with the town growing up around it, but was destroyed by the Danes around AD820 and again by Hereward the Wake 250 years later. The monastery stood where the cathedral now stands, and excavations have revealed the remains of the Saxon church, which can be seen in the cathedral, below the present floor in the south transept. In the retro-choir of the cathedral is the Hedda Stone, a very important piece of Anglo-Saxon sculpture, dating from AD800. The monastery was rebuilt by St Aethelwold, who dedicated it to St Peter. By 972, the settlement was known as Burh (a defended settlement) but subsequently the town name took up the abbey's dedication and by 1225, the town was referred to as 'Burgus Sancti Petri' and, by 1333, Petreburgh.

The present Cathedral was built by the Normans, construction beginning in 1172. It is in the Anglo-Norman Romanesque style, with an early Gothic west front. Peterborough was raised to cathedral status in 1541 when Henry VIII dissolved the monasteries and housed the tombs of Catherine of Aragon, first wife of Henry VIII and Mary, Queen of Scots. The latter's son James I, however, later arranged for her body to be removed to Westminster Abbey. The cathedral was effectively destroyed by Cromwell's soldiers in 1643 and not fully restored until the 1890s.

The Nene at Peterborough was first bridged by Godfrey of Croyland in 1308. The present bridge on this site, beside the Customs House, dates from 1934. Until 1801 Peterborough was a small town but the Industrial Revolution and the coming of the railway, together with the development of the brick industry following the discovery of Oxford Clay, stimulated growth. In 1968, the Peterborough Development Corporation was formed, the city received 'new town' designation and the population greatly increased. The latest development is the southern township, on old brick workings.

The city centre is, except for the cathedral, architecturally poor. In the cathedral environs, however, there are several interesting and important buildings. The Precincts are entered from the Market Place, by the Outer Gate and to the south of this gate, vaults connect with the King's Lodgings and the Abbots Prison. The Abbots Gate dates from 1250 and there is a Norman arch from 1180, while a late 12th-century room survives in the garden to the east of Tort Hill mound, which was heaped up by Thorold, a 11th century abbot. There are also the impressive remains of the infirmary and two small nearby detached buildings. Table Hall, dating from the 15th century and the Infirmerers' Lodging from two centuries earlier. In addition, the building known as the Vineyard marks the site of the mediaeval vineyard planted by Abbot Martin de Bec in 1140. Becket's Rest, in the cathedral grounds is a 14th-century extension to a late Norman chapel dedicated to St Thomas.

Nearby, at 41 Bridge Street, is the **Peterborough Tourist Information Centre** ☎ 01733 452336.

The Old Customs House on Town Bridge, now the headquarters of the Sea Cadets and a scheduled ancient monument, and the Old Guildhall, dating from 1671, on the market place, are also worth viewing.

Other features of interest in the centre include Peterborough United FC on London Road, Peterborough Museum and Art Gallery on Priestgate (01733 864663) and Railworld close to the Town Bridge at the Nene Valley Railway Station off Oundle Road. This provides displays and exhibits (some 'hands on'), covering present and projected future train travel, the 'Age of Steam' and local railway displays and large locomotives ☎ 01733 344240.

**Mortons Leam** was dug between 1478 and 1490 under the direction of Bishop Morton of Ely. It was modified again during the 17th century when Vermuyden was employed to drain the Bedford Levels. By 1642 several new works had been initiated, including provision of a longer straighter cut, for the quicker conveyance of flood waters, a bank on the S side of Morton's Leam and a sluice at Stanground.

**Flag Fen** is at almost the other end of the historical time scale. The site is on a gravel promontory beside the Nene and was occupied from Neolithic to Roman times. It is bounded on the west by a section of the old Roman Car Dyke and inhumations from the Beaker Period and cremations in urns from the Middle Bronze Age have been found, as well as Iron Age material.

The damp nature of the soil has acted as a preservative of much of the remains and the reconstructed Iron Age village on the site is a major tourist attraction. It was discovered in 1982, when the archaeologist Frances Pryor came across a protruding oak stump disturbed by an excavator. The site was known to be crossed by the Roman Fen Causeway, but this stump had been worked to form a post and placed three feet below the level of the Roman road. Excavation of the site revealed thousands of timbers, perfectly preserved by immersion in the acidic waterlogged peat. They composed part of a platform estimated to be about the size of two football pitches with the remains of buildings upon it, which had been built out in the shallow waters of the Fen in the late Bronze Age. Before the great drainage works of the 17th century, this had been a wild and watery landscape, but one which the 12th-century writer Hugh Candidus recorded offered an 'abundance [of] all things needful for them that dwell nearby'.

Pryor's next major discovery, in 1989, concerned a structure of posts running for over 0.5 mile in length across and beyond the platform. It became apparent that it had been constructed after the platform had been abandoned because of rising water levels. On the seaward side was unearthed a remarkable collection of metal artefacts, which included swords, daggers, tools and helmets which appeared to have been ceremonially buried as grave goods.

Flag Fen is an active archaeological park and the reconstructed village includes authentic style outhouses, round houses and a mere. Its museum contains the oldest wheel found in England, and 3,000-year-old timbers, still with the original marks of the tools that furbished them so long ago. Excavations have also revealed an intact Roman road.

To the east of Flag Fen lies **Must Farm Quarry** where eight prehistoric log boats were discovered in 2011, most of which were in an incredible state of preservation due to the wetland nature of the area. Many were virtually intact, and some have elaborate features including lifting handles, grooves for transom boards and evidence of decoration. The boats have been moved to Flag Fen for conservation and viewing.

**Flag Fen** has a **Visitor Centre, exhibition, café and gift shop** and is open April to September 1000–1700.
The Droveway, Northey Road,
Peterborough,
PE6 7QJ
☎ 01733 864468

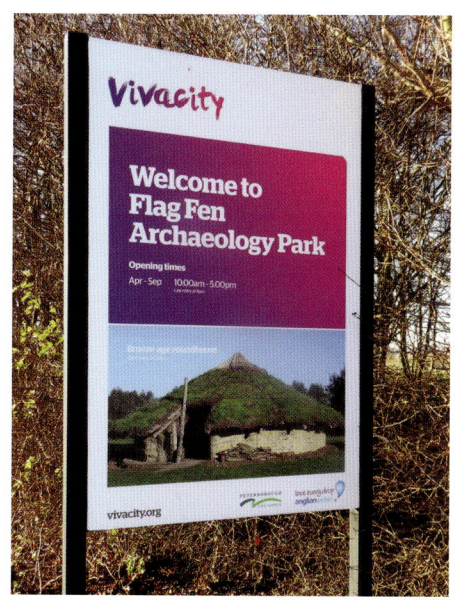

Flag Fen

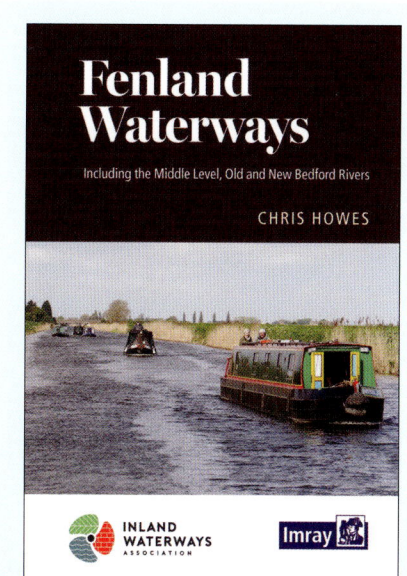

A navigation guide to the calm waters and expansive landscapes of the Middle Level.

Covering the waterways between the River Great Ouse and the River Nene, including the main link route via March and several other alternatives, *Fenland Waterways* gives all the information needed for anyone planning to navigate the area.

Includes detailed plans and route descriptions.

Available from www.imray.com.

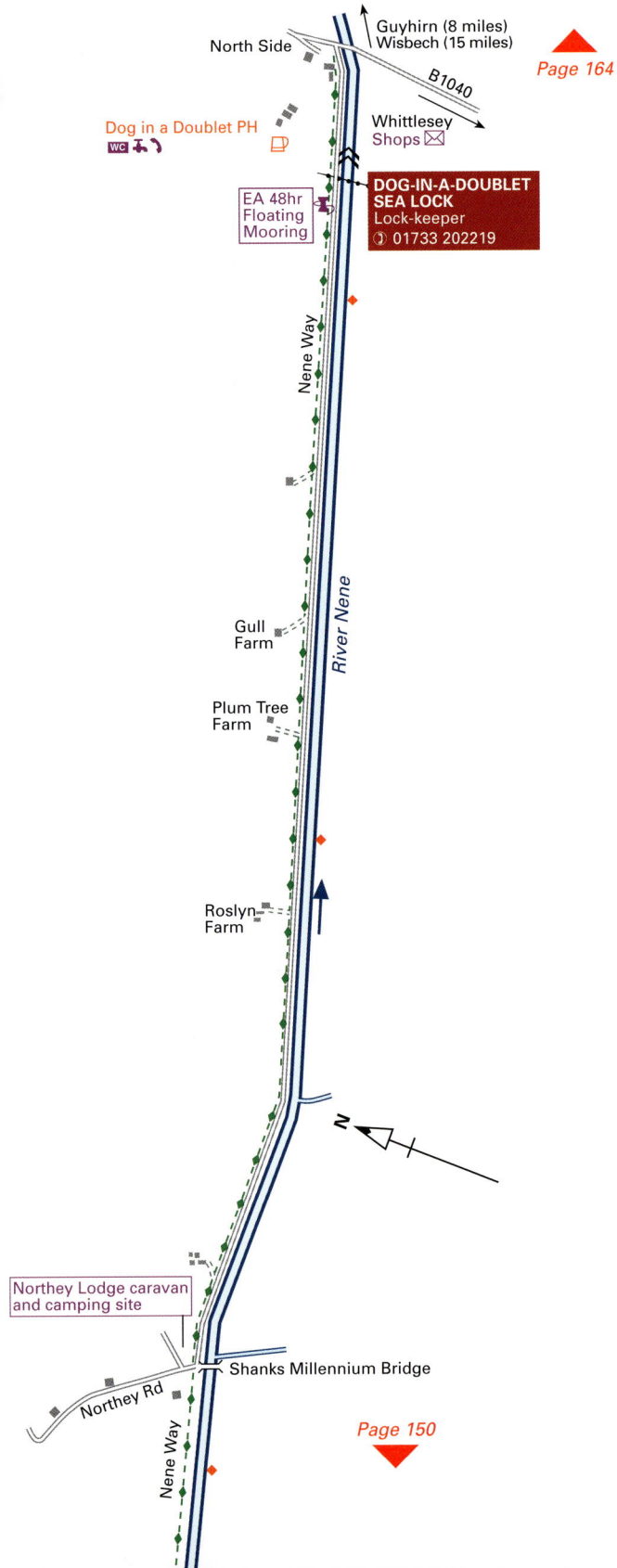

# Map 18

# Flag Fen to Dog-in-a-Doublet

| Map 18 Flag Fen (GR TL 229983) to Dog-in-a-Doublet Lock (GR:TL 271992) | | | | | | | | | | | | | | | | | | |
|---|---|---|---|---|---|---|---|---|---|---|---|---|---|---|---|---|---|---|
| Location | Miles | Locks | Lock type | Est time hours | Bridge < 2·7m | Moorings and facilities | | | | | | | Victualling | | | | Canoe | |
| | | | | | | 48hr | Long stay | Water point | CDP | Pumpout | Refuse | Diesel | Shops | Pub | Café | PO or Bank | Portage | Park & access |
| Shanks Millennium Bridge | 1·8 | 0 | | 0·4 | | | | | | | | | | | | | | |
| Plum Tree Farm | 1·2 | 0 | | 0·3 | | | | | | | | | | | | | | |
| Dog-in-a-Doublet Lock 38 | 1·1 | 1 | ☐ | 0·5 | | ♨ | | | shops and PO in Whittlesey | | | | 🛒 | 🍺 | 🍴 | £ | | |
| Map 18 totals | 4·1 | 1 | | 1·1 | | | | | | | | | | | | | | |

THE RIVER NENE

## Navigation notes

The footpath continues along the north bank, but the countryside has now changed dramatically to reflect the fenland river that the Nene has now become. The 'real Nene' can therefore be said to end at Peterborough. From now on, to the sea, the river conveys upland water through artificial cuts to its outfall. These cuts run between the steep embankments, with the flat fen lands and isolated farm buildings as scenery.

The proposed 'Boston to Peterborough Wetland Corridor' will probably join the river Nene in the vicinity of North bank and Flag Fen. This scheme a slimmed down version of the originally proposed 'Fens Waterways link'. IWA Lincolnshire and Peterborough branches are working in partnership with Lincolnshire County Council and the Environment Agency to realise what could be a really important strategic and worthwhile link.

Compared to the proliferation of wooded areas upstream, the lack of trees now is very noticeable. The embanked stretch also marks the end of the fluvial Nene as it approaches **Dog-in-a-Doublet Lock**, where the B1040 road from Whittlesey to Thorney crosses and, just off this road, is Northey Lodge Campsite and Caravan park. There are overhead lines which cross the river just upstream of the lock.

The Dog-in-a-Doublet lock and sluice complex was built in 1938 and is manned during daylight hours.

The Dog-in-a-Doublet complex protects Peterborough from tidal inundation and now marks the tidal limit of the River Nene. Previously the river was tidal up to Orton Staunch (now Orton Lock and Sluices). The sluice gates are automated and the lock, which is powered, is operated by the lock keeper. Lock passage must be booked in advance on ☎ 01733 202219 or 07384 249151. The complex also provides a fish pass, and monitoring equipment is used to gauge the numbers and types of fish travelling through.

Shanks Millennium Bridge

Dog-in-a-Doublet lock  Chris Howes

## Mooring and facilities

**Northey Lodge Campsite and Caravan Park**  where storage of boats either for long periods (six months–one year) or during the week is available.
☎ 01733 223918

Except for vessels seeking passage through the **Dog-in-a-Doublet Lock**, there is no mooring allowed within 100m of the structure.

There are **EA 48-hour moorings** at the floating landing stage, upstream of the Lock, which has a bridge to link it to the river bank. A popular location for those wishing to visit the nearby Dog-in-a-Doublet pub and restaurant.

The nearby **Dog-in-a-Doublet public house/restaurant** is a gastropub serving top quality fresh and local British food. It also offers a deli, bed & breakfast and camping.
☎ 01733 202256

There are shops and several pubs and cafes to be found in the market town of **Whittlesey**, 1·2 miles to the south of the lock. Thursday is early closing day for most shops.

THE RIVER NENE   161

## Nature reserves and features

**Kings Dyke Nature Reserve**, located on the A605 in Whittlesey, was formerly a clay extraction pit for the London Brick company. It has now been developed into an important nature reserve. It can be accessed from the river by following Funtham's Lane for 1 mile south of Northey Lodge.
www.kingsdykenaturereserve.com

## Walking and exploring

After Dog-in-a-Doublet Lock the **Nene and Hereward Ways** turn south away from the river into the town of Whittlesey:

**The Hereward Way** branches off to trudge east along the Briggate river, Twenty Foot drain and the old course of the River Nene into March.

**The Nene Way** heads north east out of Whittlesey to pick up its route along Morton's Leam on its way towards Guyhirn and Wisbech.

## Cycling

**The Fenland Trail** and **The Fens Cycleway** are routes for longer cycle exploration around the Peterborough, Wisbech, Kings Lynn area of Fenland.

**The Shanks Millennium foot and cycle bridge** is a stunning structure that provides a useful river crossing and links to several walking and cycling routes

## Local history

**Dog-in-a-Doublet**
The derivation of the name 'Dog-in-a-Doublet' is interesting. The pub was one of several erected along the Nene in the mid 1700s by the Bedford Level Corporation, then responsible for the river and one of the early publicans also served as lock-keeper and as a decoy man, working the local duck decoys. It is said that a terrier dog that he used to help him with this last-mentioned work contracted a skin disease, through which it lost its fur and that following this, the publican's wife made it a leather jerkin to keep it warm, hence 'Dog-in-a-Doublet'.

**Whittlesey** is best known for its brickworks and the towering chimneys of the kilns. Demand for the bricks made with the Whittlesey clay has declined in recent years and only one original factory remains in production. In prehistoric times the sea covered these parts and several significant marine fossils have been unearthed, including, in September 1987, that of a 160-million-year-old plesiosaur. This is now in Peterborough Museum. Four miles below Whittlesey is Poplar House Farm, where the Nene bisects the Greenwich Meridian. There is also a buried Roman causeway here, that once linked Goosetree with Eldernell.

River Nene and washland near Whittlesey

# 6

# TIDAL RIVER NENE DOG-IN-A-DOUBLET TO THE WASH

# Map 19

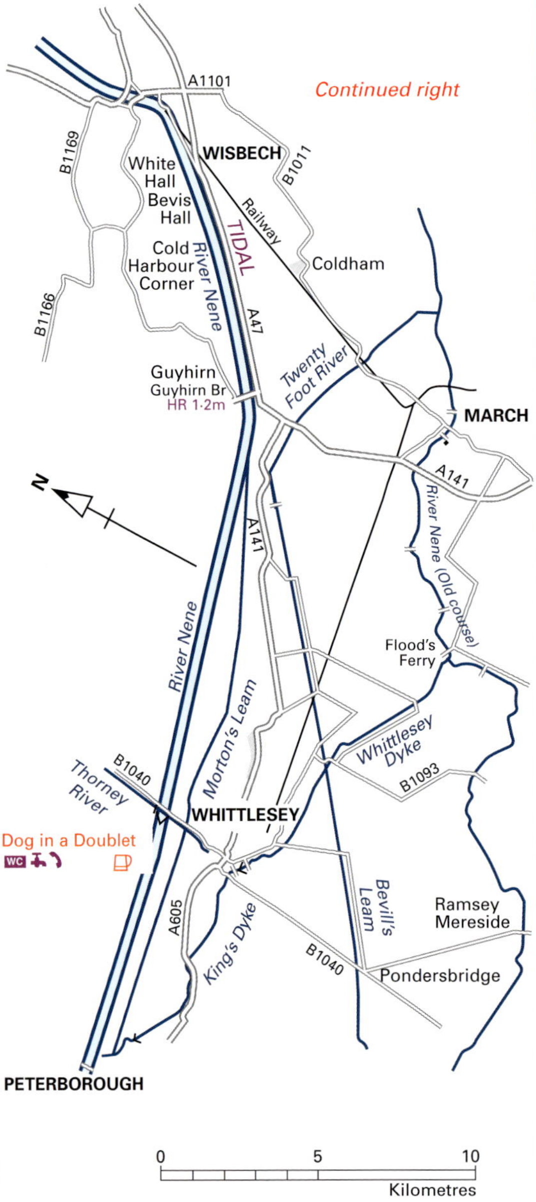

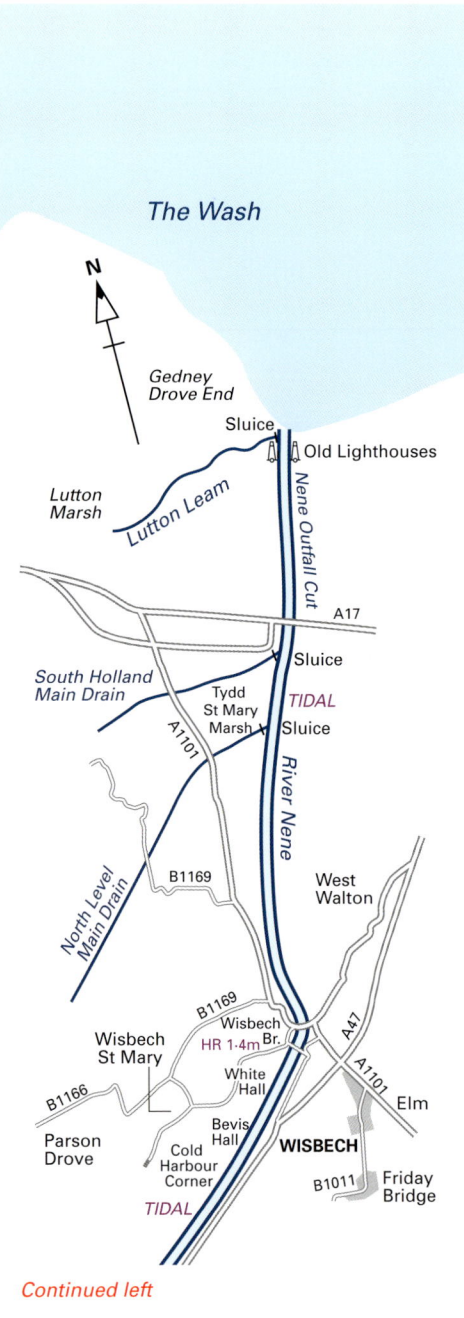

# Map 19

# Dog-in-a-Doublet Lock to Guy's Head Light

| Location | Miles | Locks | Lock type | Est time hours | Bridge < 2·7m | Moorings and facilities | | | | | | | Victualling | | | | Canoe | |
|---|---|---|---|---|---|---|---|---|---|---|---|---|---|---|---|---|---|---|
| | | | | | | 48hr | Long stay | Water point | CDP | Pumpout | Refuse | Diesel | Shops | Pub | Café | PO or Bank | Portage | Park & access |
| Guyhirn A47 Road Bridge | 8·0 | 0 | | 1·8 | ☕ | | | | | | | | | | | | | |
| Wisbech Town Bridge | 6·0 | 0 | | 1·3 | | | | | | | | | | | | | | |
| Wisbech Yacht Harbour | 0·5 | 0 | | 0·1 | | ☕ | ☕ | ⚓ | ⬇ | ⛽ | 🗑 | 🛢 | 🛒 | 🍺 | 🍴 | £ | | |
| North Level Main Drain | 5·0 | 0 | | 1·1 | | | | | | | | | | | | | | |
| Port of Sutton Bridge | 2·0 | 0 | | 0·4 | | | | | | | | | | | | | | |
| Guy's Head | 3·5 | 0 | | 0·8 | | | | | | | | | | | | | | |
| **Map 19 totals** | **25·0** | **0** | | **5·6** | | | | | | | | | | | | | | |

THE RIVER NENE

Guyhirn Bridge

## Navigation notes

Below the Dog-in-a-Doublet Lock the Nene still has a further 25 miles to travel to reach the sea, the tidal stretch is comparatively uninteresting with mooring being much more difficult due to high banks and mud at low tide.

**Guyhirn**, 8 miles downstream and just above where Mortons Leam rejoins the right bank of the Nene at the end of the Nene Washes an **EA tidal mooring** has been installed. The headroom clearance at Guyhirn Road Bridge, varies with the tide.

**Wisbech** is reached 7 miles further on. Craft should proceed through Wisbech with care as the bank is lined with steel and concrete piling, there is stoning in the bed and a strong run on flood and ebb tides, particularly in the lower stages.

Below Wisbech, the flow of the Nene through the reclaimed land divides Norfolk from Lincolnshire and, between Wisbech and Sutton Bridge, the main drains of the North Level District and South Holland Internal Drainage Boards discharge on the left bank just before the **Port of Sutton Bridge** is reached. Beyond Sutton Bridge lies the sea and for the Nene, the end of its journey.

There is a two-hour tide differential from Dog-in-a-Doublet to the West lighthouses.

For more information on the tidal Nene and passages across The Wash see *Tidal Havens of The Wash and Humber* (Imray) and its free downloadable supplement available from www.imray.com

### Moorings and facilities

**Environment Agency Guyhirn**
48-hour visitor tidal pontoon mooring

**Wisbech** - for information on the passage of craft through and moorings in Wisbech and down to the sea, the Wisbech Port Manager should be consulted. ☎ 01406 351530 or ☎ 01945 588059

**Port of Sutton Bridge**
Port Office ☎ 01406 351530

**Wisbech** town has a wide range of shops, pubs, restaurants, banks and a **Post Office**.

## Walking and exploring

**Octavia Hill Wisbech Heritage Trail** starts at Peckover House (National Trust)
www.nationaltrust.org.uk/peckover-house-and-garden/trails/peckover-house-octavia-hill-wisbech-heritage-walk

**Wisbech mini guide and Town Trail** provides an insight into the town's history and significant buildings.
www.visitcambridgeshirefens.org/documents/walks/Wisbech_Mini_Guide.pdf

**The Nene Way** crosses the river at Guyhirn to follow the north side of the river bank towards Wisbech, where it leaves the river briefly. From Wisbech it picks up the trail again on the northern bank all the way to Sutton Bridge where it crosses to the southern bank for the last 3 miles of its route to Guy's Head.

**The Peter Scott Walk** tales over from the Nene Way as it follows the river and coastline from the lighthouse along the Wash as far as Kings Lynn ferry.

## Local history

**Wisbech** has a fine display of Georgian architecture on the North Brink of the Nene, recognising the importance of the port over many centuries, although the storehouses and boat building yards that previously stood close to Town Bridge have long gone. Indeed, before land reclamation and coastal changes, Wisbech was once on the coast. It was also the home of Thomas Clarkson, who played a major part in the fight for the abolition of slavery and of Octavia Hill, co-founder of the National Trust.

North Brink, Wisbech, looking downstream

# APPENDIX

## Acknowledgements and references

| | |
|---|---|
| Nathan Arnold EA | for updating on Nenescape Landscape Partnership projects |
| CanalPlan AC | waterway gazetteer and time/distance data |
| East Northamptonshire Council | Raunds Heritage Trail |
| | Thrapston Heritage Trail |
| | Oundle Heritage Trail |
| Environment Agency | Guide to facilities on the River Nene |
| | Map of the River Nene |
| | Welcome to the Anglian Waterways |
| | Leisure and residential mooring information |
| Flag Fen Bronze Age Excavations | site plan and leaflet |
| Friends of the River Nene | Moorings guide |
| GEO Projects | River Nene map |
| Higham Ferrers Town Council | Higham Ferrers Heritage Trail |
| Inland Waterways Association | for support and endorsement of this project |
| IWA Northampton branch | The Northampton Arm leaflet |
| Long Distance Walkers Association | Notes for Nene Way, |
| | Hereward Way, |
| | Grand Union Canal Walk |
| | Peter Scott Walk |
| Marina owners and managers | for updating information about their facilities and services |
| Nene Valley | Boating, cycling and walking leaflets and maps |
| Nene Valley Railway | Visitor guide and timetable |
| Northampton Borough Council | A guide to Northampton 2018/19 |
| Northamptonshire County Council | Aldwincle and Wadenhoe riverside walks |
| | Oundle riverside walks |
| | Fotheringhay and Woodnewton riverside walks |
| | East Northamptonshire Cycle Map |
| Northamptonshire Heritage Forum | Museums, historic houses, heritage sites and societies |
| Ordnance Survey Explorer | 1:25 000 sheets 223, 224, 227, 235 |
| Ordnance Survey Landranger | 1:50 000 sheets 131, 141, 142, 152, 153 |
| Peterborough Cathedral | The Precincts Trail |
| Rushden Town Council | Heritage Trail |
| Iain Smith | for allowing use of text from earlier editions |
| Stanwick Lakes | Heritage Trail |
| | Map and guide to activities |
| Waterway Routes | for detailed mapping and distances |
| Dick Whitehouse FOTRN | for information about all aspects of canoeing on the River Nene |

# Bibliography

| | |
|---|---|
| Alderton, D, Booker, J, Batsford | Guide to Industrial Archaeology of East Anglia |
| Asher, S J, | The River Nene Navigation |
| Astbury, A K, | The Black Fens |
| Bays, J, Russell, R, | Canals of Eastern England |
| B B, | A Summer on the Nene (illustrated by D Watkins-Pitchford) |
| Cambs Federation of WI | Cambridgeshire Village Book |
| Cligman, J, Crowe, N, | Hertfordshire to Norfolk |
| Dean, C & V, | Notes for First Time Boaters on the River Nene |
| Stuart Fisher | British River Navigations |
| Hammond, C W, | Tracing the History of Place Names |
| Heritage House Group Ltd | Elton Hall and Gardens |
| Jenkins, H J K, | Along the Nene |
| Jones, J, | A Human Geography of Cambridgeshire |
| Muir, R, | The Villages of England |
| Pearsons | Canal Companion: Leicester Line and River Nene |
| Perring, F. | A Guide to the Nature Reserves of Eastern England |
| Pevsner, N, | The Buildings of England – Bedfordshire, Huntingdonshire and Peterborough |
| Pevsner, N, | The Buildings of England – Northamptonshire |
| Phillips. D, | The River Nene |
| Speed, J, | Counties of Britain – a Tudor Atlas |
| Taylor, C. | The Cambridgeshire Landscape |
| Wells, W | Bedford Level |

# Index

Page numbers in **bold** refer to maps

Abington Barrage Gate, **52**, 55, 56
Abington Lock, **52**, 53, 55, 57
Achurch, **98**, 99, 100, 103
Achurch (Wadenhoe) Meadow, **98**, 100, 101-2
*Adventure Rutland*, 133
Ailsworth, **136**, 140, 142-3
*AJ Cycles*, 82, 88
Aldwincle, **98**, 100, 101, 102-3
Alwalton, **136**, 138, 141-2, **144**, 146, 147, 149
Alwalton Lock & Moorings, **136**, 137, 138, 139, 145, 146
Ashton, 111, **114**, 115, 116, 117, 118, 119
Ashton Lock, **114**, 115, 116
Ashton Wold, 118
*Association of Nene River Clubs*, 35

Back Dike, **136**, 138, 140, **144**, 148
Back River, **150**
*backwaters*, 20
Badby Arm (Nene), 47, 49
*Barnabee*, 134
Barnes Meadow Nature Reserve, 58
Barnwell, **106**, 107, 108-9, 112
*Barnwell Boat Club*, 35, **106**, 107
Barnwell Country Park, **106**, 108, 109, 110-111, 112
Barnwell Locks, **106**, 107, 108, 109-110, 112
Barnwell Mill Bridge, **106**, 109
Barnwell Moorings, **106**, 109
*Becket, Thomas*, 59, 71, 155
Becket's Park, **46**, **52**, 54, 58, 59
Becket's Park Lock, **46**, **52**, 53, 54, 56, 58, 59
Bedford Purlieus Nature Reserve, 132
Bevill's Leam, **164**
Billing, **60**, 61, 62, 63, 65
Billing Aquadrome, **60**, 62, 63, 64, 65
Billing Lock, **60**, 61, 62
Billing Marina, 22, 34, **60**, 61, 63, 64
Billing Mill, **60**, 62, 63, 64, 65, 66
*birds*, 20, 58, 82, 88, 100-102, 126, 154

Blackthorn Lake Marina, 22, 34, **84**, 85, 87
Blisworth Marina, 43
Bluebell Lakes, **120**, 122, 124, 126
*boat clubs*, 22-4, 34, 35
*boat licensing & registration*, 8
Boat Safety Scheme (BSS), 8
*The Boater's Handbook*, 36
Boathouse Cut & Thorpe Wood, **144**, 145, 147, 148, 149
*books, maps & guides*, 20, 36, 37, 82, 168, 169
*Boston to Peterborough Wetland Corridor*, 160
Brancey Brook, **98**, 100, 101, 102-3
Briar Hill (Hunsbury) Lock, **46**, 47, 48
Briar Hill (Northampton), 50
*bridges & structures*, 14, 31
Britannia Inn, **52**, 55, 57
*British Canoeing*, 21, 35

*Cam Conservancy*, 8
*Canal Planner AC*, 35
*Canal & River Trust*, 8, 34, **40**, 43, 48
*canoeing*, 21, 25-7, 36
Car Dyke, 156
*Caravan & Motorhome Club*, **144**, 147
Carlsberg Brewery, **46**, 49, 50, **52**, 54
Castle Ashby House, 68, 70, 71
Castle Farm Mooring, **120**, 121, 123, 125
Castor, **136**, 137, 139, 140, 141, 142-3
Castor Mill, **136**, 138, 140
Cat's Water Drain, 154
Chester Farm Roman Town Heritage Site, **72**, 82, 83
Chester House & Footbridge, **72**, 73, 75, 76
*Clare, John (poet)*, 59
Claudius Way Heritage Centre, 82
Clifford Hill Fortification, **60**, 62, 65
Clifford Hill Lock & Mooring, **60**, 61, 62, 63
*closures & restrictions*, 15
Cogenhoe, **60**, 61, 63-4, 65
Cogenhoe Lock, **60**, 61, 63

170 THE RIVER NENE

*conker championships*, 119
Cotterstock, 111, **114**, 116-17, 118, 119
Cotterstock Lock, **114**, 115, 116
Cotton End Lock & Mooring, **46**, 47, 48, 49, **52**, 54
*country parks*, 20, 37
*cruising distances*, 2-3, 19
*cruising times*, 2-3, 19
*cycle routes*, 20, 58, 63, 82, 88, 95, 111, 140, 162
*cycling*, 20, 37

Delapre Abbey, 58
Delta Pit, 81
Denford, **90**, 91, 92, 93, 94, 95, 96
Denford Lock, **90**, 91, 92, 94, 95
*Denver Causeway*, 143
*deserted villages*, **84**, 86, 89
*diesel*, 23-4
*distance tables*, 2-3, 19, 32-3
Ditchford, **78**, 79, 80, 81, 82, 83
Ditchford Lakes & Meadows Nature Reserve, **78**, 81, 82
Ditchford Lock, 12, **78**, 79, 80, 81, 82
Doddington Lock & Mooring, **66**, 67, 68-9, 70
Dog in a Doublet Lock, 11, 14, 34, **158**, 159, 160, 161, 162, **164**
*Dryden, John*, 119, 149
Duck Street Footbridge, 129
Durobrivae Roman town, **136**, 138, 142
Duston Mill, **46**, 47, 48, 49

Eaglethorpe, **120**, 123, 125, 126
Earls Barton, **66**, 68, 69, 70, 71
Earls Barton Lock, **66**, 67, 68, 70
East Northamptonshire Council, 35
*East Northamptonshire Cycle Map*, 82
*eating out*, 20, 37
Elton, **120**, 123-4, 125, 127
*Elton Boat Club*, 35, **120**, 121, 123, 125
Elton Lock, **120**, 121, 124, 125
Elton Park & Hall, **120**, 124, 125, 126, 127
Elton Road Bridge, 124, **128**, 130
*Environment Agency (EA)*, 8-11, 15-16, 21, 22-4, 34, 36, 37, 48, *see also* Northampton Marina
*environmental features*, 20, 36, 37
Ermine Street, **136**, 138, 141-2

*Express Lift Tower (National Lift Tower & Abseiling Centre)*, 54, 58

*facilities & services*, 11, 20, 34-5
*feature tables*, 19
Fen Causeway, 156
*Fenland Trail (cycle route)*, 162
*Fens Cycleway*, 162
*Fens Waterways Link*, 6, 160
Ferry Meadows, Overton Lake & Moorings, **144**, 145, 146, 147, 148
*fishing*, 37
Fitzwilliam Bridge, **150**, 151, 153
Flag Fen, **150**, 151, 152, 153, 154, 156-7
Fletton Quays, 152
*Floodline (EA)*, 16, 34
*floods*, 15, 50
Flood's Ferry, **164**
*food & drink*, 20, 37
*fossil plesiosaur*, 162
Fotheringhay, **120**, 121, 122, 123, 124, 125, 126
*Four Pears PH*, **52**, **60**, 63
Frank Perkins Parkway, **150**, 152
*Friends of the River Nene (FOTRN)*, 10, 21, 22-4, 35, 36
*Frontier Centre*, **84**, 86

Gayton Junction, **40**, 41, 42, 45
Gayton Marina, 34, **40**, 41, 42, 43
Gedney Drove End, **164**
Glebe Farm Meadow & Moorings, **78**, 79, 81, 83
Goblin Brook, **106**, 107, 110
*Gorilla Firm Cycling*, **114**, 117, 118
*Grahame, Kenneth*, 127
*Grand Junction Boat Company*, **40**, 43
Grand Union Canal, 8, 21, **40**, **46**, 48-9, *see also* Northampton Arm; Westbridge Arm
*Grand Union Canal Walk*, 20, 45, 49, 58
Gravel Pit Lakes, **84**
Great Addington, 86, 87
Great Billing, 61, 62, 63, 65
Great Doddington, **66**, 69, 70, **72**, 74
Great Houghton, **52**, 53, 57, 58, 59
Great Ouse, River, 8
*Green Wheel (cycle network)*, 152, 154
*Greenway cycle route*, 88
*Greenwich Meridian*, 162

*grid references*, 19, 26-31
*guillotine gate locks*, 11, 12-13
Gunwade Lake, **144**, 148
Guyhirn, 152, 162, **164**, 165, 166, 167
Guy's Head, 7, 165, 167

Hardingstone Dyke, 62
Hardingstone Lock, **46**, 47, 48
Hardwater Road & Mill, **66**, 67, 68, 69, 70, 71
Harper's Brook, **98**, 100, 102
*headroom*, 14, 31
*Hereward Way*, 20, 138, 140, 148, 154, 162
Higham Ferrers, **78**, 79, 80, 81, 82, 83
Higham Ferrers Lock, **78**, 79, 80
Higham Ferrers Pits Nature Reserve, **78**, 81, 82
Higham Lake, 81
*history*, 7, 21
*Holiday Inn*, **52**, 55, 57
Hunsbury (Briar Hill) Lock, **46**, 47, 48
Hunsbury Hill & Country Park, 45, **46**, 48, 50

*Inland Waterways Association (IWA)*, 6, 7, 17, 35, 43, 160
Irchester Country Park, **72**, 74, 75, 76
Irthlingborough, **78**, 80, 81, 82, **84**
Irthlingborough Bridge & Viaduct, **78**, 79, 80, 83
Irthlingborough EA Mooring, **78**, 79, 81
Irthlingborough Lakes & Meadows Reserve, 81, 82
Irthlingborough Lock, 81, **84**, 85, 86
Ise River, 74
Islip, **90**, 93, 94, 95, 96-7
Islip Dave (mooring), **90**, 91, 93
Islip Lock, **90**, 91, 94
Islip Mill Footbridge, 94
Islip Mill Mooring, **90**, 91

*Jacksons*, **150**
*Jim Shead's waterways information*, 35

key to symbols used on canoe access & portage tables, 25
key to symbols used on maps, 18
key to symbols used on moorings & facility tables, 22
keys see lock keys; navigation keys

Kinewell Lake, **84**, 87-8, 89, **90**, 92
King's Dyke & Nature Reserve, 162, **164**
Kings Head (Wadenhoe) Moorings, **98**, 100, 101
King's Lynn, 162, 167
Kings Meadow Lane Bridge, **78**, 79, 80

*Landscape Partnership Scheme*, 10, 22, 35, 36, 37
*legislation*, 9
*licensing & registration*, 8
lighthouses, 7, **164**, 165, 167
Lilford Bridge, **106**, 107, 108, 111, 112
Lilford Hall & Park, 102, **106**, 108, 112
Lilford Lock, 99, 101, **106**, 107, 108
Lilford Lodge Marina, 22, 34, **106**, 107, 108, 109
Linches escarpment, **98**, 102
Little Addington, **84**, 86, 87, 88, 89
Little Billing, **60**
Little Houghton, **52**, 57, 58, **60**, 61, 62, 63, 65
Little Irchester, 54, **72**, 74, 76
*Living Landscapes*, 36, 81
*local history*, 7, 21
*lock keys*, 28, 30
*locks*, 2-3, 11-13, 14, 15, 28-33
Longthorpe, **144**, 149
*low bridges & structures*, 14, 31
Lower Barnwell Lock, **106**, 107, 109-110
Lower Ringstead Lock, **84**, 85, 86, 87, 88
Lower Wellingborough Lock, **72**, 73, 74-5, 80
Lutton Leam, **164**
Lynch Lake, **144**, 148

Mallows Cotton, **84**, 86, 89
*Malt Shovel Tavern*, **46**, **52**, 57
Manor Farm moorings, **66**, 69
*map pages in text*, 18-19, 20
*maps, books & guides*, 20, 36, 37, 82, 168, 169
March, 162, **164**
*marinas*, 9-10, 15, 20, 22-4, 34
Mary, Queen of Scots, 126
Middle Level, 8, 34, **150**, 151, 152, 153
*Middle Nene Cruising Club*, 34, 35, **98**, 99, 100, 101
*Middle Nene Sailing Club*, **90**, 93, **98**
Midsummer Meadow, **52**, 53, 55, 56, 58
Mill Cotton, 89

Mill Lakes Footbridge, 99
Milton Ferry Bridge, **144**, 145, 146, 148
Milton Malsor, 41, 43, 45
Milton Park, 143, **144**, 146, 149
*moorings & facilities*, 10-11, 20, 22-4, 36
Morton's Leam, **150**, 152, 156, **164**, 166
*museums*, 59, 71, 113, 132, 153, 156
Must Farm Quarry, 157

Naseby Arm, 49
Nassington, **128**, 130, 131, 132, 133
*National Association of Boatowners*, 35
National Lift Tower & Abseiling Centre, 54, 58
*nature reserves & features*, 20, 37
*navigation*, 7-15
*navigation authorities*, 8, 22, 34
*navigation keys*, 9, 34, 36
*navigation notes*, 20
Nene *(river name pronunciation)*, 7, 94
*Nene Extreme Canoeing*, **114**, 117, 118
Nene Marine, 35
Nene Outfall Cut, **164**
Nene Park, 20, 37, **144**, 146, 148
*Nene Valley (website)*, 20, 35, 37
*Nene Valley Boats*, 35, **106**, 109
*Nene Valley Brewery*, **114**, 116, 117
*Nene Valley Railway*, 35, 128, 132, 133, 138, 140, 141, 147, 152
*Nene Valley Ski Club*, **78**, 81
Nene Washes, 152, 154, 166
*Nene Way (general)*, 20, 49, 58, 167
Nene Wetlands, **78**, 81-2
*Nene White Water Centre*, **52**, 55
*Nenescape Landscape Partnership Scheme*, 10, 22, 35, 36, 37
New Fletton, **150**, 152
Nine Arches Bridge (Thrapston), **90**, 91, 93, 94, 95, 96
*Norbital cycle route*, 58
Normangate Field Roman Potteries, **136**, 138, 140, 141-2
North Level Main Drain, **164**, 165, 166
Northampton, **46**, 47-59, **52**
Northampton Arm, 6, 21, 28, 38-50, **40**, **46**
*Northampton Boat Club*, 34, 35, **52**, 53, 56
Northampton Central Museum & Art Gallery, 59

Northampton Marina (EA), 9-10, 15, 22, 34, 36, **46**, **52**, 53, 56, 58
*Northampton Tourist Information Centre*, 35
Northampton Town FC, **46**, 48
Northampton Town Lock 1 (Becket's Park Lock), **46**, **52**, 53, 54, 56, 58, 59
Northampton Town Quay, **46**, 56
Northampton Washlands, **52**, 56, 57, 58
*Northamptonshire County Council*, 35
Northey Lodge Campsite & Caravan Park, **158**, 160, 161

*Octavia Hill Wisbech Heritage Trail*, 167
Old Sulehay Forest Reserve, 130, 132
*Ordnance Survey (OS) maps*, 20
*organisations & services*, 34-5
Orton Lock & Moorings, **144**, 145, 146, 147, 148
Orton Longueville, **144**, 145, 147, 149
Orton Meadows, **144**, 146, 147, 148
Orton Mere NVR Station, **144**, 147
Oundle, **106**, 109, 110, 111, 113, **114**
*Oundle Boat Club*, **114**, 116
*Oundle Cruising Club*, 35, **106**, 107, 109, 111
Oundle Marina Village, 22, 34, **106**, 107, 109, 112
*Oundle Rural (cycle route)*, 111
*Oundle School Rowing Club*, **114**, 116, 117, **120**
*Oundle Town Rowing Club*, **106**, 108
Oundle Wharf, **114**, 115, 116, 117, 118
Overton Lake, Moorings & Ferry Meadows Country Park, **144**, 145, 146, 147, 148

Pear Tree Farm Moorings (Aldwincle), **98**, 99, 101
Peckover House, 167
*Peddars Way*, 140
Perio Lock & weir bridge, 115, 117, **120**, 121, 122, 124, 126
*Peter Scott Walk*, 167
Peterborough, 140, 141, 147, 148, **150**, 151, 152-7, 160, 162
*Peterborough Boating Centre (Stanground)*, **150**
Peterborough Cathedral, **150**, 152, 153, 155
*Peterborough City Council*, 34, 35, 152, 153
Peterborough City Council Embankment, **150**, 151, 152, 153, 154

THE RIVER NENE    173

Peterborough City Council Slipway (Potters Way), 11, **150**, 153
*Peterborough City Council Visitor Information*, 11, 34, 35, 155
*Peterborough City Rowing Club*, **144**, 147
*Peterborough Cruising Club*, 34, 35, **136**, 137, 139
Peterborough Greyhound Stadium, **150**, 152-3
Peterborough Museum & Art Gallery, 156
*Peterborough United FC*, **150**, 152, 156
*Peterborough Yacht Club*, 34, 35, **144**, 146, 147
Pilton, **106**, 108, 112
Plum Tree Farm, **158**, 159
Poplar House Farm, 162
Port of Sutton Bridge, 34, 165, 166, 167
*portage & access tables*, 25-7
*postcodes*, 19
Potters Way Slipway (Peterborough), 11, **150**, 153
Prebendel Manor House & Tithe Barn Museum, 132, 133
*Proteus Canoe Club*, **144**, 146
Pudding Lane Moorings (Alwalton), **136**, 137, 139
*pump out facilities*, 11, 20, 22, 23-4

Queen's Head Arm, **128**, 129, 130

*radial gate locks*, 11-13
*Railworld*, 152, 156
Raunds, 82, 86, 89
*red flag system*, 16
*refuse sites*, 22, 23-4
*reversed locks*, 15
*Richard III, King*, 126
Ringstead, **84**, 86, 87, 89, **90**, 92
Ringstead Grange Trout Fishery, 87
Ringstead Locks, **84**, 85, 86, 87, 88
*River Advice for Boaters (Strong Stream Advice)*, 10, 16, 36
*River Canal Rescue*, 35
*River Nene Regional Park*, 36, 37
Rock UK Frontier Centre, **84**, 86
Rockingham Forest, 96, 102, 119, 126, 132, 134
Roman remains, 86, 89, 133, 140-44, 149, *see also* Chester Farm; Normangate Field
Roman roads, 76, 126, 127, **136**, 138, 141-2, 143, 156, 162
Rothersthorpe, **40**, 45
Rothersthorpe Locks, **40**, 41, 42-4, **46**
*Rothschild family*, 117, 118, 119
Rush Mills Lock, **52**, 53, 55
Rushden, **78**, 80, 81, 82
Rushden Lakes & Mooring, **78**, 79, 80, 81, 82, 83
Rushden Lakes Shopping Outlet, **78**, 79, 80
*Rutland Cycling*, 148
Rutland Water, 131

Sacrewell Farm & Country Centre, 132, 134
*safety*, 8, 10, 16, 36
St Crispin's Hospital Tower, 44, **46**
*sanitary facilities*, 11, 20, 22
Sculpture Park, **144**, 147
*services*, 11, 20, 34, 35
*sewage disposal*, 11, 20, 22, 23-4
Shanks Millennium Bridge, 154, **158**, 159, 160
Ship End Pits, 130
*shopping*, 20, 37
*short stay moorings*, 10
Sibson, **128**, **136**, 139
Sibson Marina, 34, **136**, 137, 138, 139
Skew Bridge Lake, **78**, 80, 81
*slipways*, 11, 34
South Holland Main Drain, **164**, 166
Southwick, 119
*speed limits*, 9
Stanground, **150**, 151, 153, 156
Stanground Lock, 34, **150**, 151, 152
Stanwick Lakes, 20, 35, 85, 86, 87, 88
Stibbington, **128**, 130, 131, 133, 138, 139
*Stibbington Boatyard*, 34, **128**, 129, 138, 139
Stibbington Hall, **128**, 141
Stoke Doyle, 108
Stone Pit Common (Woodford Shrubbery), 95, 96
Storton's Pits Nature Reserve, **46**, 48, 49
*Strong Stream advice & restrictions*, 10, 16, 36
Summer Leys Nature Reserve, **66**, 70, **72**
Sutton, **128**, 131, **136**, 140, 141
Sutton Bridge (port), 34, 165, 166, 167
Sywell Country Park, **66**, 70

Tansor, 117, 119, **120**

*telephone contacts*, 34-5
Thorney River, **164**
Thorpe Waterville, **98**, 99, 100, 101, 102, 103
Thorpe Wood & Boathouse Cut, **144**, 145, 147, 148, 149
Thrapston, **90**, 92-4, 95, 96
Thrapston Bridge & Mooring, **90**, 91, 93, 94, 95, 96
Thrapston Lagoon, **90**, 94
*Thrapston to Stanwick cycle trail*, **90**
*Thrapston2Rushden boots & bikes route*, 88
tidal river Nene, 14, 160, 163-7, **164**
*timings*, 2-3, 19, 33
Titchmarsh Lock & Moorings, **98**, 99, 100, 101
Titchmarsh Nature Reserve, **98**, 101
*tourist & visitor information*, 11, 34, 35, 37, 155
Twenty Foot River, 162, **164**

Upper Barnwell Lock, **106**, 107, 108, 112
Upper Nene Valley Gravel Pits SSSI & SPA, 81
Upper Ringstead Lock, **84**, 85, 86, 88
Upper Wellingborough Lock, **72**, 73, 74
*useful contacts & links*, 34-5

*victualling services*, 20
*Viking Way*, 140
*visitor information*, 11, 34, 35, 37, 155
*visitor licence agents*, 34, 36
*visitor moorings*, 10

Wadenhoe, **98**, 99, 100, 101, 102, 103
Wadenhoe Lock, **98**, 99, 100
*walking & exploring*, 20, 37, 140
Wansford, 124, **128**, 129, 130-31, 132, 133, 134, 139
Wansford Lock, **128**, 129, 130
Wansford NVR Station & Moorings, **128**, 131, 132, **136**, 137, 138, 139, 140
Wansford Old Bridge, **128**, 130, 131, 133, 134
Wansford Picnic Area, 133
Wansford Pumping Station, **128**, 131
Wansford & Standen's Pasture Nature Reserve, 130, 132
Warmington, **120**, 122-3, 126
Warmington Lock, **120**, 121, 123, 125
*Washington family*, 96, 97

*water levels*, 15
Water Mill Tearooms, **84**, 87
Water Newton, **136**, 140, 141, 143
Water Newton Lock, **136**, 137, 138
*water supplies*, 11, 20, 23-4
Watersports Centre, **144**, 148
*Waterway Recovery Group*, 17
*Waterway Routes*, 35
*websites*, 20, 35-7
*weirs*, 20
Wellingborough, 11, 22, 54, 69, **72**, 73-6, 76
Wellingborough Bridges, **72**, 73, 74, 75, **78**, 79, 80
Wellingborough Embankment, 22, 73, 75, 76
Wellingborough Locks, **72**, 73, 74-5, 80
Wellingborough Prison, **72**, 74
Wellingborough Viaducts, 83
West Cotton, 89
West Walton, **164**
Westbridge Arm, **46**, 47, 48, 49, **52**
Weston Barrage Gate, **52**, 56, 57
Weston Favell, **52**, 53, 57
Weston Favell Lock & Mooring, **52**, 53, 54, 56, 57, 62
Whiston, **66**, 69, 71
Whiston Lock, 61, 64, **66**, 67, 68
White Mills Lock, **66**, 67, 68, 70
White Mills Marina, 22, 34, **66**, 67, 68, 69, 70
*Whitehouse, Dick*, 21
Whittlesey, 143, **158**, 161, 162, **164**, 169
Whitworth's Mill (Wellingborough), 74, 76
Wigsthorpe, 111
*Wildlife Trust for BCN*, 35, 36, 49, 58, 81-2, 101, 132
Wilgar Footbridge, **128**, 129, 130, 131
Willow Brook, **120**, 124
*willow pollards*, 124-5
Willy Watt Marina, 22, 34, **84**, 85, 87
Willy Watt (Woodford) Mill, 88, 89
Wilson's Pits Reserve, 81, 82
*windlass*, 9
Wisbech, 14, 34, 162, **164**, 166, 167
Wisbech Yacht Harbour, 165
Wollaston, 76
Wollaston Lock, 69, **72**, 73, 74
Wood Newton, 125
Woodford, **90**, 91, 93, 95, 96

Woodford Lock & Mooring, **90**, 91, 92, 93, 95
Woodford Riverside Marina, **90**, 91, 92, 93
Woodford Shrubbery (Stone Pit Common), 95, 96
Woodford (Willy Watt) Mill, 88, 89
Woodston, **144**, **150**, 152
Wootton Lock, **40**, 41, 44, **46**

Yarwell, **128**, 130, 131, 132, 133
Yarwell Junction NVR Station, **128**, 132, 133, 141
Yarwell Lock, **128**, 129, 130, 131, 132
Yarwell Mill & Country Park, 34, **128**, 129, 130, 131, 133